JOHN DICKSON &
CHUCK D. PIERCE

Bestselling Author of *The Future War of the Church*

WORSHIP
AS IT IS IN
HEAVEN

WORSHIP THAT ENGAGES

EVERY BELIEVER AND

ESTABLISHES GOD'S KINGDOM

ON EARTH

Regal

From Gospel Light
Ventura, California, U.S.A.

D0289947

Published by Regal
From Gospel Light
Ventura, California, U.S.A.
www.regalbooks.com
Printed in the U.S.A.

Library of Congress Cataloging-in-Publication Data
Pierce, Chuck D., 1953-
Worship as it is in Heaven : worship that engages every believer and establishes God's kingdom on Earth / Chuck D. Pierce, John Dickson.
p. cm.
Includes bibliographical references.
ISBN 978-0-8307-5543-1 (trade paper)
1. Public worship. 2. Apostolate (Christian theology) I. Dickson, John, 1951- II. Title.
BV15.P54 2010
264—dc22
2010016011

1 2 3 4 5 6 7 8 9 10 11 12 13 14 15 / 20 18 17 16 15 14 13 12 11 10

Rights for publishing this book outside the U.S.A. or in non-English languages are administered by Gospel Light Worldwide, an international not-for-profit ministry. For additional information, please visit www.glww.org, email info@glww.org, or write to Gospel Light Worldwide, 1957 Eastman Avenue, Ventura, CA 93003, U.S.A.

To order copies of this book and other Regal products in bulk quantities, please contact us at 1-800-446-7735.

Contents

Worship as It Is in Heaven: The Ladder from Earth to Heaven!

Chuck D. Pierce

The Lord has used me in many ways throughout my 30 years of ministry. I have served as a building and operations superintendent, a business administrator, a pastor of mercy and benevolence, an executive director and financial officer, a vice president, an apostle, a senior pastor, a prophet, a president and CEO, a prayer leader, an intercessor and Harvest Watchman. Through all of my assignments and missions, the one key identity that I have maintained is that of a *worshiper*. A *worshiper* is one who bows down and prostrates himself or herself before God in order to serve and sacrifice with a reverential attitude of mind and body. This act includes adoration and obedience. The word for worship in the New Testament is *proskuneo,* or "to kiss." This is such an intimate expression of two meeting together intimately.

Worship is not only an act. A worshiper is one who has relationship with the one worshiped. One of my favorite meetings in the Bible is the account of the Samaritan woman and Jesus at Jacob's Well. Jesus needed to go to this place in Samaria to bring heaven's plan into the earth. Here, a woman who was making her daily routine visit to the well to get water was confronted by Jesus. He told her everything about her life. Most importantly, He began to reveal to her who He really was. He did this in the context of worship.

Jesus replied, "Believe me, dear woman, the time is coming when it will no longer matter whether you worship the

Father on this mountain or in Jerusalem. You Samaritans know very little about the one you worship, while we Jews know all about him, for salvation comes through the Jews. But the time is coming—indeed it's here now—when true worshipers will worship the Father in spirit and in truth. The Father is looking for those who will worship him that way. For God is Spirit, so those who worship him must worship in spirit and in truth."

The woman said, "I know the Messiah is coming—the one who is called Christ. When he comes, he will explain everything to us."

Then Jesus told her, "I AM the Messiah!" (John 4:21- 26, *NLT*).

The Samaritan woman changed instantly. She shifted her faith to the one who was the Messiah. Worship must have an object, and faith must be expressed to that object. Immediately, the woman was lifted out of her last identity and the will of heaven was displayed in the earth to a Samaritan woman with a bad past.

This was a major shift! No longer would worship be limited to the Jewish temple. True worship would now be able to lift anyone out of his or her past or present identity and reveal heaven's greater plan. In just one moment, this woman went from being a harlot to being an evangelist. Instead of being a woman with a bad reputation, she started speaking from her new identity and led all of the men in her city to be transformed. The knowledge and revelation that she received by worshiping in Spirit and truth covered her city. The glory she experienced infected an entire culture. She had ascended. She had moved from a routine dark existence into a new dimension of reality. Living water was now flowing in the core of her being. Not only was she drinking, but others were also drinking from her. She was experiencing heaven on earth in Samaria.

There Is a Place "Out There"!

When I was young, one of our family traditions was to watch the *Wizard of Oz* each year. This event fascinated me. I always loved when the movie turned from black and white to Technicolor. When the color came, I knew that we had made our way "over the rainbow." Once there, I loved the strange Munchkins, the flying monkeys, the false wizard and, most of all, the melting of the witch. I knew that Oz was not real, but I did enjoy thinking about what was real "over the rainbow."

This movie always seemed to set some things in motion in my life. I would spend days looking into the heavens and imagining what really existed "out there." I would spend much time talking to God (who I had been taught was in heaven) about what He had to give, the power He had and wondering what sort of evil existed. I knew there was "a place" beyond. I knew the place was not "Oz," but "out there" became my place of escape and seeking.

Not until I was 18 did someone introduce me to the Holy Spirit. The Third Person of the Godhead began to open my eyes to a world that was "out there." He could teach me and help me see what was "out there" now. The Person of Christ came alive. The Word came alive. The spiritual realm came alive. Faith came alive. Bible stories became relevant. My eternal place came alive. The heavens were no longer fiction like a place called "Oz." The "out there" became a place I could go boldly and access the best my Father had for me. This was not a place of escape, but a place where I could commune and worship. This became the place I could go boldly in time of need to obtain help.

That place is what we want to connect you to as you seek what you are looking for in life. May this book help you understand the reality of worship and the power of ascending beyond the world that encircles you. In John 14:1-3, Jesus says:

DO NOT let your hearts be troubled (distressed, agitated). You believe in and adhere to and trust in and rely on God; believe in and adhere to and trust in and rely also on Me. In My Father's house there are many dwelling places (homes). If it were not so, I would have told you; for I am going away to prepare a place for you. And when (if) I go and make ready a place for you, I will come back again and will take you to Myself, that where I am you may be also (*AMP*).

This place is one that you can only get to through worship. When you get there, all you can do there is worship.

Create and Comprehend

Genesis 1:1 is an amazing word that is foundational to the belief system of many individuals. This word is not just pertinent to Christianity, but it is woven into many religious ideologies. In my and John Dickson's belief system, this word is foundational to what we believe: "In the beginning God created the heavens [notice the *s*, denoting more than one heaven] and the earth." There is more than one heaven but only one earth. The key word is *created*.

In the New Covenant, which is a written history of God coming as man to resist everything that had defiled man through time, and then redeem man, there is a similar word: "In the beginning was the Word, and the Word was with God, and the Word was God. He was in the beginning with God. All things were made through Him, and without Him nothing was made that was made. In Him was life, and the life was the light of men. And the Light shines in the darkness, and the darkness did not *comprehend* it" (John 1:1-5, emphasis added). The key word is "comprehend."

There is a connecting force between *create* and *comprehend*. This is a simple but complex connector: *you and me!* God has chosen to dwell in man to connect the heavens and earth. Within man is the ability to process God's plan, hear His sound and bring God's plan of continuous creativity into fullness from generation to generation.

To "create," *bara*, is to form, fashion or produce. This word has the idea of carving and cutting out a plan to be fashioned and brought into fullness. The word is linked to "clearing out" anything that would stop this plan from fully materializing so that God's hand and character are reflected and His ultimate purpose and best are demonstrated. *Bara* describes how something is brought into existence and then fashioned and formed so the divine capacity of that object is seen in all of its glory!

The word "comprehend," *katalambanoh* in the Greek, means to overcome, lay hold of, seize, perceive or lay hold with your mind. This means that there is a mental and moral effort to obtain or occupy. Darkness cannot lay hold of the light and life of God. But man, who can embrace and receive the light, not only can lay hold of the light but can also communicate and work with the light— and even extinguish the darkness that opposes this light from producing and creating God's plan in the earth.

Today, we can understand how to "clear out," fashion, form and bring to fullness God's creative purpose in every season of life as long as life exists. As the connector between heaven and earth, we can overcome any darkness that is trying to stop God from being seen in our generation. Jesus, when asked by His disciples in Luke 11:2-4 if He would teach them to pray, answered by saying:

> Our Father Who is in heaven,
> Hallowed be Your name,
> Your kingdom come. Your will be done [held holy
>   and revered]
> On earth as it is in heaven.
> Give us daily our bread [food for the morrow].
> And forgive us our sins,
> For we ourselves also forgive everyone who is indebted
>   to us [who has offended us or done us wrong].
> And bring us not into temptation
> But rescue us from evil.

Therefore, we can connect into heaven with all that Father is and makes available to us. When we connect, we reverence and honor His name. Then we bring the power and authority of that name and all of His divine purposes into the earth. We agree with Him! When agreeing with Father in heaven, we who are in the earth will see heaven's will demonstrated on earth. Our perspective will become eternal. The earth will reflect Father's dwelling place. We will see His presence abiding in our midst.

This is what we've written about in *Worship as It Is in Heaven.* The Lord says, "You comprehend and then you work with Me to fashion, form and bring to fullness My plan today—My will being seen in the earth realm. You can clear out anything that enters the atmosphere that I have given you to rule. You can understand anything you need to understand in order to take dominion over the space and land I have given you. The resources you need to accomplish My purpose, you can create. I am moving in your midst and My voice is alive all around you. Hear and see Me, and make Me a dwelling place in earth with you!"

His Word Guides!

The Lord is leading us step by step in His perfect timing by His Word! I agree with the psalmist: "Your word is a lamp to my feet and a light to my path. . . . Forever, O LORD, Your word is settled in heaven. Your faithfulness endures to all generations; You established the earth, and it abides" (Ps. 119:105,89-90). The Word of God was written in a time frame for every generation to understand, and the only way to comprehend the Word is through worship. The Word was written to a people who were called to form covenant or agreement with God, to sacrifice to Him, to love Him as He loved them, to receive His blessings on a daily basis and to worship Him.

God inspired the Word. The Word was. The understanding and revelation of the Word are activated when you stay in God's time, or *abide.* To *abide* is to stand! The earth will stand based upon the relationship and interaction that is occurring between heaven and earth. Abide also means to dwell, inhabit, settle down, stand firm and rest, and is key from generation to generation. Every generation should abide in God's Word on earth as it is in heaven. When we abide in the Word, the earth abides. When we violate the Word, the earth sorrows, moans and cries out for justice and reconciliation. When we worship, the earth experiences the blessings of mankind, who is in contact with its Maker.

The Heavens Declare!

One of my favorite passages is Psalm 19:1-4:

THE HEAVENS declare the glory of God; and the firmament shows and proclaims His handiwork. Day after day pours forth speech, and night after night shows forth knowledge. There is no speech nor spoken word [from the stars]; their voice is not heard. Yet their voice [in evidence like a cord (as connecting), especially for measuring; creates a rule likened to a musical string or accord] goes out through all the earth, their sayings to the end of the world (*AMP*, with added paraphrased Hebrew interpretation).

The heavens declare. The lines of the earth carry the declaration. We can connect to this declaration—reverberate the words that are being released by faith—and create what God wants created today in the earth realm.

I recently read an article in *Scientific American* that caught my attention:

Earth's robust magnetic field protects the planet and its inhabitants from the full brunt of the solar wind, a torrent of charged particles that on less shielded planets such as Venus and Mars has over the ages stripped away water reserves and degraded their atmospheres. Unraveling the timeline for the emergence of that magnetic field and the mechanism that generates it—a dynamo of connective fluid in the Earth's outer core—can help constrain the early history of the planet, including the interplay of . . . processes that rendered the earth habitable.[1]

This field keeps the solar wind at bay but allows mankind at the same time to connect to the atmosphere and enjoy the benefits around us. I believe that if we listen to the voice of God as He declares His will from heaven, and agree with His voice, we can see earth kept as it is in heaven.

His glory rides these lines that encircle the earth. If we hear and receive the glory realm of the heavens into earth, we will continue to keep the earth habitable and prosperous. Also, I believe that if we reject that voice that is coming from heaven on the lines and the cord that connects heaven and earth, we will eventually decay.

His Word Framed the Earth!

His Word formed and framed the earth by faith (see Heb. 11). Because of this, we seem to be the only recorded planet in our galaxy that can hear by faith the earth's frame, speak it and keep the earth moving forward into the full purposes of the Creator. His voice rules this earth. The heavens declare!

> Of the heavens has God made a tent for the sun, which is as a bridegroom coming out of his chamber; and it rejoices as a strong man to run his course. Its going forth is from the end of the heavens, and its circuit to the ends of it; and nothing [yes, no one] is hidden from the heat of it (Ps. 19:4-6, *AMP*).

Psalm 19:7-14 goes on to say:

> The law of the Lord is perfect, restoring the [whole] person; the testimony of the Lord is sure, making wise the simple. The precepts of the Lord are right, rejoicing the heart; the commandment of the Lord is pure and bright, enlightening the eyes. The [reverent] fear of the Lord is clean, enduring forever; the ordinances of the Lord are true and righteous altogether. More to be desired are they than gold, even than much fine gold; they are sweeter also than honey and drippings from the honeycomb. Moreover, by them is Your servant warned (reminded, illuminated, and instructed); and in keeping them there is great reward. Who can discern his lapses and errors? Clear me from hidden [and unconscious] faults. Keep back Your servant also

from presumptuous sins; let them not have dominion over me! Then shall I be blameless, and I shall be innocent and clear of great transgression. Let the words of my mouth and the meditation of my heart be acceptable in Your sight, O Lord, my [firm, impenetrable] Rock and my Redeemer (*AMP*).

His Word is perfect, right and causes our hearts on earth to rejoice. His Word restores us to wholeness and makes us wise. His ordinances are true and righteous. They make us rich. His Word tests us and makes us gold. His Word warns us of adverse strategies of the enemy on our path. His Word makes us *abide* and *stand* when others falter. His Word allows us to connect by His Spirit into the place of His dwelling and then dwell like Him in the earth. The Word will endure forever (see Ps. 119:89; Isa. 40:8).

Unless we reject the active, energizing authority, the power of the Word cannot be broken. This power is meant to go from generation to generation. Even if a person's bloodline has rejected the Word of God three generations before, today anyone still has an opportunity to recoup the blessings that have been postponed. Because from the beginning the Word came, He has now made this available to all mankind. The deeds of the Word can be shared as a testament from one generation to another. The Word produces works and causes us to see a manifestation.

This Word is synonymous with speech, command, promise and prophecy. In other words, if you believe that He was, if you believe that He is and if you believe that He is the same forever, then today you will see a manifestation of His goodness. He has spoken. The Word has been recorded. However, in any generation He speaks. He reiterates His Word to a generation that will embrace His sound in the earth. His voice breaks and destroys the power and the works of the enemy! He does this through you!

The Word divides between our soul and spirit (see Heb. 4:12), and that's what makes our conscience come alive in Him. From a clear conscience, you can see by the Spirit into the heavenly realm. You can also see clearly and discern in the natural soulish realm.

You can see how the god of this world is working in the atmosphere around you. When we ascend, we see!

If We Won't, Satan Will!

If we don't take the authority that was wielded by the Lord Jesus Christ through His submission on the cross, Satan will illegally rule. This is the only way that he can re-cover the earth with darkness. If we do not worship in our cities, he will cover them with darkness. He covers nations with darkness and rules people. He has no legal right to do this, but we must remember, he opposes God in us and doesn't play fair. He doesn't play by the rules. He's a legalist and uses rules or makes rules that benefit his purposes.

In the beginning, he was the angel who "covered." If we do not ascend and worship, he creates an iniquitous grid that is like a shield where the iniquities give right to demonic hosts to influence us and the society in which we dwell. When we commit an iniquity in the earth, we bring our atmosphere into agreement with Satan's rule in the air. After a while, we are walking in an evil atmosphere. That grid is called a "veil." The veil was rent by the shed blood of the Lord. However, we've allowed the veil to be rebuilt, reformed and to cover our region, which we were given to worship God in and fill with His presence.

What is happening in your area is a reflection of how you are interacting from heaven to earth. Understand that Satan has a strategy. Satan has a position. He's the god of this world. He's the prince of the power of the air. He occupies atmosphere. His headship in the atmosphere was broken by the power of the cross and the shed blood of the Lord Jesus Christ, and at that moment, mankind was redeemed! Satan's headship over mankind was broken. Does that mean Jesus cleared the air so Satan would never be present again? Absolutely not!

It's true that Satan's headship was broken. Jesus ascended, was seated in the heavenlies and made it possible for us to go boldly into the heavenlies—into the throne room of God. While He was ascending, He gave gifts to mankind (see Eph. 4). But if mankind does not align those gifts properly, Satan's headship still rules in a territory. Even though the headship of Satan has been broken, if we refuse to align the gifts we were given when the headship of Satan was broken, then we cannot take dominion in the cultures of our society. If mankind is resisting what God did for us in the heavens, then we are cooperating with Satan's thoughts or headship in our region. If we resist the power of the blood of Christ that was shed on our behalf, we are not keeping the headship of Satan broken in our area.

Satan doesn't have legal authority over us anymore! However, he does have power to operate in our lives and regions if we won't take authority over him. When Paul went into Ephesus, even though Jesus had broken the headship of Satan, Paul had to realign what was going on in the earth realm and break the headship of Satan in that city. This produced the greatest revival recorded in the Word of God. In that particular city, the people disassociated with darkness, got freed and their consciences came alive to Christ. Paul showed them who they were in Christ. He showed them where they were seated in the heavens and how they could rule.

In the history of the early church, from city to city, apostles would take their authority, lead the corporate group in worship, live with the spirit of revelation guiding them and overcome the powers and principalities that ruled the area. However, something shifted. We began to legalize our worship, rationalize our power and water down our revelatory stance. This is what the Spirit of God is restoring today—our right position in the heavenlies and our proper, righteous condition in the earth. We are a nation above all nations. If we will *be* who we *are*, we will change any nation in the earth. Ascend and begin!

Come Up, Ascend and Boldly Enter In!

Because God is the same yesterday, today and forever, this reveals to us that within the earth realm in every generation there is a people who know how to use the Word that is spoken in heaven to demonstrate God's will in the earth in time. *The Word in time!* That is an interesting concept. Many of us do not understand how the Lord speaks and connects heaven and earth. First of all, look into eternity. See a throne room. If you read the book of Revelation, this is easy to visualize. Likewise, in Hebrews 4:14-16, we read, "Seeing then that we have a great High Priest who has passed through the heavens, Jesus the Son of God, let us hold fast our confession. For we do not have a High Priest who cannot sympathize with our weaknesses, but was in all points tempted as we are, yet without sin. Let us therefore *come boldly* to the throne of grace, that we may obtain mercy and find grace to help in time of need" (Heb. 4:14-16, emphasis added). To "come boldly" means that we are not reserved but come in with frankness and full-open speech.

Many of us do not come into the throne room boldly because we forget we are approaching a throne of grace. We think of the throne room as judgment, but when we come before Him, we are obtaining mercy for everything we have ever done in the past. We gain new grace and faith for our present circumstances. We also gain so much faith that it propels us into the future. Faith should be growing and steadfast. Faith should be abiding and continuing. Faith should be producing work in God's kingdom.

See Your Ladder!

We have entered a season in which the sound of heaven is coming into the earth realm. As heaven enters earth's atmosphere, the land responds and resounds with change. You can hear the Lord say, *"I'm opening up a new way for you. Where you walk, I will reconcile heaven and earth through you."* We find a similar biblical precedent in the life of Jacob (see Gen. 28). Jacob struggled and at times manipulated to gain what he felt was God's best for him. He fled from one season of his life to an unknown, unfamiliar land to establish his future. In Jacob's fleeing quest, he traveled three days to Bethel. That night, he took "one of the stones" to rest his head and sleep. This was not just any stone, but a worship stone. This was the same place where Abraham had worshiped and sacrificed the ram in place of Jacob's father, Isaac. Now in Jacob's exhausted state, God reveals to Jacob a vision of a ladder (or staircase, as some translate it) from heaven to earth.

Stop and Rest!

Many of you are exhausted from all the strife, contention and trials that have been linked to the promise that you have been pursuing. Be like Jacob—stop and rest! "Then he dreamed, and behold, a ladder was set up on the earth, and its top reached to heaven; and there the angels of God were ascending and descending on it" (Gen. 28:12). This was really a visitation from God. In this visitation, God revealed to Jacob a ladder. This ladder was not just any ladder but represented that God is the Lord of the past, the present and the future. This brought Jacob into a relationship with the Lord. This caused him to have faith that he could actually grab hold of the promise and blessing that had been spoken over him. This also gave him confidence that he could have a relationship with holy God just as his father and grandfather (Isaac and Abraham) had. From this experience, Jacob began to worship God personally in the following ways:

1. He acknowledged that the Lord had been in the place with him, even though before that point he could not see Him.
2. He memorialized the place, set up a stone and poured oil on it.
3. He renamed the place Bethel, the House of God.
4. He recognized God as provider.
5. He had a desire to give a portion of what he had back to the Lord.
6. The fear of God began to be a part of his life.
7. He declared that a "gate of heaven" had opened forever in that place.

This would link his purpose on earth into eternity. This heavenly ladder appeared suddenly. As you read what lies ahead in the pages of this book, may you hear the invitation to come up into His presence, see your future, realign your present and reconcile your past.

Through worship, we can come before God. When Jacob saw angels, he responded to worship with worship. Angels were first ascending and then descending. Angels ascend as we worship God. Not only do we enter His throne room with boldness, but once a portal is opened between heaven and earth, the angels who ascended come back to serve God's purpose and help us accomplish His will. We must be creating this ladder in many areas of the earth—first over our lives, then over our family; next the territory we live in and, finally, in the societal structure where we have been positioned to bring Kingdom change.

As angels ascend, meet and worship before God, they can then descend to go throughout the earth to help us. Our submission creates this ladder. This ladder allows all the spiritual blessings in heavenly places to come into our atmosphere. Ask the Lord to make you aware of His presence, of angelic presence and the blessings that are very near you this season. Jesus is our Mediator who gives us access to Father. Angels work on our behalf to serve and assist us in accomplishing His best purpose for our lives. This is what happened with Jacob: a portal formed and there was an opening between heaven and earth. Angels were ascending and descending, and God was reiterating by revealing to Jacob what would happen with His people for the generations to come.

A Moment of Divine Connection: Heaven, Earth and You!

Jacob's Ladder was a *generational moment of connection*. The same principle is stated in Ephesians 1:3, where the Lord says we have all spiritual blessings in heavenly places. In 1978, I was on a bus traveling from North Houston to work downtown. As I read the above verse, faith began to fill me. Suddenly, God opened the heavens and showed me all the blessings that my dad didn't apprehend in his lifetime. I then saw all the blessings that my grandfather had not been able to obtain because of fear. I then saw his father's blessings that were stored and abundant but never activated. Suddenly, I heard the Lord say, *"These are yours, if you want to come and receive. You can see these promises manifest in your life and pass them on to your children to come."* My life was changed that day.

When we ascend into the heavens, the atmosphere in earth changes. The land transforms. A gate opens for our revelatory access. Just as in the day of Pentecost, the Spirit comes and releases new power. As Jesus ascended, He gave gifts to mankind. Those gifts were to be passed on from generation to generation. We, too, can ascend.

Ascension is available to each one of us. When you submit your spirit to the Spirit of God, you are seated in heavenly places. Your position gives you the right to ascend. You can go up in heavenly places because you already live in heavenly places. You live in heavenly places and you walk in the earth with the revelation of heaven. When you learn to believe that, you begin to see things differently from what you've seen before. What is produced in you is glory! Glory has the final word of operation in your life in the earth (see Heb. 2:7-9) because you have experienced this glory in the heavens. The goal in our life is to experience His glory and walk in this glory until glory covers the earth (see Hab. 2:14; 3:3).

When we worship, we ascend, and heaven becomes a reality in the earth. God has always had worshipers in every generation. He is developing an army that will march in synchronization with heaven. This army will ascend, hear, descend and then restore the waste places of the earth. They will walk in earth as if they were in heaven! As you read *Worship as It Is in Heaven* may you ascertain your place in the heavens and experience all that heaven has for you.

Heaven's Worship Establishes God's Will on Earth

What do the words "apostolic worship" mean? Does this term describe the latest fad in contemporary Christian music? Is it a new catchphrase to capture people's attention? No, it is neither of these. Apostolic worship is a developing phenomenon occurring at the grassroots level in the Body of Christ that corresponds with the new Church Age that has been unfolding during the last few decades. Apostolic worship means worship that engages every believer and goes forth into the atmosphere and into the community to establish God's will on earth as it is in heaven. Greek *apostolos* means "one who is sent out," so apostolic worship means worship that goes forth to establish God's will on earth.

This kind of worship includes speaking forth in intercession and prophetic declaration what God is saying in the midst of worship over specific problems and areas of warfare in a community, city, region, state or nation. Dr. C. Peter Wagner, who has studied and chronicled many of the developments in the Body of Christ since the late 1970s, calls it "the New Apostolic Reformation."[1] He believes that this reformation has been "changing the shape of Protestant Christianity around the world" on a level with the Protestant Reformation of Martin Luther and John Calvin 500 years ago.[2] In explaining his terminology, Dr. Wagner says:

> I use "Reformation" because, as I have said, I believe it at least matches the Protestant Reformation in its overall impact; "Apostolic" because the most radical of all the changes is the widespread recognition of the gift and

office of apostle in today's churches; and "New" to distinguish the movement from a number of denominations that use the word "Apostolic" in their official names yet exhibit patterns common to the more traditional churches rather than to these new ones.[3]

What then has brought the resurgence of the word "apostle" into our twenty-first-century vernacular? The answer comes when we take note of the extraordinary developments that Christianity has undergone in the decades approaching this new millennium. Most Christians can agree that something different has been happening in the worldwide Body of Christ, from the myriads of charismatically oriented house fellowships in the 1970s to the emergence of independent mega-churches—also charismatically oriented—with unprecedented attendance rolls in the tens and even hundreds of thousands, first in Korea in the 1980s, then in Argentina in the 1990s and in Nigeria and other places in this millennium. All this has been outside of the mainline denominations that have contained most of Christendom for the last five centuries.

If we look at what has developed in this segment of Christianity called the New Apostolic Reformation, one thing we note is that it has experienced phenomenal growth. Rick Joyner, in his book *The Apostolic Ministry*, says:

> The fastest growing part of the church over the past two decades has been what is now being called "the new apostolic movement." Not only does it now appear that the majority of Pentecostal charismatic Christians are embracing this truth, but many evangelical, and even those who are often referred to as "old line" denominations, are now embracing it. Where this is happening there is an obvious, new, spiritual energy and excitement created that is helping church life in the twenty-first century become what God intended it to be.[4]

Dr. Wagner says this growth has been, "much more than any other area of Christianity, even more that Islam."[5] Statistical data assembled on the Church at large shows just how dynamic this growth phenomenon is. Dr. David Barrett, the foremost authority on the statistics and trends of global Christianity, has set down his research in a massive two-volume work entitled *World Christian Encyclopedia*, published by Oxford University Press in 2001. Peter Wagner summarizes Dr Barrett's findings on the growth in different segments of Christianity:

> David B. Barrett, one of the most accomplished statisticians of the Christian church, has divided world Christianity into six "megablocks." Roman Catholics compose the largest megablock, but of the five non-Catholic megablocks, the one embracing the New Apostolic Reformation (Barrett uses the terms "Independent," "Postdenominational" and "Neo-Apostolic") is the largest. It is larger, for example, than Anglicans, Orthodox, Protestants and Marginals (Mormons, Jehovah's Witness, etc.).[6]

When I was growing up, those Christians outside of the denominational churches were just small groups "on the other side of the tracks." No one thought they would ever amount to anything, but now they are the largest and fastest-growing segment of non-Catholic Christianity. Dr. Barrett updates his statistics annually in the *International Bulletin of Missionary Research*. In the 2008 update, the megablock embracing the New Apostolic Reformation contained more than 422 million Christians around the world.[7]

The New Apostolic Reformation is changing the face of Christianity in the world and can no longer be relegated to "that bunch of crazies on the other side of the tracks." As a matter of fact, the churches of this new reformation are coming out of their hiding places and affecting the world around them. Rick Joyner believes these new apostolic churches will shake the world in the same way the first one did:

> Just as the apostolic church of the first century was extremely powerful and accomplished more for the spread of

the gospel than possibly any generation since, the apostolic church at the end will again shake the entire world with its truth and power.[8]

If the apostolic Church represents the government of God, it should affect the world around it. God does not want to be contained in the four walls of a building. Dr. Jonathan David, in his book *Apostolic Blueprints for Accurate Building,* says:

> Our quest is to understand the fundamental kingdom dynamics behind apostolic churches in the New Testament writings. These churches lived and grew in their environments only to influence and impact their communities. They had within them the dynamics to prevail over their limitations and create dramatic changes to the spiritual, political and economical landscapes of their cities. The dynamic grace that was within them made them consistently effective for the next 100 years after the Pentecost. Very few institutions have had similar success.[9]

As the years went on, however, the gift of apostle was the first gift to disappear from the Early Church. In our day, the gift of apostle has been the last gift to be restored. The twentieth century saw the development of the spiritual gifts mentioned in Romans 12, 1 Corinthians 12 and, over the last few decades, the fivefold spiritual gifts mentioned in Ephesians 4: apostles, prophets, evangelists, pastors and teachers.

The last of these gifts to be established—and indeed the pivotal gift of the five—has been the gift of apostle. The reason the apostolic gift is pivotal is that it represents the government of God—government that brings the other four gifts into their maximum economy. Although Church leaders down through the ages have represented God's government in varying measures, the gifting that God Himself fashioned to administer His government on earth in this New Testament age was that of apostle.

Where we have, in effect, used a shoe in the past to drive in a nail, even though it has worked, God has now given us a tool specifically designed to hammer a nail with accuracy, efficiency and power. The apostolic giftings that are arising are bringing the Church into a place of unprecedented accuracy, efficiency, power and growth. In the process we have been finding out that the way we have "done church" over the years has not always been God's way. Our "ways" have more often come from our traditions, our ingenuity or our personal perceptions of what God wants rather than from the revelation of God. Dr. Wagner says:

> We are now seeing before our very eyes the most radical change in the way of doing church since the Protestant Reformation. In fact, I think I could make a reasonable argument that it may actually turn out to be a *more radical* change. I am not referring to doctrinal changes: nothing has or likely ever will match the profound doctrinal insights that the Reformers surfaced, such as the authority of Scripture, justification by faith and the priesthood of all believers. The changes we are currently experiencing leave essential doctrines like this intact while at the same time reengineer the way that churches operate and carry out their daily activities.[10]

One "way" that has undergone tremendous change has been worship. We have seen a veritable explosion of worship over the past 40 years or so, and as this new millennium has dawned, the rising apostolic government has started to bring the Body of Christ into a new understanding of what God is doing through this explosion. In establishing His government in the earth, God is enthroning Himself on the praises of His people, and from that throne He is intervening in the affairs of man, from the bringing down of kingdoms to, on a more personal level, drawing home the long-prayed-for prodigal.

As the gift of apostle represents the government of God, apostolic worship is worship that facilitates the government of God as

He enthrones Himself on our praises. It is worship that brings us into the Lord's governmental process on the earth: "Thy will be done on earth as it is in heaven." It is not that the songs of this worship are necessarily about government or use the word "apostle" in their lyrics. Rather, it is that the worshipers lend themselves to the purposes of God in their worship.

You might ask, "Isn't that what we do now?" I think what we do now is love and adore the Lord with all our hearts. I believe we are fulfilling the depiction of the bride and the Bridegroom in the first part of the Song of Solomon. What I believe we are coming to is where the Bridegroom invites the bride out into His kingdom. This is where the Bridegroom enters into His apostolic function. As He calls back to us, "Come away, My beloved," we will have to come to an understanding of how we must facilitate His apostolic functioning in our worship. We can no longer allow our worship to be limited by our traditions, our culture or our personal preferences. It is time to move past these limitations and into an apostolic understanding of worship.

The purpose of apostolic worship is not to take the place of our passionate, heartfelt worship. We must never allow our intimate worship in the Bridegroom's chamber to be diminished. Instead we must discover how to take that zeal in worship into His governmental perspective. Just as I mentioned earlier that the gifting of apostle brings the other giftings to their maximum economy, apostolic worship brings all of our aspects of worship into their maximum expression.

This book will examine the phenomenon of worship from its original home in heaven to its first real explosion on earth in David's tabernacle, to it's rebirth in the New Testament Church, its fall into the earth during the Dark Ages, its rebirth again in the Reformation, its continual unfolding during the last 500 years, and, finally, its ascent into the present purposes of God in this new apostolic age.

WORSHIP
AS IT IS IN
HEAVEN

What Happens When We Worship

You are holy, O You who are enthroned upon the praises of Israel.
PSALM 22:3, NASB

The Essence of Worship

I am a worship leader, but first I am a worshiper: whether the music is playing or not, whether the circumstances are favorable or not, and whether I feel "in the mood" or not. Matt Redman, in his book *The Unquenchable Worshipper*, describes what we should be like as worshipers of our God:

> Enter the unquenchable worshipper. This world is full of fragile loves—love that abandons, love that fades, love that divorces, love that is self-seeking. But the unquenchable worshipper is different. From a heart so amazed by God and His wonders burns a love that will not be extinguished. It survives any situation and lives through any circumstance. It will not allow itself to be quenched, for that would heap insult on the love it lives in response to.[1]

Matt gives us the essence of our relationship with God: unquenchable worship. God has saved us, empowered us and given us purpose in life. We are His worshipers. Nothing can dissuade us from our worship; it is our communion with God, and He loves the time we spend with Him.

Just as our individual worship is the essence of our personal relationship with God, our corporate worship is the essence of our collective relationship to God as Christ's betrothed bride here on earth. When we worship corporately before the Lord, we become more than just a collection of individuals. We become something greater. This phenomenon is called "synergism," which the *Merriam-Webster Dictionary* defines as "conditions such that the total effect is greater than the sum of the individual effects."[2]

Together we demonstrate the combined passion and fire of many individual worshipers and become greater than just the sum of our individual parts. Because of this it is important that we guard our personal times with the Lord and never let the fire go out, so that when we come together we can enter into the power that corporate worship is supposed to be. In our book *The Worship Warrior*, we enumerated several unique things that occur when we worship corporately:

- **An increase of strength.** One can put 1,000 to flight, but two can put 10,000 to flight (see Deut. 32:30). This is a valuable principle of multiplication.

- **The power of agreement.** Jesus told us, "Again I say to you, that if two of you agree on earth about anything that they may ask, it shall be done for them by My Father who is in heaven" (Matt. 18:19, *NASB*). This is the power of agreement that increases the effectiveness of our prayers. The word "agree" means to come into harmony with. It actually means we make the same sound on earth that is coming from heaven. Therefore, our sounds are in harmony.

- **The Lord's presence.** We have a special promise from Jesus that He, Himself, will show up when we gather together in His name. "For where two or three have gathered together in My name, I am there in their midst" (Matt. 18:20, *NASB*). When we come together, He is there with us.[3]

Another picture the Lord gives us is that together we become the Body of Christ. "Now you are Christ's body, and individually members of it" (1 Cor. 12:27, *NASB*). He is the head; we are the body. This image should become evident in our corporate worship. What the head is thinking, the Body should respond to in its worship. If the Lord is celebrating, His body should be celebrating. If He is warring, we should be warring. This is how it is in heaven: a sea of individual worshipers who, when joined together, synergistically bring forth the awesome experiences we read about in the book of Revelation. Whatever God is doing, His worshipers in heaven respond to it in their worship.

In heaven their corporate worship plays a central role in God's ruling process. The same is true of our corporate worship here on earth, but many have not understood this aspect of worship.

What Takes Place When We Worship

God Is Enthroned

Psalm 22:3 tells us that God enthrones Himself on our praises. All of us are familiar with that Scripture, and I, like many others, always get a picture of God coming down during our worship and snuggling into the big overstuffed easy chair of our praises. I love this picture. I know how God loves us and loves to visit us when we praise Him, but one day I began to think of some of the pictures of thrones that I had seen—none of them looked like an overstuffed easy chair. As a matter of fact, most of them didn't look comfortable at all. They were usually sturdy, straight-backed chairs whose function was not comfort. Then I began to think about what the function of a throne was.

The *Merriam-Webster Dictionary* says a throne is "the chair of state of a sovereign or high dignitary."[4] A throne represents sovereignty and royal power: it is a seat of authority. It is a place where edicts are decreed, laws are made, orders are issued, proclamations are declared, commissions are awarded and rewards are given. It is the place where sovereigns do business.

The word "enthroned" is from the Hebrew word *yashab*, which means to sit down as judge.[5] What David understood, that much of the Church today does not, is that God chooses the atmosphere of our praises on which to establish His throne of authority. It is on our praises that God sits as judge.

For many this comes as a bit of a surprise. The word most associated with worship in our day has been "intimacy," not "authority." As we will see in chapter 9, God associates both of those words, "intimacy" and "authority," with worship. It is we who have separated the two. We tend to let God handle that "authority" end of things by Himself, while we concentrate on giving Him our hearts of adoration in worship. But Psalm 149:6 tells us that God wants us to not only have the high praises of God in our mouths, but at the same time have a two-edged sword in our hands. This psalm says it is our honor to have a part in the enforcement of His authority through our worship as well as release our hearts in adoration to Him. Cindy Jacobs wrote in her book *Possessing the Gates of Your Enemy*, "We are enforcers of His will."[6]

This is the apostolic or governmental aspect of worship that we first see through the ministry of King David. God brings us into His throne room by bringing His throne into our praises. Whether we realize it or not, God enthrones Himself on our passionate praises in order to rule, to reign, to issue laws, decrees, edicts and proclaim His purposes in the earth and to determine the very course of history.

Chuck Pierce wrote the following in his book *Interpreting the Times*:

> Praise can change any atmospheric warfare around us. Praise can break us out of dry and wilderness times in our lives. The power of our voices with the breath of His Spirit will break the conformity of the enemy's blueprint of the world around us.[7]

Once, Chuck told us the Lord wanted our church to spend three days in worship. After we finished this assignment, we read in our local newspaper a statement from our local abortion clinic that they were going to close down because the atmosphere in our city was not conducive to them. Praise had changed the atmosphere over our city. God had enthroned Himself on the praises of His people and decreed from that throne that the abortion clinic was finished in our area.

It was with this understanding of enthronement that David called upon the Lord during his worship to "Rise up for me to the judgment You have commanded!" (Ps. 7:6). This was a pattern of worship that God first established in heaven. It was David who was given the charge of bringing it about on earth.

As It Is in Heaven

In heaven God clearly establishes His throne on the praises of His worshipers there. In the fifth chapter of Revelation we see God in His throne room. In subsequent chapters we read of some serious things that are about to issue forth from this place of ultimate authority. The Lamb is going to break the seven seals; the four horsemen of the apocalypse are going to ride; the sun is going to be turned black; the moon is going to be turned red as blood; there will be earthquakes, famine, war, a plague of locust; the seven trumpets of judgment are going to be sounded; and much more.

But first God calls the elders before Him with their harps and bowls. These harps represent worship, and the bowls are filled with the prayers of the saints, which is our intercession. A tremendous worship service then erupts as the elders, the living beings, the angels and the hosts of heaven fall down before the throne and the contents of the bowls go up before the Lord as incense.

But why have a worship service when we have apocalyptic business to do? The end of the earth has to be brought about. The kingdom of God has to be brought in. Some awesome stuff has to be attended to. Our minds can't wrap around the concept of war and worship joined together. But we see in Revelation that God chooses this very atmosphere of worship and intercession to war and to launch His acts of authority. God's throne rests on the praises of His worshipers. God does not walk out the back door of our worship services in order to shield us from having to see the authoritarian business He has to do. He chooses instead to do that business when we are engaged with Him in worship.

Hosanna! Hosanna! Hosanna!

We see the same pattern in the life of Jesus. Jesus generally assumed the character of the Lamb of God while in His earthly ministry. Although Jesus took authority over nature, demons and sicknesses, He generally did not exert His authority over mankind. In the garden of Gethsemane, Jesus told His disciples that He could have called 12 legions of angels to save Himself from the Roman soldiers that had come to take Him away (see Matt. 26:53), but He specifically chose not to exert that authority.

On one occasion, however, we see Him act quite differently. In Matthew 21, Jesus came into the temple in His authority as King of kings and Lord of lords and drove out the money changers, proclaiming, "My house shall be called a house of prayer; but you are making it a robbers' den" (Matt. 21:13, *NASB*). Robert Gay, in his book *Silencing the Enemy,* comments on this incident:

> I do not believe it was merely the activities of the money changers, because Jesus had seen them before at the temple. It was not the selling of doves, for this had been going on for years, and Jesus had never done anything about it. What caused Jesus to arise with righteous indignation in a violent assault against these men? It was the shouts of praise that were coming from the people.[8]

What made this day different from all the other days He had entered the temple during His lifetime was that this day Jesus had entered the city amidst a worship service. This had been the day of His triumphal entry into Jerusalem. "Behold, your King is coming to you; He is just and having salvation, lowly and riding on a donkey" (Zech. 9:9). The crowds waved palm branches and laid down their coats before their King. They broke into praises and called out to Him, "Hosanna! Hosanna! Hosanna!" Jesus was enthroned on the praises of His people, and from this throne He operated in a different manner than He had the other times He had entered Jerusalem. It caused Him to take up His kingly authority over mankind; and as He walked into the temple, He drove out those with evil intentions. Although the hosanna singers did not realize it, their worship loosed Jesus into His governmental position as King of kings. Our worship is to accomplish the same thing, but we are not to remain in ignorance in our enthroning. This is the age that we are to come into understanding and agreement as we enter into our apostolic worship.

In Psalm 110:1, God told Jesus to come and sit at His right hand while He made His enemies a footstool for His feet. Then God said in verse 2 that it would be out of Zion that He would send forth Jesus' rod of strength. That "rod," in the Hebrew, is used for ruling and chastening.[9] Zion, as we will see, is the place where God is enthroned on His people's praises. It was during the "hosanna" worship service (out of Zion) that God gave Jesus the rod of strength to chasten the moneychangers of the temple.

Tambourines and Lyres

In the Old Testament, God calls for worship as He prepares to deal with a principality that ruled over the kingdom of Assyria: "And every blow of the rod of punishment, which the LORD will lay on him, will be with the music of tambourines and lyres" (Isa. 30:32, *NASB*). Here, again, God calls for His people to enthrone Him on their praises in order for Him to carry out this act of kingly authority. Why should we as modern-day Christians care what God chooses to do to some dusty old Middle Eastern principality? Assyria, to the ancient Hebrews, represented the military power that was coming to destroy Israel. God enlisted the Hebrew people to participate in their own salvation from Assyria by enthroning Him on their praises so that He might bring judgment on the destructive powers facing them. God invites us to do the same thing—enthrone Him on our praises so that we might participate in the judgment He desires to bring on those things that come to bring destruction on us.

Although we don't always know what we are participating in, we sometimes sense an "urgency" in worship to address a certain issue or come against a certain spirit or mindset or injustice. The closer we are to our intercessors, the more likely we will be to sense what God is doing as we enthrone Him. That loved one that we have interceded for might be addressed from the throne in our next worship service, or God might deal with some issue in the nation. The timing is God's. He stores up the prayers of the saints in bowls of incense to be brought before Him with harps of worship.

As we look at the Scriptures in this light, we see more and more instances of God being enthroned on His people's praises to carry out His acts of authority. Therefore, we need to understand the role that our worship plays in addressing those powers and bringing them down. Sometimes, God is just waiting for the music to start.

Jailhouse Rock

Paul and Silas clashed with the spiritual powers over Philippi, but it wasn't until the music started that God shook the earth and opened the doors of evangelism in that region. As the two men—bloody, bruised and shackled—began to sing praises to God in the bottom of that jail, God enthroned Himself on those praises and broke the power of the enemy. Chuck Pierce says this:

> Most Christians focus their worship on relationship and adoration, which is both excellent and right. However, our adoration and quest to know God must also move to a higher level—that of exercising His will on Earth. What God is doing and saying in Heaven must be manifested on Earth. As we worship, our adoration ascends to His throne. It is through this process that we are able to then descend in effective warfare. In turn, this call is releasing a sound from Heaven that is being embraced by people all over the world. The call to worship draws us nearer in intimacy—and its sound causes us to go to war![10]

This Honor Have All His Saints

As I mentioned earlier, it is God who joins worship and the sword. We are the ones who have tried to separate them. Psalm 149:6-9 says:

Let the high praises of God be in their mouth, and a two-edged sword in their hand, to execute vengeance on the nations and punishments on the peoples, to bind their kings with chains and their nobles with fetters of iron, to execute on them the judgment written; this is an honor for all His godly ones.

What we saw in Isaiah 30:32 was this: the saints participating with God in punishing evil powers. It was to the music of our tambourines and harps that God set about His work of punishing the principality ruling over the kingdom of Assyria. The high praises of God and the two-edged sword were joined. When we worship, God goes into action. What an honor! "This is an honor for all His godly ones." Joseph Garlington sums it up like this:

When the praise of God is in our mouths, what is in our hand? A two-edged sword. What is it for? To inflict vengeance on the nations and punishment on the peoples. How do we do that? While we praise God with our mouths, we have a two-edged sword in our hands, but meanwhile God gets busy binding their kings with fetters and their nobles with shackles of divine judgment written against THEM. God sums everything up by saying "This is an honor for all His godly ones" (Ps. 149:9).[11]

Back to Revelation

Continuing on in the book of Revelation, we see this pattern over and over again: enthroning worship coming forth, followed by the tremendous acts of God.

In chapter 7 we see a "great multitude" from every nation and tongue worshiping God, joined by the angels, the 24 elders and the 4 living beings. Following this worship, God brings up seven angels to sound the seven trumpets, which bring forth more judgments.

In chapter 11, another worship service occurs: the 24 elders again fall down and begin to worship the Lord. After this worship service, signs are seen in heaven: the woman that bears the man-child, and the dragon that seeks to destroy Him.

In chapter 14, the 144,000 celibates worship, singing a new song to the Lamb. After this time of worship the Lord gives the word to reap the earth.

Then in chapter 15, those who overcame the beast took up harps and worshiped before the throne singing the Song of Moses and the Song of the Lamb. After this worship service, in chapter 16, the seven bowls of judgment are poured out amidst worship from the very angels pouring out the judgment. Then in chapter 18, Babylon falls.

In chapter 19, there is a thunderous worship service by a great multitude. After this worship, Jesus comes forth on a white horse, leading the army of heaven into the battle of Armageddon. The devil is cast into the pit and the new heaven and new earth come forth.

Most of us remember all the apocalyptic events in Revelation. What we haven't taken note of is that all of these events are woven together through the great worship services in the book. God establishes His throne in the midst of these worship services so that the worshipers always have a part in the awesome workings of God.

Out of Zion

As Goes the Tabernacle, So Goes the Nation

It was David, of course, who coined the phrase "enthroned on the praises." He, of all people, knew what happened when God enthroned Himself on the praises of His people. When God was enthroned, David knew that God's hand would be against the enemies of Israel. Isaiah reveals an insight into this principle when he says, "So will the LORD of hosts come down to wage war on Mount Zion and on its hill" (Isa. 31:4, *NASB*). Although Mount Zion was never the site of a physical battle during the time the tabernacle was pitched there, it was where the Lord came down to enthrone Himself on the continual praises there and wage war against Israel's enemies.

Therefore, when it came time to pick the worship team in the tabernacle, David did not gather the priests and Levites to make the choices. He instead gathered his military commanders. These were the men who actually had to face the physical enemies of Israel. David believed that these commanders had the right to choose the people who would be in that most critical place, the tabernacle (see 1 Chron. 25:1), while they were out commanding their troops in battle.

Imagine if that happened today: a church is about to add a couple of members to its worship team and the president of the United States sends down a Marine Corps general to make the final selection. If the president had the same understanding of what happens when we worship that David did, he would probably try.

David's military commanders wanted to make sure that serious, passionate, prophetic worshipers were ministering before the Lord. Their lives depended on it and they didn't want some shallow prima donna bringing forth a "performance" in the sanctuary. They knew that as things went in the tabernacle, so things went on the battlefield. As a result of this, David's commanders extended the borders of Israel to the fullness of what was promised to Abraham. Jim Hodges explains this attitude like this:

> What happens in heaven, in earth, and in history, is the result of the worship and intercession of the Church on earth agreeing with the worship and intercession of the Church in Heaven.[12]

This is why David ran a different worship team into the tabernacle each and every hour of the day and night. David wanted the worship to be fresh and powerful. Each of the 24 teams had waited in anticipation for their hour to come before the Lord. They were excited. They were prepared. They were eager for their turn. When their hour came, they worshiped with all of their hearts, because they only had an hour. This was the level of worship that went on in the tabernacle. Because this worship went on continually, God was enthroned continually. Many Scriptures describe God's acts of authority from His throne on Israel's praises in Zion:

- From Zion, God stretches forth His scepter of authority (see Ps. 110:1-3).
- From Zion, God issues His commands (see Ps. 133:3).
- On Zion, God installs His King (Ps. 2:6).
- From Zion, God's deliverer will come (see Rom. 11:26-27).
- From Zion, God declares blessings (see Pss. 128:5; 134:3).
- From Zion, God hears the prayer of the destitute (see Ps. 102:17).
- From Zion, God punishes His enemies and the noise can be heard all over the city (see Isa. 66:6).
- From Zion, God will remove the veil from the nations' eyes (see Isa. 25:7).

When God says He will rebuild Zion and rebuild the tabernacle of David, it is not so that He can have some good music to listen to. He intends to establish His throne on the praises of His people and from that throne remove the veil from the nations and bring in the fullness of the Gentiles and His kingdom.

By Many or by Few

God can be enthroned on the praises of a sea of worshipers or on the praises of two or three. Where two or three are gathered in His name, Jesus is there. There were only two, Paul and Silas, in the Philippian jail—praising the Lord—when God brought the earthquake. It turned out to be the key to the evangelism of the area.

Whether the worship is on an apocalyptic scale like we saw in Revelation, or just a small gathering of two or three, God is not limited to deliver by many or by few (see 1 Sam. 14:6). He might topple a kingdom or He might call a lone prodigal home that you have been praying for a long time, but His plan is always to involve us in the work of His kingdom. He gives us authority and tells us to heal the sick, raise the dead, cast out demons and make disciples of the nations. The Bridegroom in the Song of Solomon beckons us to come away with Him as He tends to the business of His kingdom. In Revelation 5, the prayers of the saints had been stored up in bowls. God had these prayers brought to Him along with worship (the harps) as He prepared to release from His throne the things that would bring about the end of the age.

On a smaller scale, I believe that as we pray to God for the harvest in our area or for Him to bind up the principalities that hold people of our area in bondage, He comes in our corporate worship to enthrone Himself and pronounce edicts against the hindrances to God's children and to the harvest that we have prayed to bring in.

How Must We Then Worship?

If God is going to enthrone Himself on our praises, what does He want our praise to be like? I believe heaven's worship is the example God gave us to pattern our worship after here on earth. If that is so, then we need to look at how our present worship measures up. Is our worship spontaneous and dynamic like it is in heaven, or is it the same old thing every week? Is our worship prophetic and intercessory like it is in heaven, or is it just good quality music? Do we war in our worship, or do we stay away from the devil, hoping he will stay away from us? Does God interact with our worship, or do we just get the crowd warmed up for the speaker to come? If our worship is not like heaven's worship, it is not apostolic. We must, therefore, ask ourselves how we came to learn our present patterns of worship.

These are questions that deserve our attention. Let's look now at worship in heaven as it isn't on earth.

LOOK FOR THE COMING WORSHIP ON EARTH
CHUCK D. PIERCE

These are intense but glorious times throughout the world. Floods, earthquakes, tornados, fires and every other kind of disaster keep occurring in the earth realm. The Church is arising from nation to nation. God's kingdom is being unlocked and His kingdom people are advancing in the earth. Cultures are transforming to reflect God's will in the earth.

There is a hunger to hear from heaven and demonstrate the power that dwells in the throne room of God. Revelation uncovers and makes clear what was hidden in our midst. We are a people who must have vision to advance (see Prov. 29:18). Without prophetic revelation, we lose our way. I am an ambassador to represent Jehovah God and communicate His will in the earth. To do so, I must remain in communion and know His voice. To remain in communion with Him, I must worship.

Worship occurs when we release the depth of our being through devotion and allegiance to something that we revere more than ourselves. Job said, "I know that my Redeemer lives!" (Job 19:25). I echo this statement. Once people have revelation of the source of their life, worship should arise from their inmost being. We were made to cultivate and produce God's plan of fullness in the earth. We are called to watch after the portion we each have been allotted. Just as man and woman communed in the Garden of Eden, we are called to watch, cultivate and commune in "our garden." We must openly express this reverence and communion through acts of adoration. There is only one who is worthy to receive our special devotion and honor. When we connect with God and become one with Him, we reflect His nature in the earth.

In Old Testament times, the patriarchs would build an altar each time God revealed Himself. Each moment of God's revelation in a place created an event. Moses turned aside from his daily chores of shepherding his father-in-law's herds to see a strange manifestation: God burning in a bush without the bush ever being consumed. This was such a life-changing moment that from that day forth, the Lord used this time to advance His covenant plan and covenant people.

Through Moses, God established the form of worship and the principles of worship that the Israelites' would follow (see Exod. 25-31; 35:1-40:38). This would set the precedent for a people to follow in order to reflect, adapt, mature, reform and align their desires in earth with worship in heaven. David shifted Moses' worship into a new level and corporately led the people in reflecting heaven's expression. New Testament worship was characterized by *joy* and *thanksgiving*! Because of God's gracious redemption of us in Christ, worship should always reflect our faith, and focus us on His unmerited grace through His Son, Jesus Christ.

A major shift is coming in the way we worship and acknowledge God corporately. God is saying that in the times of drought and crisis that will manifest in the days ahead, we will lead His people to:

- *Worship expressly on a daily basis.* There is coming a Holy Spirit movement in us and around us. We will sing songs of breakthrough. We will shout our way into victory. We will dance in ways we have never danced. We will prostrate ourselves as Hannah laid before the altar, and more.

- *Give incredibly.* Incredible giving is linked with miraculous and demonstrative acts of faith. This is not just presumptive initiatives such as emptying our bank accounts. There are coming ways in these next few months that we will give incredibly through this drought and time of crisis that we are in.

- *Be strategically creative.* This creativity is stored within us. Most of us are not aware of how deep God's well really goes. This creativity will be used over our mission and assignment. He will show us daily how to advance creatively in our mission.

These are hard times, but they are good times. These are the times that God is opening up the deep fountains in us. Be bold to advance!

Our worship will release great blessings into the earth realm. The redeemed of the Lord will say so! This is a time when the burning bush/I AM type of worship is coming into the midst of God's people. This is going to release a deliverance call across the earth. Deliverers will rise up! Entire groups of people will begin to be delivered from the bondage and oppression that has kept them prostrate, and they will begin to stand before the Lord with great shouts of victory. This is a time of much confrontation. But when the confrontation of the enemy comes forth as a result of intimate communion and worship, we are assured victory. This is a time when we must give Judah (the tribe who led, praised and warred through worship) the freedom to experiment until we come into the sound that will bring victory into the earthly realm.

Why do I worship? To know Him and the power of His resurrection and to express my love to Him. He loved Me first and gave His Son that I might be freed from the grasp of an enemy who had me bound. Because of His giving, I must give back by expressing my devotion to Him.

For Study and Reflection
Read Psalm 121. Meditate on Psalm 119:48
and memorize Psalm 63:4.

In Heaven as It Isn't on Earth

After these things I looked, and behold, a door standing open in heaven.
REVELATION 4:1

Worship in Heaven

The Door Opens

When John the apostle was called up from the Isle of Patmos to a door that opened into heaven, he found himself in the middle of an extraordinary worship service. From the moment John went through the door, as recorded in Revelation 4, he was enveloped by the worship of the 24 elders and the 4 living beings. Then in chapter 7 a great multitude from every nation and tongue worshiped the Lord. In chapter 11 it's the 24 elders again; and in chapter 14, the 144,000 sing a new song to the Lamb. In chapter 15, those who overcame the beast took up harps and worshiped before the throne; and in chapter 19, a thunderous worship service erupts from a great multitude.

The worship service John found himself in was exuberant and noisy. Some were falling down in awestruck worship, some were crying out to the Lord from the depth of their hearts, some sang songs that weren't in the hymnal and, at times, the sound of it all was absolutely deafening. It flowed and changed, and God was in the middle of it interacting with the worshipers and bringing forth things in heaven and on earth. There were prophecies given, there was shouting, spontaneous songs erupted, war broke out. Kingdoms rose and kingdoms fell, and the service didn't end at noon so everyone could go home and watch the football game. It went on for 18 chapters, ebbing and flowing and continually changing with different participants taking up the lead: sometimes angels, sometimes elders, sometimes countless multitudes. God—in the midst of all of this—answered prayers, pronounced judgments, sent the hosts of heaven into battle, brought an end to the devil's reign and issued in the new heaven and new earth.

What a worship service! Then, just as it was about to end, the *halal* was initiated: wild celebrating with boasting and raving and general un-churchlike behavior.

> After these things I heard something like a loud voice of a great multitude in heaven, saying, "Hallelujah! Salvation and glory and power belong to our God" (Rev. 19:1-2, *NASB*).

Halal

"Hallelujah" means "Praise God!" Everybody knows that. We say "hallelujah" when we get excited in church, but we also use the word to highlight our conversations when we are with other Christians. It's what some call "Christianeze": those words or expressions we use, like "glory" and "praise the Lord," when we are at church. At work we would say, "Oh, boy" or "that's great" or maybe something a little more earthy. We have watered down the word "hallelujah" to the point that when we read Revelation 19:1-2, we tend to think it is saying, "Oh, boy! Salvation and glory and power belong to our God." It is not.

"Hallelujah" is from the Hebrew word *halal*.[1] The ancient Hebrews had several words for praise, and each of those words had their own specific meaning; but the crown jewel of them all was the word *halal*. It was used more than any other expression of praise in the Bible and was the most animated of the Hebrew words for praise. In essence *halal* means "to shine." Now this is not just a normal, everyday shininess; this means a brilliant, radiant, conspicuous shininess that can't be ignored. It literally means to make a show of celebrating with boasting and continuous, noisy, foolish-sounding raving. Well, this is not what we mean when we say "Hallelujah" in church. We just mean, "Oh, boy." When the Hebrews said *halal*, it was more of an announcement: a call for everyone to enter into that highest form of praise, making a show of celebrating with boasting and continuous, foolish-sounding, noisy raving.

All of this is hard for us to imagine. That's not what we do in church. Although *halal* was the most commonly used expression for praise for the ancient Hebrews, it is the least used expression for the modern Church, except when we want to say, "Oh, boy!" in church. Because of this we don't even have an example of *halal* that we can look to in our churches today. The best picture of *halal* we can give in our society is outside the Church in the world of sports. When we see the great victory celebrations after our championship games, we see the fans expressing excitement and abandoned exuberance: jumping, hugging and screaming. They are unashamed in their show of enthusiasm: they get loud, they get rowdy, they rave, they act foolish. They "make a show of celebrating with boasting and continuous, foolish-sounding, noisy raving." We look on and say, "Oh, how they love their team!" I believe God does too. Perhaps God wonders why His children don't show their exuberance for Him like those sports fans do for their team. The Hebrews did, and they praised with reckless abandon. The inhabitants of heaven also did. Just imagine what John describes as "something like a loud voice of a great multitude" rejoicing with all their might in the *halal*.

Although *halal* is the most commonly used Hebrew word for praise in the whole Old Testament, it is not seen until the day David built his tabernacle. David set the Levites in the tabernacle with their main function being to praise God with thanksgiving *yadah* and to *halal* (see 1 Chron. 16:4).[2] They probably looked at David and said, "What's *halal*?" David probably gave them a demonstration. What we call the book of Psalms, the Hebrews knew as the book of Praise. Our word "psalm" is not Hebrew; it comes instead from the Greek. *Halal* was not just for those who liked to worship God that way. No one said, "Well, that's not the way I relate to God." Everyone *halalled*. David *halalled* (see Ps. 35:18). The Levites *halalled* (see 1 Chron. 16:4). Throughout the book of Praise (Psalms) everyone and everything is admonished to *halal*: Jerusalem, the nations, the heavens, the earth, the sun, moon and stars and everything that has breath. Jesus even said that He *halalled*. In Matthew 27:46, Jesus quoted Psalm 22:1 by heart while He was on the cross, which suggests that He had memorized and frequently praised God according to Psalm 22:22. In heaven they *halalled* as we saw in Revelation 19. David only excused one group from this kind of praise. He said, "The dead do not *halal*" (Ps. 115:17). Today, for the most part, neither does the Church.

Water Fight

I went to school at Texas A&M University in the early 1970s. In the Corps of Cadets, I had some wild experiences, one of which was called the "water fight." These water fights were not just a few guys squirting each other with water guns or cups of water. These were semi-organized water wars, on an apocalyptic scale, involving thousands of cadets and great rivers of water. They would start with an upperclassman ordering a freshman to stand on top of his dining room table during the evening meal and shout at the top of his lungs, "Water fight!" At that announcement, thousands of cadets would leap to their feet and pour out of the dining hall and race back to their dorms. In their rooms they would grab their three-gallon metal trash can and head back out in front of their dorm. Selected crews of cadets would fill 55-gallon garbage cans with water from the shower stalls and pour the water out the windows. We would gather under those windows and fill our trash-cans under the waterfall cascading down from four stories of dorm shower rooms. Then we lined up in two opposing skirmish lines directed by upperclassmen armed with bullhorns, on the roofs of the dorms. When the command to "charge" was given, thousands of cadets would raise a war cry and hurl themselves at the opposing side with reckless abandon, loosing a tsunami of water at each other. The wall of water knocked people down and swept others off their feet.

The melee of fun and frolic continued as cadets ran back to the waterfall to refill their trashcans and enter the charge again. It was noisy, clamorous, wild, undignified, exciting and tremendously fun, just like in heaven when the roaring voice shouted out *"Halal!"* in Revelation 19. Maybe there was no water involved in the heavenly celebration, but the excitement level was certainly similar. What fun they have in heaven!

On earth, however, we seem to limit our times of *halal* to the secular side of our lives. Exuberant praise is, in fact, a normal human behavior. When we receive some long-awaited good news—Jimmy passed his algebra exam—we wave our hands in the air and shout, "Way to go, Jimmy!" When we win the football game, we high five and yell and act wild. Only in church and in the public library do we restrain ourselves. We humans have the natural tendency to get stagnant in our religion and to get our worship down into a set pattern—something manageable. We don't like surprises. When we become sedentary, our zeal cools off and we become less and less effective. Our devotion gravitates toward our liturgy (whether denominational or charismatic) instead of our living relationship with God. It's all right that the dead don't *halal*, but as for the Church, it's time.

As It Is in Heaven

As wild as heaven's worship might have seemed to John, nothing could have been seen as out of order. The elders picked up their harps and bowls together as if on cue. One elder didn't start by himself and the others just think it was a good idea to join in. When it was the right time, they moved together as one. The different groups that worshiped were ordered and together. They didn't wander around and end up having a worship time with a handful of angels, an elder and a couple of guys out of the 144,000. Each group had its own strength, its own testimony, which came forth at the right time. Each group had its time in the center stage: then at the appointed times they came together in specific combinations or, at times, as a whole. It was orchestrated. There was even correction of wrong behavior during the worship when John was overcome with awe and mistakenly fell down and worshiped an angel. No one was out of place, and order was maintained. Yet it was hardly stuffy or religious.

Even though what John saw going on in heaven was orderly, it certainly doesn't sound like what went on in most of our churches last Sunday. Yet, if there is any pattern of worship that we should be following, it should be this pattern we see in heaven. Jesus prayed, "Your kingdom come. Your will be done on earth as it is in heaven" (Matt. 6:10). What we have is "on earth as it *isn't* in heaven." The book of Revelation gives us the pattern of worship in heaven, but I have not seen any major efforts of the Church today to follow that pattern. Mark Twain poked fun at the Christians of his day because they talked about how they wanted to go to heaven but didn't seem to want to do any of the things they would be doing once they got there:

> Profoundly devout old gray-headed men put in a large part of their time dreaming of the happy day when they will lay down the cares of this life and enter into the joys of that place. Yet you can see how unreal it is to them, and how little it takes a grip upon them as being fact, for they make no practical preparations for the great change: you never see one of them with a harp, you never hear one of them sing.[3]

Are we any different? We talk about how great heaven is but we don't really consider worshiping like they do in heaven. The book of Revelation offers a window, not only into the judgments of God in the earth but also into the worship that we ourselves should aspire to. We might not be able to operate on quite the apocalyptic scale that John witnessed in heaven, but surely we can get a little closer than we are at present. Barbara Wentroble, writing on how to release God's authority on earth, says:

> In the Bible, God gives us pictures of what heaven looks like. He does not give us these pictures so that we will be homesick and always wanting to leave Earth and go to heaven. He gives us pictures of heaven so that we will know what he wants Earth to look like.[4]

I believe that the only difference there should be between our worship here on earth and the worship that is in heaven is the intensity level in heaven that will require us to be in our "heavenly bodies" in order to survive. Joseph L. Garlington believes that we would not survive the glory of the worship in heaven:

> If God gave us heavenly worship right now, we would explode! . . . I believe we couldn't handle heavenly worship because we don't have heavenly bodies yet.[5]

If the worship in heaven is the example God has given us, we should be trying to see where we are falling short of it. Jim Hodges, who heads a network of churches and ministries worldwide, says that the book of Revelation is our pattern for worship today:

> If Psalms is the Hebrew hymn and prayer book, then the Book of Revelation is the Church's worship and prayer manual![6]

If the worship in heaven is our model, then let's take a look at some of the aspects of it. I have pulled out several of these aspects of heaven's worship that I believe we need to note.

Heaven's Worship Is . . .

Heaven's Worship Is Continual

In heaven the worship never stops. John noted that the four living beings before the throne of God never rest. They never take a break. They never get bored singing, "Holy, holy, holy." They might rest if they could, but each time they come to a stopping place, they just can't stop. They see no end to God's glory. They fall down again and the worship goes on and on and on. In heaven they don't have to stop for lunch or take bathroom breaks: we do, and I don't suggest that we stop having them, but I do believe we do need to break worship out of that little time slot we have limited it to on Sunday mornings. We can worship at home, at our job or while driving in the car. We can worship together as we gather for other functions in our churches. We can have special worship nights and have early-morning prayer and worship meetings: the list goes on. Worship didn't stop in the fourth chapter of Revelation; it went on chapter after chapter. It preceded every major activity throughout the rest of the book.

Heaven's Worship Is Face to Face

One of the restrictions in Old Testament worship was the veil that separated worshipers from the presence of God. In heaven there is no veil. Nothing prevents the worshipers from coming before the unobstructed presence of Almighty God. Mortal man, however, was not able to withstand the glory of God's presence. When Moses asked to see God's face (see Exod. 33:20), God set him in the cleft of a rock and covered him with His hand while He walked past. When God had passed by, He took His hand away and Moses got to see God's back. Even then Moses' face shone so brightly from his close proximity to the Almighty that he had to cover his face when he returned to his people (see Exod. 24:29-33).

Even angels coming from the presence of God in heaven cause people to fall down as dead. When Isaiah saw his vision of God, he cried out, "I am undone." Only during the brief period of David's tabernacle were the Old Testament worshipers allowed to come before the unveiled Ark of God's presence. This was because of a special grace that we will discuss later. It was only when Jesus died on the cross that the veil was torn open, making a way for us, by His blood, to come before God's presence in worship. Now we, like the hosts of heaven, can worship God face to face even though in our earthly bodies we see "through a glass dimly." A fellow worship leader, Greg Otis, explains it this way:

> Our present times of intimacy with the Lord are a mere shadow of what they will be in our glorified bodies. After all, the marriage of the Lamb has not taken place yet. Right now we see through a glass dimly, but then face to face. I believe that where we are right now in the Song of Solomon

is where the Bridegroom gazes at us through the lattice (Song of Solomon 2:9). As awesome as our times of intimacy sometimes are, they are merely His gaze through the lattice.[7]

I believe Greg is right. We would probably not be able to survive anything more than the gaze of our Bridegroom through the lattice. Then, of course, since the marriage of the Lamb has not taken place yet, it would be improper as well as deadly.

All the same, God has drawn us into His presence by the blood of His Son that we might worship Him face to face to the full capacity our earthly bodies are capable of. Imagine, then, those that are before God's throne in heaven with nothing to diminish their gaze. Because there is no veil, nothing screens any part of God's glory from them. They are in continual awe and wonder. We on earth are enthralled by our limited glimpses of God: we cry, we laugh, we fall down, we swoon and sometimes we are incapacitated altogether. But then we get up. The service is over and we go home. In heaven, they *are* home.

Heaven's Worship Is Prophetic

Imagine the worship in Revelations 5, when the Lamb is before the throne with the seven seals. We read that they began to worship and sing, "You are worthy. . . to open its seals" (v. 8). The song was prophetic. Heaven and earth had just been searched for someone that was worthy to break the seals, and no one had been found. John had wept. Then the Lamb of God appeared before the throne and took the scroll. The four living beings and the 24 elders initiated the worship, singing prophetically that the Lamb was the one who could open the seals. What they were singing was about to happen. Thousands upon thousands of angels began to take up the cry as the worship began to swell. Then every creature in heaven and earth and under the earth joined the crescendo of worship—animals, birds and insects as well as people. The sound must have been deafening. The anointing of the prophetic revelation must have been overwhelming as it spread from the throne throughout heaven and eventually to the ends of the earth.

When prophetic songs are released in worship, they have the power to penetrate more than just the fancy of our souls to the very depth of our beings, quickening our immortal spirits. Worship becomes prophetic when it makes known the heart of God or the actions that God is about to take. In the book of Revelation, we see God continually moving through the worship to announce His intentions as well as through angels or other messengers.

Heaven's Worship Is Intercessory

In heaven the worship is mixed with intercession. When the 24 elders begin to worship in Revelation 5, they bring not only their harps, but also bowls that were filled with the intercessory prayers of the saints. As the elders worship with their harps the smoke from the bowls of incense rises up and is intermingled with the worship. This is an aspect of worship we often miss here on earth. Intercession is more than just praying for needs; it is standing in the gap. The gap is the area of difference between what God wants and what is actually happening. God looks for those who will stand in that gap and intercede:

> I looked for a man among them who would build up the wall and stand before me in the gap on behalf of the land so I would not have to destroy it, but I found none (Ezek. 22:30, *NIV*).

As worshipers, we need to avail ourselves to God to stand in that gap and intercede in our worship. Revelation 5 shows us through the example of the harp and bowl that God expects us to mix our worship with intercession that will rise up as incense before Him and move Him to action. This is something we will look at in greater detail in a later chapter.

Heaven's Worship Is Spontaneous and Dynamic

In heaven the worship is spontaneous: unplanned and directed by the Spirit of God. When the Spirit of the Lord is moving in worship there is a propensity to sing impromptu songs by His leading.

The Bible calls this a "new song." These songs are not learned ahead of time. They are prophetic, Spirit-breathed songs that reveal God's heart.

We see this in Revelation 5:9, when the Lamb is holding the scroll with the seven seals. They began to sing a "new song" before the Lord. This song sprang forth spontaneously. They didn't practice it ahead of time. It was the Spirit-breathed truth that the Lamb was worthy to break the seals. In chapter 14, we see the spontaneous new song come forth again, this time from the 144,000 singing to the Lamb on Mount Zion. The Spirit of God is revealing the song to the 144,000 alone. No one else could even learn it.

The worship in heaven is also dynamic—always changing and moving in a new direction. They don't sing the same song the same way every time. In heaven they bow down, they stand up, they shout, they sing, they celebrate and they war. Their songs were many and varied. Bob Sorge makes this comment about the varied approaches we might have in our worship:

> Some people get preoccupied with the direction of their songs: "Is the song directed to myself, to my neighbor, or to God?" Songs that speak to God are not necessarily any better or more desirable than songs that speak about him. What matters to God is that we enter into sweet communion with him, regardless of whether the song is written in the first, second, or third person.[8]

I think it is important to note that in heaven they sometimes sing to God and sometimes sing about Him. Sometimes their songs are exhortations or prophecies or proclamations, and sometimes they are songs of adoration and love. In Revelation 11:15, they do nothing but shout with loud voices; another time they stand in silence for half an hour. They sing new, spontaneous, prophetic songs as well as established songs like the Song of Moses.

Worship takes on a different look as God moves into different actions. It's not always just the elders and the living beings. Sometimes they are drowned out by the myriads of angels, while at another time it is a single angel offering his praise. Then in Revelation 7, the 144,000 sing a spontaneous new song to the Lord and are the only ones who can sing the song. Immediately after that God brings forth His praise from an uncountable multitude out of every nation and tongue. In chapter 15, it is the ones who have overcome the beast who take up the lead. In chapter 16, the angels who are pouring out the bowls of judgment praise the righteousness of the Lord. In chapter 19, a great multitude brings forth a thunderous worship celebrating the marriage of the Lamb; and in chapter 5, every created thing worships God. That's not just every living thing, but every *created* thing, like rocks and mountains. Heaven never gets in a rut.

Heaven's Worship Is Warring

"And there was war in heaven" (Rev. 12:7, *NASB*). We all know the story: Michael and his angels are warring against Lucifer and his. Even when heaven was rid of its rebellious angels the war was not over. It would continue on earth for the millenniums to come. Much of heaven's attention has been given to the war that rages on the earth, because the war is against God's authority. The worship in heaven does not stop when attention is given to the war on the earth; the worship is an integral part of the war.

God directs the war from amidst the worship. God enthrones Himself on the worship, and from that throne He exerts His authority. He sends Michael to lead the angels in battle. In the book of Daniel, we read that God sent Michael to battle the spirit over Persia so that God's messenger could get through to Daniel (see Dan. 10:13). In heaven, Jesus is not only seen as a Lamb, but He is also mounted on a white horse leading the armies of heaven. Heaven is in war until the enemies of God are completely vanquished. The worship in heaven serves God's purpose in war until it is won.

God Interacts with the Worship in Heaven

In heaven the worship is never one-sided. God interacts with the worshipers. When they sing that the Lamb is worthy to break the seals, the Lamb breaks the seals. When they sing that the accuser of the brethren is thrown down, the dragon is thrown down from heaven. Obviously they don't just sing anything they want in heaven. They sing according to what is in God's heart to do at that time. That's awesome! Don't you wish we did that in our worship? I believe we are coming into a measure of that in these days.

As the book of Revelation unfolds, we see worship continually rising up, followed by God taking action to bring forth His purposes. Once Chuck Pierce said to me, "John, you need to be singing about miracles." I said, "But miracles are not happening in our services." I felt that it would be hypocritical to sing about them if they weren't happening. Chuck said, "How will they ever start happening if you don't sing about them?" In Romans 4:17-18, Paul says, "God . . . calls those things which do not exist as though they did" (Rom. 4:17-18). When God is ready to start moving in an area, He calls us to move out in faith in that area. Faith is the evidence of things not seen. In worship, we must seek the heart of God and proclaim prophetically the things He is moving us toward. So, I started writing and singing songs about miracles. We sang in faith, and then God began to bring them forth in our church.

On Earth as It Isn't in Heaven

For the Sake of Your Tradition

Why is heaven's worship so different from our own? Our modern understanding of worship is often determined more by our society and the traditions handed down to us than by the examples we see in the Scriptures.

It's not that society and tradition are all bad; they provide the characteristics by which our different ethnos groups express themselves to God. In Revelation, we see a multitude "from every nation and all tribes and peoples and tongues" (Rev. 7:9, *NASB*) worshiping God in heaven. Although they were together as one, their different ethnicities were clearly distinguishable to John. This is important. David cries out in Psalm 22:27, "All the ends of the earth will remember and turn to the Lord, and all the families of the nations will worship before You" (*NASB*), and in Psalm 86:9,

"All nations whom You have made shall come and worship before You, O Lord" (*NASB*). God has called us to make disciples of all nations, or ethnos. Each of us should bring the uniqueness of our ethnos to God when we worship.

The problem comes when the traditions of our ethnos rather than the inheritance that God has put in us determines those expressions. If the Word of God says to worship with psalms, hymns and spiritual songs, but the tradition in our church only allows us to worship with hymns, our tradition has then supplanted the Word of God. The apostle Paul said to worship with uplifted hands and sing with your spirit as well as your understanding. But we all know the trouble some of us would get in if we did that in our church—not because we have disobeyed the Scriptures, but because we have gone against the traditions of our church. Jesus told the Pharisees, "You break the command of God for the sake of your tradition" (Matt. 15:3, *NIV*). Although we might cry out in indignation about how bad the Pharisees were, we have done the same thing in the area of worship. We have broken the commands of God for the sake of our traditions.

Our traditions have often determined who we are as a church. Even though we might come to realize that the Bible has presented us with a different model than the one we follow in worship, we feel that we just can't be unfaithful to our traditions. LaMar Boschman, a leader among today's worship leaders, describes a conference he went to several years ago in which he observed this struggle to be true to the old.

> In 1994, the North American Summit on the Future of Worship convened 29 denominations in Nashville to discuss the future of worship. I was there with Robert Webber to represent some of the nondenominational churches and ministries. I was amazed that all the participants seemed to have the same concern: How can we renew our worship and be more relevant to our society? Yet the hardest thing for most of us was to be open to change. Almost everyone thought if we change what "we do" it would compromise who "we are."[9]

Even Worse

In some places worship has fallen into even worse hands. Its purpose is merely to warm up the crowd before the speaker comes: a comforting, mellowing influence, even entertainment. The music is allowed to soothe everyone's emotions, to take their minds off of their troubles and put everyone in a good mood. This, however, was not the kind of worship we see in Revelation. Although we are certainly blessed as we worship, and our hearts are opened to receive the Word when it is preached, the objective of our worship is not to warm up the crowd or to make us feel better. It is to minister to God.

Consider then the speaker who is used to waiting in the wings until the worship is done or the people who hang in the periphery of the sanctuary—in the doorways and halls—chatting and carrying on until the "singing" is over. Imagine their surprise when they reach heaven and attempt to prattle around until the worship is over. Finally, one of them leans over to an angel and asks, "How long do these worship services usually last?" "I don't know," the angel might say. "I've never seen one end. This one started before the foundation of the earth."

That's Not My Style

The pattern of worship we see in heaven might be a little scary to us. It's much louder, more active, more prophetic and spontaneous than much of our own worship today. We are not used to warfare, especially in worship, and we are not used to putting words like "intercession" in the same sentence with worship. And if anyone entered into the *halal* during one of our worship services, we would probably call 911.

But God wants to pull us out of our comfort zone in worship, and we need to let Him. If He wants us to do something that is just not our style, we need to do it. I don't always get to do my favorite songs. Sometimes I don't feel like praising or warring. But I am willing to put aside my own preferences to lend myself to God's purposes, and I always end up extremely blessed, even more so than I would have been if I had gotten to do my own thing. We must be willing to put aside our favorite styles, our natural tendencies, our traditions and our personal wants and needs in order to enter into the fullness the Lord has for us.

Many years ago, my pastor, Robert Heidler—after years of struggling through two or three hymns (first and last verse) per service—was exposed to a lively, Spirit-filled worship service. He and his wife, Linda, were amazed at the vivacious worship around them. Their spirits were excited in the joy of worship, but their minds were wondering how they could ever participate in such a thing. That night God gave Robert a dream. He was back in Florida where he grew up, on the beach that he loved so much. Out in the water people were swimming, playing, diving and surfing. When he went out to join them he was only ankle deep in the water that others were completely immersed in. When he awoke, God told him not to settle for ankle deep when he should jump in.

Football in the Future

Football games are fun and wild and full of life and free expression, but imagine if they got "religious" like church has over the years. My pastor, Robert Heidler, gives his rendition of football in the future where the original joy of the game is gone but we feel we must keep the tradition going:

> Imagine it's the year 2537, and football has become a ritual. The fans enter the stadium in silence, making their way to the same seats they have occupied for years, listening quietly to the prelude music until the game begins. Outward expressions of emotion are not considered appropriate and fans are expected to watch the game with a proper show of respect, not disturbing the others in the stands. After a touchdown, soft music is played and the fans recite in unison the age-old adage, "Go team." After the game the coach thanks the fans for coming and urges everyone to invite their friends to come the next week because attendance has been down. A pancake breakfast is

scheduled the following week to raise money for new uniforms for the team.[10]

Heaven forbid that football should ever suffer the fate that our worship has. Heaven forbid that we should allow worship to suffer it any longer! The power and the passion and the glory and the anointing of heaven's worship can be ours if we are willing to shake off the shackles of our traditions and just "jump in," as God admonished Robert Heidler to do. God wants to enthrone Himself on the praises of His people and rule and reign from that throne.

In the next few chapters we will look at how God brought worship into the earth, how He gave David the blueprint for heaven's worship and how that worship—in David's tabernacle—became the prototype for New Testament worship. We will also look at how that prototype fell into the earth and died and how God has been raising it up over the last 2,000 years.

Ask for a Window into Heaven
Chuck D. Pierce

Don't be afraid to ask God to see! In these days ahead, we must "see beyond"! We must ask the Lord to open our eyes to the invisible world around us. We must co-labor with the hosts of heaven. We, the army of the earth, and the hosts of heaven, the angelic forces, must co-labor together to bring forth God's kingdom plan in the earth. We must worship in new ways! We must release our inhibitions and ascend in worship in new ways, until we are boldly before the Lord who created us for a time such as this.

Ask the Lord to open your eyes! Ask Him to remove veils of religion and unbelief that have captivated your heart and faith expression. Ask Him to deliver you from the trauma of past circumstances. Ask Him to break a spirit of infirmity that has attached to wounded emotions because of deferred hopes. Break any wrong judgments that you have built up in your mind against God because you did not "see" the fullness of His plan for your life in the past season!

When working in the secular field of human resources, I would journey each day through intense traffic to my office in Houston, Texas. This would entail a one-hour commute each way. I finally realized that if I had someone drive me, I would be free to read and even seek the Lord during those two hours, instead of wasting energy reaching my destination (and at times, experiencing a touch of road rage). Therefore, I found a commuter bus where I could get seated and immerse myself in communion with God.

One hot summer day, as I was having my daily Bible reading on the ride to work, the following verse leapt off the page of my Bible:

> Blessed be the God and Father of our Lord Jesus Christ, who has blessed us with every spiritual blessing in the heavenly places in Christ, just as He chose us in Him before the foundation of the world, that we should be holy and without blame before Him in love, having predestined us to adoption as sons by Jesus Christ to Himself, according to the good pleasure of His will, to the praise of the glory of His grace, by which He made us accepted in the Beloved (Eph. 1:3-6).

Suddenly, a window in heaven appeared and opened. Now, remember, I am on a bus to downtown Houston, and the heavens open and I "see beyond." I could see all the blessings of my grandfathers. I could see all of the blessings that my father had been offered. I could see how the faith of my grandmother had stored blessings in the heavens for future generations. I could see my blessings for *now* and the *future*.

The Lord then spoke and said, "*All of these blessings are yours. The blessings that were never taken by your family bloodline are still there to be released to you. The blessings I have for your children and their children are stored for future release. Look now and see your call. I have spoken these blessings to you. Now you must bring those blessings into reality by faith! Faith comes! Bring My faith that is in heaven into action in the earth!"*

The Word had unlocked the heavens for me and allowed me to see into a realm that I had never seen before. Faith filled the bus. I could not contain this faith. I actually thought the bus would turn over as the atmosphere of heaven invaded. I said to the Lord, "What do I do with this faith?" He said, *"Give it away!"* Since that time, I have warred on earth for a manifestation of all of these promises. I had seen my inheritance and received faith to possess, or occupy, what God was offering me!

Like the apostle John on the isle of Patmos, I had come up and seen beyond where I was on earth. Worship causes you to ascend and see what heaven has to offer. After seeing into God's heart and dwelling place, you have the faith to bring what is revealed into the earthly reality.

For Study and Reflection

Read Revelation 4. Meditate on Isaiah 55 and
memorize Ephesians 1:3-6.

The Power of Music

Then Cain went out from the presence of the LORD.
GENESIS 4:16

Worship on Earth

Worship and Music

When the earth was created, the worship of heaven was not immediately released into it. In heaven, worship and music were one. On earth, the two would not be joined for quite some time. It is hard for us to think of worship outside the medium of music. But LaMar Boschman tells us, "Worship is not defined as music in the Bible. Not once. However, many Christians think worship is a synonym for music."[1]

For us to better understand worship, we must see it outside the context of music. Sometimes we think we have worshiped if we have sung a slow song to God. You can sing a song without ever entering into worship, and you can enter into worship without even singing one song.

In Genesis, we see worship in its essence: communion with God. Adam and Eve communed with God in the "cool of the day" (Gen. 3:8). After the Fall, the element of sacrifice had to be added to man's worship. The blood of an innocent animal had to be shed to provide Adam and Eve with the skins with which to be covered and with blood to atone for their sin (see Gen. 3:21).

This was, of course, a foreshadowing of the sacrifice that Jesus would make once for all: His sacrifice made a way for us into the presence of God, to commune with Him. So now, sacrifice and communion defined worship. In the generations to come, God would add music, singing, dancing, celebration, prophesying, interceding, warring, and more. But the essence of worship—sacrifice and communion—would never change.

Even in the New Testament, though Jesus is our sacrificed Lamb, we are still admonished to bring a sacrifice of praise (see Heb. 13:15). And Paul tells us in his letter to the Romans, "Therefore I urge you, brethren, by the mercies of God, to present your bodies a living and holy sacrifice, acceptable to God, which is your spiritual service of worship" (Rom. 12:1, *NASB*). Jack Hayford explains that "sacrifice has always been involved at the heart of all worship of the Most High; it is the bite in worship. By bite I mean the cost."[2] If our worship does not contain the aspects of sacrifice and communion, we are just singing a slow song to God.

That's Where I Used to Worship

After Adam and Eve, the Bible shows us Cain and Abel coming before God. Obviously they knew from their parents that they needed to come with a sacrifice. Cain, however, decided he didn't want to bring an animal sacrifice as his parents had. Cain wanted to bring a sacrifice that did not require the shedding of blood. He felt his sacrifice of garden produce should be just as good. Here we see the beginning of a contention that has not abated throughout history: the issue of how to worship. Today it has become one of the greatest contentions among the people of the earth, permeating politics, social life, music and world affairs. Where two or more are gathered it seems that a disagreement over worship will eventually ensue.

Sometimes it doesn't even take two or more to have a disagreement. There is a story of the man who was rescued from a desert island. The man was a builder and had spent his years on the island building different structures. By the time he was rescued he had built a complete village. His rescuers looked around them in awe as the man pointed out the different buildings he had constructed: "That's my house, that's the general store and that building with the tall steeple is where I go to church." One of the

rescuers noticed another building on the other side of the village
with a similar tall steeple, and asked, "What about that building
over there?" The man frowned and finally replied, "That's where I
used to go to church."

Go Yonder and Worship
Worship is first mentioned in Genesis 22:5, in the story of Abraham and Isaac. Through Abraham, God would show the true nature of worship, once again apart from music. Abraham took Isaac
to the mountain and said to his servant, "Stay here with the donkey; the lad and I will go yonder and worship." We all know the
story and we know that Abraham was not intending to go up with
Isaac and do anything that we would associate with worship. Abraham took no worship team, not even a CD player. How would he
worship? What Abraham was intending to do was offer to God the
most precious thing in his life—his son Isaac.

By this, God demonstrates to us once again the essence of worship—sacrifice and communion. While we have perfected the musical part of worship, we sometimes have lost the "essence" of it.
Some might say, "But Abraham was Old Testament, we are New."
David was also Old Testament, but he understood the heart of the
matter: it was not the sacrificed animals that pleased God, but a
broken and contrite spirit (see Ps. 51:17). The sacrifice is in the
heart. Abraham's son was not what God was after; He was after
Abraham's heart. God, through Abraham, gives us a picture of the
real meaning of worship before He allows music to be joined with
it. God also lets us see that music alone is not what He is after, but
our hearts. Music can stir the realm of our soul, but worship
comes from our broken and contrite spirit.

Enter Music

Music Makes Its Earthly Debut
When music first came to earth it had quite a bumpy landing.
From eternity past music had been the exclusive possession of
heaven. There, it was not used for many of the purposes we have

seen it used for here on earth: Its sole function had been to facilitate worship. Worship is music's highest purpose, and until the earth was created music had never been used for anything else. Now, as it made its entry into the earth, it would face the fancy of man's discretion. The father of music on earth was Jubal (see Gen. 4:21). Jubal was a descendant of Cain who, as you remember, had his own ideas about worship. Because of this, Cain killed his brother, Abel, and was forced to go "out from the presence of the LORD" (Gen. 4:16). Music, then, made its entry on earth "out from the presence of God" and remained in that estranged state for generations before God began to bring it back to the purpose for which it was created—worship.

The Power of Music

Music is a powerful medium whether used "out from the presence of God" or under the presence of God. Richard C. Leonard observed, "Music has a powerful effect on human experience. Students of religious phenomena have long recognized that music transcends our understanding and appeals to our intuitive nature."[3]

Music makes us laugh or cry or dance or swoon. It causes us to reminisce or peer into the future. It stirs us to fight and go to war. One of the deadliest weapons of warfare on the earth is the bagpipe. To its music men have marched, against all odds, into hails of bullets or thickets of swords. Music also soothes the savage beast. Music consoles us when we are down or empowers us when we are driven. Music can disable our resistance or fortify our convictions. It can carry us to the heights or depths of our emotions. Martin Luther said:

> Next to the Word of God, music deserves the highest praise. She is a mistress and governess of those human emotions . . . which control men or more often overwhelm them . . . Whether you wish to comfort the sad, to subdue frivolity, to encourage the despairing, to humble the proud, to calm the passionate, or to appease those full of hate . . . what more effective means than music could you find?[4]

What's Love Got to Do with It?

Music tears down resistance and inhibition and enables its message to penetrate the deepest recesses of the human heart. It has been said that music will be sitting on the living room couch while preaching is still knocking on the front door. You get the picture. A person who is dead set against the gospel might interestingly enough find his heart being touched by a gospel song. The mental barriers might melt away with the music and the heart open up to the wooing of the Spirit of God.

But it works the other way as well. Do you ever catch yourself singing some catchy phrase of song, the message of which you don't agree with or even understand? But there you are humming that tune or singing that phrase that got stuck in your mind. In the music industry that catchy part of a song you end up humming or singing is called the "hook." The hook is something that repeats or is catchy enough to make you want to repeat it. It stands out in a song, drawing you into it. Songwriters look for the hook that will make people come back to their music, singing it over and over again. If someone tried to convince you of the message of the song, you would say, "Oh, I don't believe that message, and I am totally against it." But there you are raking the leaves in your backyard, bouncing your head and maybe dancing around a little bit, singing, "What's love got to do, got to do with it." Your better judgment was dismantled by the song. That's the power of music.

Peter, Paul and Mary

Peter Yarrow, of Peter, Paul and Mary fame, while a student at Cornell University, in the late fifties, led a folk music sing-along for the students on Saturday mornings. Peter saw the power that music had to break down barriers among the students and open them up to the messages of the songs. Later in his life he commented on that experience: "In a very innocent way, the simple act of singing a song cut through the logical preconceptions, and went straight for their hearts."[5] Peter went on to say that it was this realization that caused him to pursue a career of "reaching people's hearts through music."[6]

Everyone knows the rest of the story. The music of Peter, Paul and Mary and others like them set fire to our nation during the turbulent years of the Civil Rights movement in the sixties. People who had rejected the message of that movement and locked their front door to its insistent knocking found themselves sitting on their living room couches singing the catchy songs of that movement: "Blowing in the Wind," "If I Had a Hammer," and many more. The music had disabled their defenses and doctrines.

God can use music to sweep away people's fears and doubts and open their hearts to His truth, bringing them into the intimate communion of worship. You can also see the ability the former worship leader of heaven, Satan, has in music to stir the baser instincts of fallen man and lure people into behavior they wouldn't otherwise engage in. The decision is always in the realm of our soul, which chooses between our flesh and our spirit.

Worship in the Grip of Music

The Great Escape

The thing we have to be aware of in our worship is that music has a power all its own that we must not fall prey to. The Lord taught me a valuable lesson early in my Christian walk. It was the early seventies, when many charismatics dutifully went to their denominational churches on Sunday morning but during the week found homes to gather in for some prayer and worship. I was one of those charismatics, and each Sunday I almost died trying to endure the service at my church. But I loved the informal Spirit-led get-togethers many of us enjoyed at our choir leader's home during the week. These meetings were my refuge in a trying world as we gathered to pray and sing and fellowship.

One night during one of our midweek meetings, God spoke to my heart that I was merely using these gatherings as an escape. An escape whisks you away from reality so that you don't have to deal with your real-life situations. It was not the power of worship that I was entering into but the power of music to ease my frustrations. The music touches our soul and soothes our emotions, and we escape into that warm fuzzy place. It all seems so spiritual. We sing the Christian words, we feel so close to Jesus, we can almost feel Him stroking our hair and saying, "There, there, everything will be all right." But when the music stops, we go home and nothing has changed in our lives: we have the same problems, the same weaknesses and the same attitudes. There was no sacrifice in our worship. We have not really come before the Lord in faith and trusted Him to show us our way of deliverance. We have just escaped into the comforting power of music.

As for me, instead of touching God, I was touching a picture of God I had built up in my mind. What the Lord showed me specifically that night was that I was just "crying in my beer," trying to do with Him what I had done in college with booze before I got saved. Back then I had looked forward to the weekends when I could escape from the pressures of school and the troubles of life and get drunk with the guys. My escapes were short-lived though. In the morning, when I woke up, my troubles and pressures were there again.

But now I was a Christian. I truly loved the Lord, and I truly thought I was worshiping Him. The problem, however, was that I was not coming to sacrifice and commune; I was coming to escape. Because of this there was no reality in my worship. There was no revelation of the God who is the answer to all of my problems, who is my deliverer, who has a way of escape for me and a way to victory. I like Robert Gay's understanding of this revelation of God we need in our worship:

There is a difference between celebrating and having a revelation of your celebration. Praise and celebration without a revelation of its power have little effect in the realm of the spirit. Let me give you an example. We could take a drunken man off the street and bring him into the church. This man could say the sinner's prayer simply by repeating what he was told. But if there was not first a revelation of the lordship of Jesus and the fact that God raised Jesus from the dead, that man would go away just as unsaved as he was before he said the sinner's prayer. Why? Because he said words without understanding and revelation. Unfortunately, much of the church is like that. We come to church and praise the Lord with no understanding and revelation of the power God has put in our praise. Consequently, nothing happens.[7]

That revelation that Robert talks about comes from our communion with God. That communion comes when we come before Him with a sacrifice of praise. "He who comes to God must believe that He is, and that He is a rewarder of those who diligently seek Him" (Heb. 11:6). We must come to Him believing that He is our deliverer, our salvation and the one who is the answer to all of our problems.

When God reproved me that night at our midweek gathering, it changed my whole understanding of worship. After that I came to Him not to escape but to acknowledge Him and praise Him in the midst of my difficulties and trust Him for all my needs. As I praised Him, God began to give me my strategies for victory while I was in His presence. Without understanding worship apart from music, we can fall into the trap of letting music become our escape from reality instead of our aid for expressing our hearts to God.

No one in the Bible ever came away from a face-to-face encounter with God without being changed, and that's what our worship should be: a face-to-face encounter with God from which we come away changed. The problem is that our worship often does not involve presenting ourselves as a living sacrifice to the Lord. Escape does not require sacrifice. Instead of true worship we have only imagined ourselves in "the chamber" with the Lord pouring out His sympathy on us because of the difficulties we have experienced. We have merely been "crying in our beer." LaMar Boschman explains this problem that exists in his description of some of our contemporary Christian worship:

It speaks in the voice of our time and it represents a powerful penetration of the global culture. However, it is also a reflection and celebration of who we are and not of who God is. We're simply looking at ourselves in the mirror. The result is narcissism.[8]

Narcissism is the undue dwelling on our own self. The word "narcissism" is derived from the Greek myth of Narcissus who fell in love with his own reflection in the water and ended up wasting away as he gazed at himself. Worship, when it ends up being more us-centered than God-centered, is nothing more than narcissism: It is merely music with Christian words that we use to escape into our imagined "chamber" with our own picture of Jesus stroking our hair and saying, "There, there, child, everything will be all right." Instead of coming out from the presence of the Lord, saying like Paul, "I can do all things through Him who strengthens me" (Phil 4:13, *NASB*), we waste away in our self-pity and go back home unchanged, as I did in the seventies.

Does God Really Need All that Praise?

The red flag for me is when I hear people say, "I don't like all that praise. I just like to worship." What they are saying is that they don't want to expend the effort it takes to praise. They are not in the mood. It is not a part of their personality. They are more laid back and mellow. In other words, it would be a sacrifice for them to do such a thing. Praise is indeed often a sacrifice. That's why God calls for it and requires it of us. So is God some sort of egomaniac who has to be praised all the time? Bob Sorge says:

> No, it is not that God needs our praise, but he knows that we need to praise him! Ultimately, praise does not benefit God (he is God, whether we choose to praise him or not)—God has commanded praise for our own good. Not until we praise him are we able to come into proper relationship with him. Without a thankful and praising heart, we will never grow in the grace of Christ Jesus.[9]

When we praise, it changes our entire atmosphere. If it was cloudy before, the sun soon comes out in us. Praise determines our perspective: God gets bigger and our problem gets smaller in comparison. Our faith rises; our determination grows. We make a habitation for God in our hearts (*navah*). We offer a sacrifice of praise, lifting our hands in thanksgiving (*towdah*). We begin to remember all the things God has done for us and throw our hands up, thanking Him for every single incident (*yadah*). We begin to speak out the magnificent qualities of our God and tell of His mighty exploits (*tehillah*), and then we start to get really loud (*shabach*). Our passion rises up and we begin to rave and boast and celebrate (*halal*). All this we do with singing and music (*zamar*). Now we are confident in our God. We are full of faith. We have the high praises of God in our mouth and a two-edged sword in our hand, and we are ready to do whatever God wants and to face any force that opposes us.

Singing Like We Are on Valium

David said to bring your sacrifice of praise before the Lord. This takes an effort, sometimes a tremendous struggle for our flesh. We don't feel like praising; we'd just like to slip into some easy music and imagine the Lord stroking our hair.

Praise, however, is the very thing that clears away the obstacles that keep us from that true "inner chamber" and sincere worship. Praise is what redefines our perspective in the midst of adverse circumstances. Praise is what breaks us through to the presence of God. Jim Hodges, from the Federation of Ministries and Churches, says:

> We are singing too many non-breakthrough songs. We are singing like we are on valium. *May the Lord help us to break out of our introspective, pietistic, and private focus in our corporate worship services!*[10]

Although music is a powerful aid, we should be able to praise God with or without it. I remember a worship service I once attended. I had looked forward to it all week. I always enjoyed the worship services at this church. I got there early to get a good seat, and while I was sitting there waiting for everything to begin, the Lord spoke to my heart, "Praise Me." I said, "Lord, that's what I came here for. I'm just waiting for the music to begin." The Lord said, "Praise Me now." I was taken aback, but I stood up and raised my hands and began to praise the Lord—no music, no projected lyrics, no warm fuzzy feelings—just the stark reality of my heart of love to my God. When I did, the heavens opened and God flooded my heart. When the worship team got there they had to catch up with me. Bob Sorge says:

> Those of us who use musical instruments in praise must be careful not to become too dependent upon those instruments so that when the music stops, the praise and worship immediately cease! Our praise should ascend to God even when no instruments are readily available.[11]

The Lights Go Out in Texas

The technology of our age has greatly aided us in our worship, but that same technology can cripple us if we allow ourselves to become dependent on it. Recently, I was leading worship for a conference in our church. As I opened my mouth to sing the first word of the first song, the power went out: the lights went out, the sound system went down and we all gasped together in darkness. The power grid for the whole area had gone down. We were without technology. When I gathered my senses I looked out over the shadows of the hushed crowd and began to sing "All Hail the Power of Jesus' Name." Immediately the saints joined in singing a deafening a capella. This continued for an hour as we pressed into God in intercession and worship. God began to reveal the source of the darkness and the strategy to come against it. In one hour to the minute the power came back on and we cheered and celebrated before the Lord. It was the best worship service of the whole conference. The lack of technology had spurred the hearts of true worshipers into an even higher level of worship.

The "Wow" Factor

The world seeks experiences. We seek the Lord. If a technology failure wrecks our worship, then it was not really worship; it was just warm fuzzy feelings. If there is no sacrifice in our worship, then it is only an "experience" that we are after.

In these days of ever-advancing technology, we can easily find ourselves seeking more and more things to enhance our experience: lighting, visual effects, sounds—all of which thrill and excite our soul but do not quicken our spirit. LaMar Boschman, in his book *Future Worship,* makes a pertinent statement about this:

> When feelings become the purpose and goal of worship, emotional stimuli and external aids will be used to reach that goal. . . . When our desire and intent are simply to attain good feelings, we lose the reality and purpose of worship. Our worship then becomes humanistic and is a mere by-product of electronic manipulation.[12]

I am not against technology. I need all of it I can get, but my real thrill is when God touches my heart. My spirit jumps. No amount of sensory stimulation can compare with that. I was surprised recently when I read this in a Christian magazine:

> The use of pyrotechnics during worship services and programs has been gaining in popularity in the last 10 years. Increasing the "wow" factor of worship services and youth programs, and increasing attendance therefore continues to be a motivation factor when deciding to incorporate pyrotechnics.[13]

As beneficial as technology can be for us, it can also become a substitute for the manifestations of the Holy Spirit. Our worship then becomes just an emotional experience. Pastor Bob Rognlien gives this warning: "One of the pitfalls of technology in worship is losing sight of the fact that worship is first and foremost a human experience with God."[14]

The Early Church faced somewhat the same problem as it was accepted into the Roman Empire in the fourth century. The Romans didn't have electronics. Their "wow" factor was in their grand buildings and majestic rituals for worship. Christian historian Phillip Schaff says:

> The public worship of God assumed, if we may so speak, a dramatic, theatrical character, which made it attractive and imposing to the mass of the people, who were as yet incapable, for the most part, of worshiping God in spirit and in truth. It was addressed rather to the eye and the ear, to feeling and imagination, than to intelligence and will.[15]

The Reality of God

In the Scriptures, people were not affected by electronics or grand buildings. Their "wow" factor was God Himself. When they came face to face with Him they were swept off their feet. They were smitten by the reality of God. They couldn't help but fall down and worship. Chuck Pierce sums it up in this short statement: "Worship occurs when the reality of God manifests."[16]

It's as simple as that. The people of the Bible didn't analyze the facts and determine the best course of action. They responded to the reality of God. Ernest B. Gentile puts it this way:

> Christian worship depends on God revealing himself through the Lord Jesus Christ to man. Man simply responds to the revelation. Man cannot initiate suitable worship. He cannot fully comprehend his own inner workings, let alone the wonder of God.[17]

Who can behold the Lord without falling down to worship Him? Here is where music plays its part. It removes our barriers: the walls we put up to shield ourselves. What we often end up doing is shielding ourselves from God. As music dissolves these barriers we come face to face with Him: our spirits broken and contrite, our sacrifice to God. Music then can be an aid to express our love to God and enter that sweet communion with Him.

In heaven they didn't have to be taught the difference between worship and music because in heaven there is only "spirit." In heaven music cannot incite the baser nature of the soul. On earth we need to understand the difference between music and worship because down here our spirit and our soul war within each of us. Even though we would not intend to use music for evil, still we need to discern between soothing our soul and quickening our spirit. Without the aspect of sacrifice in our worship we are only soothing our soul. Music alone can do that.

Worship, however, brings us face to face with God in communion, and no one can see God and live. Some part of our flesh must die and some part of our spirit must increase when we worship before our God. Jack Hayford describes God's outlook toward our worship like this: "He is not looking for something brilliant but something broken."[18]

Like Abraham showed us, our worship is not dependent on music or the wow factors we have added to it over the centuries. It doesn't have to be brilliant, but it does need to be broken, like Abraham's was when he came to offer to God what he valued the most, his precious son.

Music is a wonderful medium that God has given us to disable our inhibitions and loose the depths of our spirit to Him in worship. Although music had a bumpy landing on earth and worship had its small beginning, God intended, in the fullness of time, to bring the very worship of heaven down to His small planet. The place where God intended to bring heaven's worship was a little hill in Judah on the border of Benjamin. This small mountain had been prepared ahead of time, and for centuries it had waited for its day.

You Will Sing the Sounds of Heaven
Chuck D. Pierce

My life is filled with music. My family loves music. We go to plays, concerts and all kinds of musical performances. We attend jazz festivals and outdoor music gatherings. We watch musicals. All of my children are musical. For some, music seems to be their goal. Sound and music play a great part of our lives. The people I minister with are musical. If they are not gifted musicians, they are worshipers. In heaven, worship and musical sound are one.

Wherever I minister, music and sound set the stage for the release of God's will into the place I have been called. Recently, I had a team ministering in Paris. Key leaders and influencers from the city were with us. In my heart I had this desire arise to go through the city and *sow joy*. During our worship, I kept hearing the Holy Spirit saying, *"The sound of joy is in you!"* He kept saying this over and over again. Then He showed me that we, the people of God, must release the sound of joy! No matter what our natural circumstances or situations dictate, and no matter what we feel physically, we have a sound of joy to release. We must employ the law of sowing and reaping, and sow from the joy in us, which is a fruit of the Holy Spirit. As we release the sound of joy from the earth, He releases His joy from heaven: "In Your presence is fullness of joy; at Your right are pleasures forevermore" (Ps. 16:11). That joy becomes our strength to produce supernatural victory! I knew that I could find the sound in heaven that would produce joy in the people of Paris as I ministered and visited the city.

Heaven is filled with sound, because heaven is filled with worship. When we enter the throne room and come boldly before the Lord, we have access to the same worship sounds of heaven. We also have access to the same emotion of heaven. Sound creates movement. Worship, sound and music are important. Your conscience is like a window between your soul and spirit. Make sure nothing is clouding your conscience. Sound that leads you into movement and worship will cause your conscience to remain in alignment with God. The conscience is one of the absolute authorities of our life. When our conscience is aligned and interacting with the Word of God, the "window" remains clean and open. The conscience is the lamp of the body. The conscience is the eye of our spirit that causes us to see into the heavenly realms. Clean and open your window and receive the sound of the Lord! Let the wind of the Spirit bring the sound that you need through the window of heaven and into the place where you are standing.

"Weeping may last for the night, but a shout of joy comes in the morning" (Ps. 30:5, *NASB*). Unshakable praise must keep going forth in your life. Unshakable praise plows through the hardest ground. When the ground is hard, when the circumstances are adverse, God's favor is on the one who will praise. Fallow ground will break up. Declare the plow of praise that will cut through the ungiving earth and make a way for the good seed of the Word to be planted. The Word of God tells us to submit ourselves to God, to draw near to Him and then resist the devil. I believe that as we worship and submit ourselves to a holy God, we can come into intimate contact with Him. Even though we walk here on the earth in our worshipful submission, at the same time, we ascend into heaven. As we individually seek God and ascend into the throne room, we can hear the sound of heaven in our spirit man on earth.

Recently, in a worship service, LeAnn Squier, an amazing musician and psalmist, began to prophesy. I began to hear and release revelation along with her. The Spirit of God began to speak to us the following:

> *I am creating a unique identity in My people. Even in searching for the sound of your sound, your identity is found in the unique sound within you. I am removing from you the noise of the world's confusion. This noise has made you something that I never intended you to become.*
>
> *I am going to begin to pour such a pure stream of sound from heaven around you that you will hear who you are to become. You won't sound like any other individual, and the place on earth where I have positioned you will not sound like any other location. You are in My time, so you will not sound like another day, century or decade. You will have a sound for now. You will have an identity that is so unique, that is so unmistakable. There are ten thousand of ten thousands of voices that are going to begin to join with your sound. This sound will be poured from heaven but then rise back from the earth.*

I am tipping My golden chalice from My heavenly palace and disseminating and depositing thousands and thousands of songs and sounds in you, the sanctuary of your dwelling and the land around you. You will birth words that express and sounds that impart and deliver the voice of what I have done and what I am doing to the societal culture around you. This will not be a sound that has one local expression but will be linked together with harmonies of others around the world. This sound will produce a joy in the lands of the earth.

There is a voice. The sound of My voice is going to come in an unmistakable clarity. Begin to look for the new expression. Begin to look for the new words. Begin to look for the new sounds that are going to accurately express the sound of this pouring out of this drink offering that I am delivering. I am giving assignments! Some will sing! Some will orchestrate! Some will create the movement of dance to the sound. You will bind the enemy in chains and break the back of principalities that are controlling and resisting the movement of My Spirit in the earth. I am reordering your day with sound and the music of heaven. This day will not sound like or look like any other day.

For Study and Reflection
Read Revelation 5. Meditate on Psalm 149 and memorize Matthew 6:21-23 (*AMP*).

Bringing in the Ark

He raised up David to be their king; of him He bore witness and said,
I have found David son of Jesse a man after My own heart, who will do all
My will and carry out My program fully.
ACTS 13:22, *AMP*

Carrying Out God's Plan

After God's Heart

It was Paul who spoke these words to the Jews in the synagogue at
Pisidian Antioch. I like what Charles Swindoll has to say about
Paul's words:

> What an epitaph! Not, "I found David to be a great war-
> rior," or "I found David to be a faithful shepherd," or "I
> found David to be a brilliant king"—none of those things.
> It says, "I found David to care about the things I care
> about. He's a man whose heart beats in sync with Mine.
> When I look to the right, David looks to the right. When
> I look to the left, David looks to the left. And when I say,
> 'I care about that,' David says, 'I care about that, too.'"
> That's being a man, a person, after God's heart.[1]

The Unseen Root

We can see then that the unusual things David did were not just
the workings of an incredibly creative mind; David was carrying
out God's heart, "God's programs fully." He was acting in accor-
dance with God's will and was fulfilling what was in God's heart.

There are several things about David that were unique because of his call to carry out this program of God's. First, David was singly noted in the Scripture as having Jesus as his root (see Rev. 22:16)—that unseen, underground part of David from which he drew his "sap." No other person in the Bible is noted as having Jesus as his root. David's purpose on earth was more than just to bring revival or deliver Israel again; it was to unveil a heretofore-unknown aspect of heaven: worship.

The Keys of David

Another unique thing about David was that he was the sole owner of a set of keys. There is no mention of these keys in the chronicles of David's life. We don't see these keys until God gives them to a man named Eliakim in Isaiah 22:20-22. The capability of these keys was to open things that no one will shut and to shut things that no one will open. The keys were specifically called "The keys of David." Even though they were given to Eliakim to use, they were not Eliakim's keys; they were David's. What David unlocked that no one could lock was the worship of heaven released into his tabernacle. When the days of David's tabernacle were finished, this same worship was locked back in the heavens for 1,000 years until it was released again on the New Testament saints with the promise that God was raising up again the tabernacle of David.

Although certain aspects of the worship in David's tabernacle were carried over into Solomon's temple, the fullness of it was not. Even those certain aspects of worship did not last long in the temple. They were revived under different kings throughout Israel's history, but by the time Christ was born there was nothing left but dead rituals. When Jesus appeared to John on Patmos, He proclaimed that He had the Keys of David with Him (see Rev. 3:7). I believe that Jesus was signifying that what David had opened with those keys we would be opening in the Church Age.

The Priesthood of Melchizedek

David was also unique in his understanding of the priesthood of Melchizedek. This order is explained in Hebrews 5–7. Melchizedek, a contemporary of Abraham, was both the king of the ancient city of Salem and the priest of the Most High God (see Heb. 7:1). The mysterious Melchizedek had no beginning or end; he was an eternal being, a type of Christ (see Heb. 7:3) whom God set up as a king/priest in Salem, the very place that was later called Mount Zion where David set up his tabernacle. Jesus was the "Root and the Offspring of David" (Rev. 22:16, *NIV*) and went before David—in type as Melchizedek—to pave the way as king/priest on the site where the tabernacle would later be raised (see Ps. 76:1-2). After Abraham's encounter with Melchizedek, recorded in Genesis, no one in the entire Old Testament even makes reference to the old king/priest except for David. No one but David needed a revelation about Melchizedek in his or her Old Testament paradigm. But David, in order to prototype a New Testament paradigm, had to understand how to operate as a king and priest at the same time, and he cries out in Psalm 110 his revelation that the coming Messiah would be a priest according to the order of Melchizedek.

Mount Zion
Also unique was David's drive to possess Mt. Zion as his capital. No other Israelite in their history had cared enough for the site to permanently secure it. Although everyone probably thought Hebron was a fine capital city, David alone knew that he would not be able to "carry out God's plan fully" in Hebron. Because David was a man after God's own heart, he knew that he must acquire Melchizedek's old hill. That hill was one of the places the Children of Israel had never been able to permanently possess over their centuries in the Promised Land. But when God was ready for it, David was able to take the hill against all odds.

Nobody Else
When we put all these "uniques" together, the picture is staggering. Nobody else but David was noted as a man after God's own heart. Nobody else but David had Jesus as his unseen root. After Abraham's visit with Melchizedek, nobody else but David in the Old Testament expressed an understanding of Melchizedek or

walked in that king/priest order. It was not lawful for Old Testament saints to walk in that priestly order except for David. Nobody else was chosen to carry out God's plan fully and nobody else had the special keys to accomplish those plans. From all of this we see that David was more than just a great guy and a wonderful king and the sweet psalmist of Israel. He was brought on the scene at this time in history to accomplish God's purpose in bringing the very worship of heaven down to earth.

The Back Door to Success

Of Whom Much Is Given Much Is Required

Although David was a man after God's own heart, he was not perfect. Much was given him—he was given the responsibility of carrying out God's plan—and much was going to be required of him as well. David had a burning desire to find a place to house the Ark, but God's plan was greater than just a suitable place for the Ark to dwell. So as David set out with the best of intentions concerning the Ark, it was inevitable that God would have to break into those plans to bring forth His greater purpose: " 'Let us bring the ark of our God back to us, for we did not inquire of it during the reign of Saul.' The whole assembly agreed to do this, because it seemed right to all the people" (1 Chron. 13:3-4, *NIV*).

With great joy David brought the people together to bring in the Ark, which had been neglected for so many years. They celebrated with all their might. They brought their trumpets, their harps and their tambourines. It was a happy day. But, alas, tragedy struck. Oxen upset the cart on which the Ark was carried, and the Ark almost fell off. When Uzzah reached out his hand to steady the Ark, God struck him. The tragedy about Uzzah's death was that he never knew the danger he was in. And, though no one realized it at this point, the responsibility lay with David. Caz Taylor says:

> Though they danced, sang and played instruments with great joy during the first attempt at bringing the Ark to Zion, the priests had not been properly sanctified, assigned

or instructed about their duties. David didn't make it clear to them exactly what their responsibility was in this due order. In fact, he was only learning of it himself.[2]

The Ark came with very specific instructions and warnings, and David should have known them. He was in charge. The Ark was not to be transported on an oxcart in the first place. It was only to be carried on the shoulders of consecrated Levites. If it had never been put on the oxcart, it never would have been in danger of falling off. David was in a new level of responsibility now. "To whom much is given, from him much will be required" (Luke 12:48, *NKJV*). David was coming to a new level: even though his relationship with God was more awesome than anyone else's on earth, it was not enough now. That which was great for yesterday was not going to make it for today. When we are young in the Lord, He sometimes lets us get away with things that, as we mature, He does not. A toddler in the throne room of a great king might be allowed some liberties that the established court officers are not.

Good Intentions

Although the journey ended in tragedy, David was not doing something particularly bad by attempting to bring the Ark to Jerusalem. It had seemed a good idea to everyone, and it was. It would have been bad if David had neglected the Ark and left it in a place where it was not accomplishing the purpose for which it was given. The issue here was not about doing something good or bad. The issue was that God had a plan that was beyond David's good intentions.

Sometimes our good intentions get in the way of God's plan. Adam and Eve had good intentions when they determined to cover their nakedness with leaves they had sewn together. But God knew that mere leaves could never cover the shame of their fall. They had eaten from the tree of the knowledge of good and evil, and though they had chosen the good over the evil, there was another tree in the garden, which God took back up into heaven. It was the tree of life.

This life is beyond the knowledge of good and evil, and it is only in God. When we do no more than choose "good" over evil, we sometimes miss the "life" that God has for us. Adam and Eve could only come up with that which was good, but God's plan of life foreshadowed the redemption of Christ's blood by shedding the innocent blood of an animal and using its skin to replace the leaves. David had chosen the good, but in the process had run up against God's plan. God's plan was not just to upgrade his living quarters but also to bring the worship of heaven down to earth.

The New Cart

There was nothing disrespectful about using the oxcart to transport the Ark. Israel was an agrarian society, and an oxcart was a valuable asset. And this one was a *new* cart: very likely the equivalent of a stretch limo in our present day. I'm sure that many folks along the roadside looked longingly at that nice new cart. Whispers began to arise: "*Aw-baw` naw raw-aw` ag-aw-law`, em!*" (translation: "Would you look at that new cart, Ma!"). But whether or not the Ark was being transported on a classy vehicle was not the issue. The cart was a good thing, but it was not God's method. God had said the Ark could only be carried on the shoulders of consecrated Levites. It was the heart that God was after. His presence would be transported on nothing less than dedicated hearts. Good intentions or not, the consequences for doing otherwise were lethal.

Lest Ye Die

In the fourth chapter of Numbers, God gave explicit directions on how to move the Ark. Three times in these instructions He gave the warning to do things a certain way "lest they die." We see similar warnings today in dangerous places: Don't touch the electrical wires, lest you die; don't hang over the railing, lest you die. We expect our government officials to post these warnings for us. They are responsible. But no such warning was made known about the Ark, and soon enough disaster struck. "When they came to the threshing floor of Kidon, Uzzah reached out his hand to steady the ark, because the oxen stumbled. The LORD's anger burned against

Uzzah, and he struck him down because he had put his hand on the ark. So he died there before God" (1 Chron. 13:9-10, *NIV*).

We all understand if someone gets hurt when he disregards the warnings about dangerous electrical wires or something similar. He was warned. He chose to take a chance and test the laws of nature, and suffered the consequences. What we need to understand is that all true laws are God's whether we find them in nature or in Scripture. Some people get mad at God when they read of Uzzah's fate. Even David did. Why did God take such drastic measures against this man when he was only trying to keep the Ark from falling off the cart? We need to see that Uzzah's death from violating a scriptural law was no different than someone suffering the consequences of defying the natural law of gravity by jumping off a cliff. The laws that God lays down in the Scriptures are just as sure as the ones He lays down in nature, and the consequences are just as certain.

David, however, didn't know all that he was responsible for; so when Uzzah was struck dead, David got mad. David had held a celebration for God, and God had ruined it: right there in front of the whole nation. But then David, more wisely, became afraid. Then he fell into depression. "How can I ever bring the ark of God to me?" (1 Chron. 13:12, *NIV*). He thought he understood God, but he didn't understand this. It was all very confusing.

Get Over It

David's bubble was burst. It was a very difficult time for him. But David had weathered difficult times before. He had been anointed king of Israel and then been sent back to tend his father's sheep. He had defeated Goliath and had become a military leader, then found himself running for his life. In his exile, raiders burned his city and carried off his family. In all these things and more David found a place of victory. All of us will have to get past our "bubble" if we want to go on with God. The state of our "bubble" does not affect the progress of God's kingdom. The plans of God do not stop when we get disappointed or embarrassed or upset or confused. We get embarrassed and think the Spirit is quenched.

Actually, the Spirit might be doing just fine. All that got quenched was just our flesh, which is at war with the Spirit anyway.

Read the Fine Print

When Moses got his commission and took off back to Egypt, who do you suppose stopped him along the way? It wasn't the devil; it was God:

> At a lodging place on the way, the LORD met Moses and was about to kill him. But Zipporah took a flint knife, cut off her son's foreskin and touched Moses' feet with it. "Surely you are a bridegroom of blood to me," she said. So the LORD let him alone (Exod. 4:24-26, *NIV*).

Moses, like David, had not read the fine print. Anytime you are in a big-time contract situation, you need to read the fine print. Moses should have circumcised his son as a sign of covenant connection with God. The covenant is for our protection, just like a contract. His son was unprotected, and Moses was about to go in with a stick and take several million slaves away from the strongest military power on earth. We need to know the Word of God. As the magnitude of our ministry increases, we desperately need to know the Word and stand on it. And we can't let our little disappointments get in our way. Deal with them and go on. David parked the Ark and began to deal with his disappointment.

The Oxcart that Couldn't

When David brought the Ark in the first time, all he knew was that he wanted to honor God and provide a place for the Ark of His presence. If God had let David succeed in his own strength and understanding, it probably would have still been the best thing Israel had ever seen. They would have had great worship. They would have had wonderful celebration. They would have had dedicated ministers. God, however, was after something more than just "the best thing Israel had ever seen." God was bringing a portion of heaven down to His little planet. Man would taste worship as it was in heaven and as it would be in the dispensation of the New Testament to come.

The oxcart could not accomplish the glory that God intended. So David had the Ark put in the home of Obed-Edom while he recovered and reevaluated his situation. The next three months proved to be very significant.

WORSHIP THAT RESETS OUR DESTINY CLOCK
CHUCK D. PIERCE

Have you ever made a mistake, or tried to do a thing in your flesh or at the wrong time? Have you ever known the will of God but not listened for His way to accomplish His will? I think we all have done this at one time or another. When we make a wrong move, get trapped by falling to a temptation of the enemy, ignorantly get seduced from God's perfect way or even willfully choose to take a path in life that leads to destruction, there is a way of escape.

Because there is an escape route from our wrongdoings does not mean that we will forget all of the hurt or confusion that came into our life during our time of deviation. However, if we survive and learn from our season of wandering, we can use that revelation to overcome the enemy's plan for others. Once we start again, we can actually use our experience to overcome. Our heart can be made clean, our spirit renewed and our destiny clock reset. God's redemptive plan is activated and the horizon line of our future can be seen again. I believe many of those who have been a mess in the past will triumph and overcome in the future.

God has a triumphant plan for those who will worship Him. Here's what Revelation 5:1-9 tells us:

> And I saw in the right hand of Him who sat on the throne
> a scroll written inside and on the back, sealed with seven
> seals. Then I saw a strong angel proclaiming with a loud

voice, "Who is worthy to open the scroll and to loose its seals?" And no one in heaven or on the earth or under the earth was able to open the scroll, or to look at it. So I wept much, because no one was found worthy to open and read the scroll, or to look at it. But one of the elders said to me, "Do not weep. Behold, the Lion of the tribe of Judah, the Root of David, has prevailed (triumphed) to open the scroll and to loose its seven seals."

And I looked, and behold, in the midst of the throne and of the four living creatures, and in the midst of the elders, stood a Lamb as though it had been slain, having seven horns and seven eyes, which are the seven Spirits of God sent out into all the earth. Then He came and took the scroll out of the right hand of Him who sat on the throne.

Now when He had taken the scroll, the four living creatures and the twenty-four elders fell down before the Lamb, each having a harp, and golden bowls full of incense, which are the prayers of the saints. And they sang a new song.

God is aligning the generations to express heaven's sound. He is a tri-generational God who longs to hear three generations of a bloodline worshiping, sounding and triumphing in the earth as He has triumphed in both earth and heaven. I love the next generation. I enjoy making them communicate with me and listening to what they have to say. Hannah Pierce, my son Joseph's daughter, and my oldest grandchild, works in the media and sound department of my ministry. She is in her second semester in college.

Recently, she came to me and said, "Grandpa Chuck, a few months ago, Aaron [Aaron Smith, one of our worship pastors] asked me to write a song for the movie *13 Going on 30*. Every time I sat down to work on the song, I found myself fighting a horrible case of writer's block. Finally, after wrestling with myself for a few weeks, I wrote something the day before the meeting. I felt like what I wrote was a good song, but I was unsure, because it wasn't where I felt that I was in my spiritual life. I was relying on my own writing and trying to fit a song into the theme instead of asking God what He wanted. I performed the song and it was a mess! I am extremely discouraged by this flop."

I said, "Well, honey, pull aside, wait and look for another opportunity to redeem yourself. The Lord already has your next time in place."

Three weeks later, Aaron came to Hannah again and asked her to do a song. When I heard the song on Sunday morning before the congregation and those joining us on the Web, I was amazed! I asked her what she did when writing it. She replied, "I was quick to ask God what to do. For the next few days, I kept humming the song that I had done before and had grown to dislike. I then asked Aaron what the theme for the night was, and he told me, 'Recovery!' I continued to try to write something else. I tried fast songs and slow songs, but nothing seemed to be right. Finally, I said, 'Okay God!' I felt that I was supposed to change the song from what I had originally written to what the Lord wanted it to be. This meant that I had to come up with new music (which was tough, considering it was my self-reliance that got me into the 'song mess' in the first place)! I reworded some of the lyrics to go with what God was saying in my life. When the song was finished, I felt good that God was trying to show me that where I have tried to rely on myself in the past and do what I wanted to do or what I think other people will like, He wants to restore my faith in Him and my reliance on Him for what I desire and need."

Hannah's song was one of the most incredible Songs of Recovery that I have heard. Remember when David brought in the Ark of God's Covenant the wrong way? Because of this debacle, he postponed the Glory from entering the city. However, God redeemed his mess and reordered his steps. He did the same for my granddaughter Hannah, and He will do the same for you!

For Study and Reflection
Read 2 Samuel 6:1-11. Meditate on Exodus 3
and memorize Proverbs 16:25.

Bringing in the Ark Again

*You are the heads of the fathers' households of the Levites; consecrate
yourselves both you and your relatives, that you may bring up the ark of the
LORD God of Israel to the place that I have prepared for it. Because you did
not carry it at the first, the LORD our God made an outburst on us,
for we did not seek Him according to the ordinance.*
1 CHRONICLES 15:12-14, NASB

A Significant Three Months

A Comprehensive Plan
When David recovered from the Uzzah fiasco, he realized that he
had not inquired of the Lord like he should have. Therefore, as
David sought the Lord over the following three months, God was
able to download into David the plan that He had intended for
the Ark. In that short amount of time, David developed a comprehensive plan to put 38,000 Levites to work serving the Lord as
ministers, gatekeepers, judges, officers, instructors, teachers,
guardians, and more. Four thousand alone were instrumentalists
(see 1 Chron. 23:2-5). There were 288 singers.

At the end of that three months, David knew that the Ark was
to be carried, who was supposed to carry it and why. He knew what
he was to wear to bring the Ark in: not only the fine linen robe of
a king, but also the linen ephod of a priest—bringing together the
two offices of king and priest (see 1 Chron. 15:27). And he knew
exactly what the Levites and priests were to do in both his tabernacle and in the tabernacle of Moses. Pretty good organizational

skills for a man whose résumé, up to this point, included such things as sheepherder, fugitive and part-time bodyguard to a Philistine king.

It is obvious that David did not just think all these things up in three months. This was God's intended purpose, which He had placed David on the earth to perform. David's own well-meaning attempt to bring in the Ark had met with disaster. David suffered great frustration and embarrassment because of the failure; but because he would not be turned from his desire to take care of the Ark, God was able to give David a plan that was beyond his understanding or imagination—a plan to bring the worship of heaven down and establish it on the earth.

David was a type of the New Testament gift of apostle. We are told in Ephesians 2:20 that the Church would be built on the foundation of apostles and prophets, with Jesus being the chief cornerstone. Man's wisdom cannot build God's Church. Through God's prophets He releases His intentions to the Church. Through His apostles He gives wisdom to implement those intentions. After David did his best with his own wisdom, God prophetically showed him His intentions for the Ark. Then David was given wisdom, like his New Testament apostolic counterparts, to implement God's plan.

A Unique Structure

There was already a tent specifically built for the Ark to dwell in— the tabernacle of Moses. It was just down the road from Jerusalem in Gibeon (see 2 Chron. 1:4-5). The logical thing for David to do would have been to bring the tabernacle of Moses into Jerusalem and put the Ark back in it. The tabernacle of Moses had been built for the purpose of housing the Ark. Moses had been given the blueprint directly from God as to how to construct the tabernacle and how to handle the Ark itself. For 500 years the Ark had known no other dwelling place except the tabernacle of Moses. It was the prescribed place for the Ark to dwell.

But David knew this was not the destination God had in mind for the Ark at this time. He did, however, honor the former dwelling place of the Ark by setting up the original bronze altar in front of the tabernacle of Moses and assigning priests and Levites to perform the burnt offerings, the morning and evening sacrifice, and every other thing that the Lord had commanded in the Law for them to do. In addition, David assigned worship leaders to minister there in worship and thanksgiving (see 1 Chron. 16:39-42).

No Rituals

David, with his new revelation, knew that his tabernacle was to be different from the one that Moses had built. Moses was given the pattern of worship for the old covenant. There was a process that the worshiper went through to come before God in worship, most of which was done for him by the priest. The brazen altar was for their sacrifice, and a laver represented their cleansing by washing. Then in the holy place was the lamp stand, the bread of the presence and the altar of incense. Finally, once a year, the high priest alone entered through the veil into the holy of holies with blood to sprinkle on the mercy seat of the Ark of His presence.

David's tabernacle contained none of the sacred trappings that stood between the worshiper and the presence of God. The strict rituals prescribed for Moses' tabernacle were not to be observed in David's. Instead they came boldly before God's presence by faith. The pattern of worship in David's tabernacle was what Jesus referred to in the New Testament as "spirit and truth"—the "truth" of the Old Testament rituals brought to life, not by formal rituals but by the Spirit of God. Their sacrifices were not those prescribed by law but were sacrifices of praise. Jim Hodges explains this in his comparison of David's tabernacle at Zion and Moses' tabernacle five miles away at Gibeon:

> At Gibeon, there was sacrifice: on Mt. Zion, there was song! It is interesting to note in the Book of Revelation, there is no more sacrifice, but there are songs to the Sacrificed One, the Lamb![1]

The pattern of worship that was in heaven was now being released by God on the earth in David's tabernacle.

No Veil
David did not provide a veil to put the Ark behind. In doing this he was specifically going against the instructions the Lord had given Moses about the Ark. No one was permitted to see the Ark except the high priest, and that only one time each year on the Day of Atonement when the priest entered behind the veil with the blood of the sacrifice to sprinkle on the mercy seat of the Ark. Even when the Ark was transported, the Levites who transported it were not permitted to see it. The priests carefully covered the Ark before the Levites were brought in to carry it out.

Only three months earlier David had seen the life of Uzzah lost because the ordinances concerning the Ark were not observed. Now he set the tabernacle up in direct violation of those same ordinances. Every other instruction concerning the Ark was carried out in detail, so we must deduce that David was acting on God's instruction. Surely he would not otherwise have dared such a move. This was not just a creative way David thought up to spice up the worship in the tabernacle. And the fact that no disaster occurred during the years the Ark sat unveiled in the tabernacle just makes us believe all the more that this was God's call, not David's.

What was happening? God was bringing down the worship of heaven, and in heaven the worship is face to face with no veil. The same would be true of worship that the New Testament saints would experience. Since Jesus made a way for us, by His blood, into the presence of God, we have the privilege of worshiping Him face to face.

David's brilliant organization of the thousands of priests and Levites for service was not from his own organizational skills but from the heart of God. When David set up his tabernacle in a different manner than Moses' tabernacle, it was not a passing fancy; he was carrying out God's program. Even naming the hill Zion couldn't have been David's idea. It was the name of God's holy hill in heaven but was not known on earth until David gave it as the name of the hill he would set his tabernacle on.

David's Worship Leaders

Something Old, Something New

David did something very interesting for which there was no earthly precedent. David installed Levites in the tabernacle whose job it was to direct the singers and musicians as they worshiped before the manifested presence of God. Today we call this type of minister a worship leader. This had never been done on earth before David, but there was once a worship leader in heaven. In Ezekiel 28:11-16, we see that God anointed a special cherub named Lucifer to lead the worship of heaven. Derek Prince says:

> Lucifer is described as the "anointed cherub who covers." It seems that Lucifer had covered with his wings the place of the manifestation of God's glory in His heavenly temple, just as the cherubs in the tabernacle of Moses covered the mercy seat and the place where the visible glory of God appeared.[2]

Lucifer was established on God's holy mountain in heaven, Mount Zion, eons before there had ever been a Mount Zion on earth. Lucifer's very being was inlaid with precious stones. Just imagine the brilliance of those stones as Lucifer hovered over the manifested presence of God, reflecting God's glory. Lucifer's very name meant brightness. In Isaiah 14:12, Lucifer is referred to in some Bible translations as "morning star" or "daystar." The name Lucifer comes from the same root word from which we get the word "hallelujah," the Hebrews' most exuberant form of praise.

Lucifer was God's hallelujah, and he didn't have to pick up a musical instrument to lead the praise; he *was* a musical instrument: harps and pipes were also inlaid in him like the precious stones. This was the purpose for which he was created—to lead the worship on God's holy hill, Mount Zion. He was anointed for the task. The anointing of God enables you to accomplish God's call in a manner that is beyond your own abilities. Lucifer was awesome in his calling. He was the very seal of perfection. What could represent perfection more than leading the host of heaven in God's praises? He was full of wisdom, he was beautiful and he was perfect. But Lucifer also had the capacity to choose. Billye Brim says:

> God gave Lucifer—as He gave all the angels—a free will in the day of his creation. He must have used it to worship and please God for some measure of eternity. How long the Bible does not reveal. But it does reveal that he was the first to turn his will against the Father's and it caused his fall.[3]

Lucifer the Beautiful

Lucifer, at some point, allowed his pride to get a foothold in him. He became all too aware of his own beauty and splendor. Even the great wisdom that was given him was overcome by his fixation on his own magnificence. Ezekiel 28:17 says, "Your heart was lifted up because of your beauty; you corrupted your wisdom for the sake of your splendor." It's interesting to note the contrast in Jesus' attitude mentioned in Philippians 2:5-8:

> Christ Jesus, who, although He existed in the form of God, did not regard equality with God a thing to be grasped, but emptied Himself, taking the form of a bond-servant, and being made in the likeness of men. Being found in appearance as a man, He humbled Himself by becoming obedient to the point of death, even death on a cross (*NASB*).

Lucifer began to wonder why he—as magnificent as he was—was not getting the attention he deserved. God was God, and no one could replace Him. But Lucifer could see that he was the most marvelous of God's created beings, obviously, and in his own eyes, God's favorite.

In Isaiah 14:13, God says that Lucifer wanted to exalt his throne above the stars of God. The "stars of God" refer to the angels, and Lucifer wanted his place to be distinguished above the other angels to show his preeminence. He wanted to be right up there with God. He wanted to be worshiped. We see this even in the New Testament, when Satan tempted Jesus with the kingdoms of the world if only Jesus would bow down and worship him. Lucifer wanted to be "like the Most High" and so embarked on a campaign to accomplish this. His method for attaining his goal became the modus operandi for which he would be known for the rest of eternity.

Satan, the Accuser
In Ezekiel 28:16,18, God speaks to Satan: "By the abundance of your trading you became filled with violence within, and you sinned. . . . You defiled your sanctuaries by the multitude of your iniquities, by the iniquity of your trading." Derek Prince says:

> This word *trading* is also applied to someone who goes about as a *talebearer* or a *slanderer*. In other words it could describe someone who peddles both goods and gossip. In various other books of the Bible—e.g., Leviticus, Proverbs, Jeremiah—this word is translated as either a "talebearer" or a "slanderer." For example, Leviticus 19:16 says: "You shall not go about as a talebearer among your people."[4]

Lucifer became a slanderer. I'm sure it was slyly done: "I love angel Bob. He's the greatest, but he just shouldn't have been put in a leadership role so soon. I mention this only so you can be praying for him." And apparently Lucifer slandered a great deal. God said that by the abundance of his trading, or slandering, he became filled with violence. In the Hebrew, this word "violence" carries with it the implication of unjust gain.[5] The slander was working. Lucifer was amassing his "unjust gain" in influence and power. Eventually, one-third of the angels would fall under his sway. That's quite an accomplishment if you think about it: angels in the very presence of God being turned from His glory to take up the cause of this worship leader who wasn't getting his supposed just recognition.

But by now, Lucifer had lost his effectiveness as a worship leader. God told Lucifer that his sanctuaries had been defiled because of his slandering and tale-bearing. Lucifer was ruined. His sin was found out. The very place that had been consecrated for him to minister was now corrupted. Still he gathered the angels that supported him to try to take back his place by force. It was futile. He was cast out of heaven along with the angels he had deceived. He would no longer be called Lucifer, God's bright morning star, God's "hallelujah." The slander and accusation in which he had engaged so heavily now determined his name for the ages to come, Satan, which means adversary or accuser.

Glittering Lights

When David installed his worship leaders in his tabernacle, he had an interesting name for them. In the English Bible this word has been translated "chief musician," and you would think it came from the two ancient Hebrew words for "chief" and "musician," but it does not. It comes from a single Hebrew word, *natsach,* which means a glittering light in the distance used as a beacon to travel toward.[6] Lucifer had been the bright light of heaven, but he had fallen because of his pride. David's worship leaders were glittering lights that served as beacons pointing the way to the presence of God. Although these Levites were leaders, their intention was not to outshine God, just to glitter enough to point the way to Him.

Included in the definition of the word *natsach* is the aspect of overseeing or administration. Worship leaders have the responsibility of overseeing and administrating a worship service. This is more than just leading songs and directing the worship team. It is finding the heart of God and His desire for the service. If God begins to put an anointing on one of the musicians or singers, the worship leader needs to perceive it and bring that out. If a prophetic mantle descends upon the service, the worship leader needs to make room for it. A "bright light" can be a one-man show and carry the whole service, but a "glittering light" needs to draw in the other participants as the Spirit moves on them: "When you assemble, each one has a psalm, has a teaching, has a revelation, has a tongue, has an interpretation. Let all things be done for edification" (1 Cor. 14:26, *NASB*). This Scripture is not just for home groups or cell groups. The largest of churches can operate in this principle if the worship leader is in a position to administrate the worship service as well as lead the worship.

David's glittering lights were chiefs, leaders, and they had the responsibility of overseeing or administrating the worship in the tabernacle. Often the Lord stops me from going to the next song in a service. Sometimes He lets me know why, but sometimes I just feel a restraint in my spirit not to move on to the next song or even to do anything at all. It is like the Lord is saying, "Hush for a minute, son." I know I have the physical ability to start into a song and "keep the service going," but my spirit just won't go in that direction. It used to frustrate me, and I would say, "Lord, I'm stuck. I can't move, and everyone is staring at me! I have to do something." But everyone wasn't really staring at me. They were just caught up in the presence of the Lord the same as I was, and I didn't really need to do anything. The Lord was restraining me so He could bring forth something from someone else.

I have no problem with worship leaders that show a little glitter. The problem is when they revel in that glitter and fail to serve as beacons pointing the way to God. That beacon is what sometimes connects us to the worship of heaven. What starts off focused on the "stage" ministry of the worship leader should usher us into the glory of heaven's worship in which God is the focus. The beacon was not an end in itself; it just led the saints into the presence of God.

To Minister, to Commemorate, to Thank and to Praise
"And he appointed some of the Levites to minister before the ark of the LORD, to commemorate, to thank, and to praise the LORD God of Israel" (1 Chron. 16:4). David's objectives were fourfold.

1. To minister: *sharath* (shaw-rath'); *Vine's* says, " 'to minister, serve, officiate' . . . to be distinguished from the term for more menial serving, *'abad*, from which the word meaning 'slave' or 'servant' is derived. *Sharat* is characteristically used of 'serving' done by royal household

workers. . . . In the manner of the modern 'public servant' idea, the word is used in reference to court officials and royal servants."[7] So this "ministry" before the
Ark of the Lord that the Levites were commissioned to
do involved an administrative aspect to it.

2. To commemorate (*Webster's* defines as to recall to
   mind, to serve as a memorial of): *zakar* (zaw-kar'); a
   primitive root; properly, to mark (so as to be recognized), i.e., to remember; by implication, to mention.[8]

3. To thank: *yadah* (yaw-daw'); a primitive root; used only
   as denominative from OT #3027; literally, to use (i.e.,
   hold out) the hand; physically, to throw (a stone, an
   arrow) at or away; especially to revere or worship (with
   extended hands); intensively, to bemoan (by wringing
   the hands).[9]

4. To praise: *halal* (haw-lal'); a primitive root; to be clear
   (orig. of sound, but usually of color); to shine; hence, to
   make a show, to boast; and thus to be (clamorously)
   foolish; to rave; causatively, to celebrate; also to stultify.[10]

What picture does "to minister before the Ark of the LORD, to
commemorate, to thank, and to praise the LORD God of Israel"
bring to our twenty-first-century mind? Does it bring war, recompense or intercession to mind? Does it make us think of groaning
out our frustrations to God, or asking how long He is going to
take to answer our prayers? It made David think this, and the
psalms are filled with such things. How long, O Lord? Break the
teeth of my enemy, O Lord! Paralleled in the book of Revelation,
the martyrs cry the same thing from underneath the throne of
God, and God does not rebuke them. He comforts them and tells
them it will be soon. Psalm 149 says it is our honor as saints to
bring recompense on the evil rulers in our worship. Each of us
might have our own idea of how the Lord would want to be min-

istered to, but if we look at the psalms we can get a good picture of how David did this: interceding, warring, testifying, prophesying, praising.

Worship in the Tabernacle

It Was Face to Face, Just Like in Heaven
In heaven they worshiped face to face, but during David's time that manner of worship was expressly forbidden. The presence of God in the Old Testament was always behind a veil. So in order to bring the worship of heaven down to the earth, God had to suspend this regulation for the 40 years that David's tabernacle was in operation. The New Testament saints that would follow David's prototype a thousand years later would be able to worship God face to face because of the sacrifice Jesus made to bring them through the rent veil, which was His flesh. Kevin J. Conner, in his study of David's tabernacle, says this:

> The tabernacle at Zion had a functioning priesthood in relation to the ark of God, but had no outer court or holy place. In type, it was the transfer of the holiest of all, symbolizing worship "within-the-veil" kind of access and worship before the presence of the Lord.[11]

Worshipers for the first time entered "within the veil" to worship face to face with the presence of God, just like the worshipers in heaven.

It Was Continual, Just Like in Heaven
In heaven, God is enthroned on praises 24 hours a day, 7 days a week, 52 weeks a year. Not having earthly bodies, those who are praising God in heaven don't need to eat or sleep. They don't need to mow their yard or pay bills or take the kids to soccer practice.

In order for David to bring heaven's continual worship to earth, he had to overcome these human frailties. He did this by staffing his tabernacle with 24 worship teams. Thousands of

Levites were divided into 24 courses. They drew lots for the hour of the day they would serve. Each hour a new team would come in that was fresh and rested and prepared to give it their all for that hour. Psalm 134 is specifically addressed to the Levites who served in the night shifts: "Behold, bless the LORD, all you servants of the LORD, who by night stand in the house of the LORD! Lift up your hands in the sanctuary, and bless the LORD" (Ps. 134:1-2). David wanted God to be enthroned continually on the praises of Israel so that day and night God would be ruling and reigning from that throne. Chuck Pierce seizes on this thought in his book *Interpreting the Times*:

> This was a revelation that David had capitalized on in his tabernacle. If God establishes His throne on our praise, then imagine how beneficial it would be to maintain that praise all the time. God would be continually enthroned, and from that throne, He would be continually ruling in favor of Israel.[12]

It Was Intercessory, Just Like in Heaven

"Give ear, O LORD, to my prayer; and give heed to the voice of my supplications! In the day of my trouble I shall call upon You, for You will answer me" (Ps. 86:6-8, *NASB*). Intercession is a common theme in the psalms that were sung in David's tabernacle as David and the other writers call out to God for His intervening hand. One of the most heartrending examples is when Asaph, one of David's worship leaders, stands in the gap for God's people when he sees prophetically the coming destruction of the temple at the hands of the Babylonians:

> Remember Your congregation, which You have purchased of old, the tribe of Your inheritance, which You have re-deemed—this Mount Zion where You have dwelt. Lift up Your feet to the perpetual desolations. The enemy has damaged everything in the sanctuary. Your enemies roar in the midst of Your meeting place. . . . They have set fire to

Your sanctuary; they have defiled the dwelling place of Your name to the ground (Ps. 74:2-4,7).

The Babylonians would not be a threat for hundreds of years. The temple that Asaph saw destroyed had not even been built yet. But Asaph, seeing these events prophetically, came into great intercession and travail, praying for a people not yet born, interceding for a calamity that he would never live to see. When we allow the worship of heaven to come into our midst, we are able to take up the harps and bowls along with the 24 elders and present them before God on His throne. God is able to throw us into the gap to stand for His purposes and worship there until those purposes are accomplished.

It Was Prophetic, Just Like in Heaven

The worship in David's tabernacle was very prophetic, as so many of the psalms reveal. David, in Psalm 22, prophetically spoke the words that Jesus spoke when He was on the cross; Asaph, as we just saw, prophetically viewed the destruction of the temple by the Babylonians. But the psalms were not just prophecies of the future; they also sang prophetically the purposes and intentions of God into the situations they were presently in. In Psalm 50, God sings to His congregation through Asaph: "Hear, O My people, and I will speak, O Israel, and I will testify against you; I am God, your God!" (Ps. 50:7). God goes on to take His people to task concerning their attitudes in worship.

In David's tabernacle, even the musicians prophesied on their instruments. Jeduthum (also known as Ethan) was particularly known for his ability to prophesy on his instrument (see 1 Chron. 25:3, *NASB*). In our church, it is our lead guitar player, Thom Rana, who is the strongest in prophesying on his instrument. It is nothing he set out to do, but as we spent time before the Lord in our worship, we would experience a prophetic mantle descending on us, and Thom would begin to play. Many times one of us would sing the interpretation in a song. Other times, Chuck Pierce would come up on stage and say, "I hear what the guitar is prophesying," and he would speak the interpretation.

The Bible doesn't say that an instrument's prophesying must be interpreted. Sometimes our spirit quickens in us as God speaks to our innermost being through the prophesying of an instrument. But sometimes those with the gift of interpretation can hear the words that God is saying through the instrument. Moreover, "David and the captains of the army separated for the service some of the sons of Asaph, of Heman, and of Jeduthun, who should prophesy with harps, stringed instruments and cymbals" (1 Chron. 25:1).

It Was Spontaneous and Dynamic, Just Like in Heaven

We often wax sentimental about David's tabernacle and think what wonderful worship must have been there and how awesome the presence of the Lord must have been. Indeed, the worship was wonderful, and the presence of the Lord was awesome; but what we should be doing is examining what they did that we might be falling short of. In David's tabernacle the worship was dynamic, always moving and changing. Just like heaven's worship, it never got in a rut. A look at the first few psalms in Scripture reveals the span that their worship covered. Psalm 1 is like a proverb to teach God's people:

> Blessed is the man who walks not in the counsel of the ungodly, nor stands in the path of sinners, nor sits in the seat of the scornful; but his delight is in the law of the LORD, and in His law he meditates day and night (Ps. 1:1-2).

Psalm 2 is a prophetic treatise on the majesty and power of God and the futility of those who resist Him:

> Why do the nations rage, and the people plot a vain thing? The kings of the earth set themselves, and the rulers take counsel together, against the LORD and against His Anointed. . . . He who sits in the heavens shall laugh; the LORD shall hold them in derision. . . . "Yet I have set My King on My holy hill of Zion" (Ps. 2:1-2,4,6).

The next few psalms are meditations and cries for help, and then Psalm 8 is a grand song of praise: "O LORD, our Lord, how excellent is Your name in all the earth" (Ps. 8:1). Just like we saw in the worship of heaven, the songs in David's tabernacle were many and varied. Sometimes they sang their songs to God and sometimes they sang about Him. Sometimes their songs were exhortations or prophecies or proclamations or warring, and sometimes they were songs of adoration and love.

The worship was also spontaneous, springing forth from the creative nature of God. The worshipers sang spontaneous prophetic songs: "He put a new song in my mouth, a song of praise to our God" (Ps. 40:3, *NASB*). A "new song" is one that had not been sung before. It was fresh and new from the Lord that came prophetically while they were before the Lord in worship. The psalmists admonish us in several places to "Sing to the LORD a new song" (Ps. 149:1). It was the same thing that we saw in the worship service in heaven:

> And they sang a new song, saying: "You are worthy to take the scroll, and to open its seals; for You were slain, and have redeemed us to God by Your blood out of every tribe and tongue and people and nation, and have made us kings and priests to our God; and we shall reign on the earth" (Rev. 5:9-10).

Spontaneity was such an important part of the tabernacle worship that they had Levites assigned to record the songs that came forth in their worship: "And he appointed some of the Levites to minister before the ark of the LORD, to commemorate, to thank, and to praise the LORD God of Israel" (1 Chron. 16:4-5). This word "commemorate" in Hebrew (*zawkar*) means "to mark" in order to remember. In the *KJV* it is translated "record," which is what the Hebrews did; they recorded for posterity their spontaneous prophetic songs.

Imagine, if you will, the awesome, free-flowing, Spirit-led worship that David's worshipers experienced, always moving and changing and with fresh expressions of praise continually bubbling up. Even the word "praise" could have any number of meanings to the worshipers in David's time. There are several Hebrew words that convey a panorama of expressions in worship to God. We translate them all as one word: "praise." If we look at these Hebrew words, we can get a picture of where we, as sophisticated moderns, might fall short of our Old Testament counterparts. We have already looked at the crown jewel of praise words, *halal*, but here are a few more to consider:

Navah: The first Hebrew word we want to look at is *navah*. This word is very simple: it just means to make a habitation for the Lord with our praises. Exodus 15:2 says, "He is my God, and I will praise [*navah*] Him." The *King James Version* actually translates this as "I will prepare him an habitation." This is always the first step in worship; just making room for God. Sometimes in our busy lives we simply crowd God out. We are busy; we are occupied; we have things to do. We gave Him room on Sunday, but now it is Monday, and we have business to attend. Monday, however, is a time when God greatly wants us to make room for Him. We, therefore, have to create a framework in which God can come and dwell. God longs to inhabit our praises, but if we are too busy to praise Him, we leave no place for Him to dwell. We have to say, "God, it's Monday, and I have a lot of stuff on my plate, but I'm just going to take time to praise you right now and make a habitation for you in my heart before this busy day begins." That's *navah*.

Towdah: *Towdah* is simply thanksgiving and adds a physical expression of lifting your hands to God. *Towdah* means, then, to openly declare thanksgiving to God, lifting up your hands in adoration. With *navah* we could quietly sit at our workstation on Monday morning and open our heart to God as a habitation, but with *towdah* our praise becomes noticeable to those around us as we lift our hands and give thanks.

Indeed, there is an aspect of sacrifice in *towdah*. It is used to denote a sacrifice of praise or a thank offering. Jeremiah says, "They will come in from the cities of Judah . . . bringing sacrifices of thanksgiving [*towdah*] to the house of the LORD" (Jer. 17:26, *NASB*). Jeremiah uses the same word again, speaking of people "who bring a thank offering [*towdah*] into the house of the LORD" (Jer. 33:11, *NASB*). When we offer our thanks to the Lord—even when we are in the midst of adverse circumstances—we are very pleasing to God. Peter puts it like this: "For what credit is there if, when you sin and are harshly treated, you endure it with patience? But if when you do what is right and suffer for it you patiently endure it, this finds favor with God" (1 Pet. 2:20, *NASB*). This is a sacrifice of praise, and God says, "Whoso offereth praise [*towdah*] glorifieth me" (Ps. 50:23, *KJV*). Whoever offers God an open show of thanksgiving with uplifted hands glorifies Him. Others can see our thankful hearts to God.

Yadah: *Yadah* is another word the Hebrews used that meant to give thanks with raised hands. A couple of things, however, set it apart from *towdah*. *Yadah* is used more to thank God for specific deeds He has done. When Jehoshaphat set the Levite singers out in front of his army, they were to "praise [*yadah*] the LORD; for his mercy endureth for ever" (2 Chron. 20:21, *KJV*). Isaiah said, "I will praise [*yadah*] Your name, for You have done wonderful things" (Isa. 25:1). David said, "Hope in God, for I shall yet praise [*yadah*] Him for the help of His countenance" (Ps. 42:5), and again, "Oh, that men would give thanks [*yadah*] to the LORD for His goodness" (Ps. 107:15).

The list goes on: *yadah* is offered because of God's lovingkindness (see Ps. 138:1), because He has heard us (see Ps. 118:21), because His anger was turned away (see Isa. 12:1), and because we are fearfully and wonderfully made (see Ps. 139:14). Another distinguishing aspect of *yadah* is the intensity that it carries. There is a passion in it: groaning and wringing the hands and throwing them up in fervent thanksgiving and praise. Our little prayer, "God is great. God is good. Let us thank Him for our food," will not count as *yadah*. Our thanksgiving praise is to be intense. It is to be full of ardor and zeal.

An interesting thing about *yadah* is that it is related to *Yehudah*, Judah. Judah was Leah's son. Leah was the unloved wife of Jacob, who only loved his other wife, Rebecca. Leah kept thinking that if she produced sons for Jacob, he would love her. He didn't. Finally, after three sons and no results, "She conceived again and bore a son and said, 'This time I will praise [*yadah*] the LORD.' Therefore she named him Judah" (Gen. 29:35, *NASB*). She praised God for His love for her instead of man's love.

Zamar: *Zamar* means to make music and sing: literally to pluck the strings of an instrument. Most of the times when it is used it is coupled with the word "sing." This, to the Hebrew people, was synonymous with celebration. In almost every instance of its use in Scripture, *zamar* is accompanied with the word "singing." Psalm 104:33 says, "I will sing praise [*zamar*] to my God while I have my being" (*KJV*). Psalm 108:1 tells us, "I will sing and give praise [*zamar*]" (*KJV*). Psalm 138:1 says, "I sing praise [*zamar*] unto thee" (*KJV*).

Tehillah: Not to be confused with the popular Mexican libation (tequila), *tehillah* is a Hebrew word that denotes a quality or a deed that is deserving of praise. Other Hebrew words focus on thanksgiving, or actions like kneeling, raising hands, celebrating, dancing, and the like; but *tehillah* focuses on declaring the attribute of God or the things He has done. "God, You are merciful and You have saved me from destruction." This can be times when we are struck with the overwhelming magnificence of God and we gush forth our praise in response, like the living beings before the throne of God in heaven continually crying out, "Holy,

holy, holy." This can also be at times when we speak out the things God has done for us in the past in order to establish our heart's attitude about an upcoming situation, as Jehoshaphat did in 2 Chronicles 20:5-12.

But *tehillah* is more than this. God wants to actually *be* our praise. Here's how that works: Say there is a guy you know who has a very expensive, exotic car. He is very proud of it, and everyone is in awe of him as they see him zipping around town in that car. When people see this guy, the first thing they think about is his car. It is his praise, his *tehillah*. God wants to be that to us.

Moses said, "He is your praise [*tehillah*] and He is your God, who has done these great and awesome things for you which your eyes have seen" (Deut. 10:21, *NASB*). Jeremiah said, "Heal me, O LORD, and I will be healed; save me and I will be saved, for You are my praise [*tehillah*]" (Jer. 17:14, *NASB*). When people see us, the first thing they should think about is the great God that we have.

God also wants us to be His *tehillah* (see Jer. 13:11). Whereas the guy with the car would ask you, "Have you seen my car?" God would ask, "Have you seen My servant Job?" (see Job 1:8). God was proud of Job: he was God's *tehillah*. He wanted to talk about Job and point him out to everybody. God wants us to triumph in our praise of Him (see Ps. 106:47) and show it off to everyone (see Ps. 51:15; Ps. 9:14). He wants us to wear it like a coat (see Isa. 61:3). He says it looks good on us (see Pss. 33:1; 147:1). David told God that *tehillah* awaited Him in Zion (see Ps. 65:1) and that we should all make God's *tehillah* glorious (see Ps. 66:2).

Shabach: *Shabach* means to praise the Lord in a loud tone. When we raise our voice it is usually because we are in doubt that our message is understood or heeded at our regular tone. *Shabach* increases the intensity of our message and draws attention to it that it might not have received before. It gets our message across in the midst of tumult or confusion. The recipient of our message is left with little doubt of our intention toward them. Others within earshot of our voice are also left with little doubt of our intention toward the recipient of our message.

Shabach means figuratively to pacify with a loud tone of voice. We can draw a couple of different perceptions from this. One is that if God doubted the sincerity of our praise, our loud tone would make our praise sound more convincing, soothing His misgivings. It's like the drill sergeant, when he hears a halfhearted "Yes, sir" from his troops. He shouts, "I don't hear you!" which brings a resounding, loud "Yes, sir!" This thunderous response assures the sergeant. He knows exactly where the troops stand.

The other perception we can draw is that everyone else knows exactly where the troops stand. The fervor we show in our loud, vibrant praise can have a pacifying effect on the enemy. God is soothed by the assurance of our display of praise; and the wind is taken out of our enemy's sails as they are convinced of our determination.

After Nebuchadnezzar spent a year under God's judgment, he wanted God to have no doubt where he stood when he said, "I Nebuchadnezzar praise [*shabach*] and extol and honour the King of heaven, all whose works are truth, and his ways judgment" (Dan. 4:37, *KJV*).

David said, "One generation shall praise [*shabach*] Your works to another" (Ps. 145:4). David used the word *shabach* because he knew the importance of the older generation praising God loudly and definitely to the younger generation, leaving no doubt as to the message.

Jerusalem is exhorted to praise (*shabach*) the Lord (see Ps. 147:12), and the nations are told to do the same (see Ps. 117:1). Let's get loud in our praise.

It Was Warring, Just Like in Heaven

We saw that God's holy hill in heaven was His command center in the war against the devil on earth. In Psalm 78, we saw that God made His sanctuary on Zion just like the one in heaven. I believe that God was moving His command center from His heavenly Zion to the earthly one where David pitched his tent. From that earthly command center, God was enthroned on Israel's praises (see Ps. 22:3, *KJV*) to hold court. From Zion, He then sent forth His word (see Mic. 4:2), roared at all contenders (see Joel 3:16), and sent forth His rod to rule (see Ps. 110:2). The psalms give us countless references to warring worship. God is called upon to destroy our adversaries, train our hands for war, and give us strength in the battle and deliverance from our enemies. David was so aware of the warring aspect of their worship that he drew his military leaders into the affairs of the tabernacle.

God Interacted with Their Praise, Just Like in Heaven

One thing we can see by reading through the books of 1 and 2 Samuel, 1 and 2 Kings and 1 and 2 Chronicles is how God interacted with His worshipers during the time of the tabernacle. It was as if they were the throngs that dwelt before the Lord in heaven itself. This was the high point of Israel's history.

In the generations before David, the people of Israel were renowned for their stiff-necked resistance in the wilderness and their continual falling away during the season of the judges. In the generations after David, Israel drifted steadily away from their God. Many prophets were sent to call Israel back, but they fell further and further away until destruction overtook them.

But for those 40 years that Israel worshiped their God face to face in the tabernacle, the Lord was their God and they were His people. They called and He answered. They strayed and He chastened, but they always returned to worship in His presence. He answered their cries and interacted with their worship as if they were in heaven with Him.

This had been God's plan that He had called upon David to "carry out fully": to bring the apostolic worship that was in heaven down to earth. It was the plan that God intended to restore and eventually bring us into. Zion was where it all came about, and Zion would be where God would bring it all about again.

DIVINE RECOVERY OF WHAT HAS BEEN LOST
CHUCK D. PIERCE

Recently, I heard the Spirit of God impressing me with the following exhortation:

> *There is a cry deep within My people that is arising. This cry will begin to cover the land. They will cry loud and long! Join in this worship cry throughout the earth. Allow this cry to come from deep within you. Cry "Restore! Restore!" Cry "DIVINE RECOVERY!"*
>
> *If you will sound this cry, I will come and act. Divine recovery will be loosed and your atmosphere that is holding the losses of your past will change. This cry has been stored within you, but you have been afraid for the cry to be sounded. Your past disappointments and lost hopes have captured this cry. I can see where the cry has been held captive in you. But I am releasing a sound from heaven that is stirring this cry.*
>
> *Deep within your bones there is a burning. The burning is creating a sound that needs to be released into the earth and the heavens. Now I need to hear your cry! When this cry comes up into the heavenly realm and penetrates My throne, divine recovery will begin.*
>
> *Shout loud and then celebrate recovery! Shout seven times. Seven times produces a completion and creates an entryway into your Promised Land. This land has been waiting for you to recover the treasures that have been held captive by the enemy! Shout now! "Recovery! Recovery! Recovery! RECOVERY! RECOVERY! RECOVERY! RECOVERY!" Shout now, for lives and lands hang in the balance.*
>
> *Shout these words over your family! Shout long and hard for your children. Shout these words over your bloodline! Shout these words over your neighborhood! Shout loudly over your city! Shout recovery even louder over your state. This shout must be extended into your next season of maturing. Shout over the supply lines that you need to see opened! Shout until your provision is released.*

Shout over your businesses! Shout! I long for you to recover what was lost!

Recovery is coming! I will recover your lost integrity. I will recover your identity that has been submerged. I will recover your hardened heart and create within you a new heart. I will make your heart soft and your spirit new again. I will recover your spirit that has been wounded, and break the power of your fragmentation that has scattered your faculties and made you think that you would never be whole again.

I will cause you to rejoice over your return! I will recover you from the shame of mistakes and unwise decisions. I WILL! I WILL! I WILL! So shout loud and long! You will dance and rejoice like you have been set free from a confined prison cell. So shout now, for the door of your captivity is opening! You will then establish My glory in the place of your freedom!

Some of your friends around you will say, "This cry and your expression are offensive!" Some of your enemies will rise up and say, "We must stop this sound!" Nevertheless, let My sound in you arise, and I will scatter your enemies. The friends who only appeared to be your friends will disperse! You will be seated in a new place to receive the best that I have waited to give you! So, do not be quiet. Cry until you see Jerusalem established as a PRAISE in the earth! Sound My sound of return and you will see My glory established in the place that I have given you to occupy!

For Study and Reflection

Read Isaiah 42. Meditate on Psalm 39
and memorize Psalm 28:1.

6

The Glory of Zion

For the LORD *will rebuild Zion and appear in his glory. He will respond to the prayer of the destitute; he will not despise their plea. Let this be written for a future generation, that a people not yet created may praise the* LORD.
PSALM 102:16-18, NIV

For a Future Generation

Zion was not just for David's generation. It is not just for the Jews. God wanted all of the information about Zion written down so that we, the "future generation," would know, and it would give us cause to praise the Lord. The future generation can expect God to build up Zion and appear there in His glory. He will respond to our prayers and will not despise our plea. Although it started with David, it did not end there. It ends with us. I hope these next few pages will give you cause to praise the Lord.

The Safekeeping of the Ark

David, early in his reign, knew that besides his kingly responsibilities of protecting the kingdom and ruling the people there were some things he needed to do. One thing David knew was that he needed to attend to the Ark. For decades it had remained at Kiriath-jearim in the home of Abinadab. Here the Ark was respected and taken care of. During the months before the Ark's arrival at Kiriath-jearim, it had suffered the disrespect of Eli's two decadent sons who had taken it into battle in an attempt to gain an advantage against the Philistines. But the Ark is not a good luck charm.

The battle was lost and the Philistines captured the Ark, though they soon suffered as a result of their mistreatment of it. Eventually they sent the Ark back to Israel on a wandering oxcart that ended up in Beth-shemesh. There the Ark suffered the indignity of the curious inhabitants of Beth-shemesh who just had to take a peek inside. The outcome was, of course, fatal for the curiosity seekers. Finally, honorable men from Kiriath-jearim came to remove the Ark to the safety of Abinadab's home. David knew he needed to do something with the Ark, and though his understanding of this responsibility was not complete in the beginning, he knew he was the one who must find a resting place for it.

Zion

Another thing David knew was that he needed Mount Zion. "Zion" is a word that brings different pictures to different people's minds, and to some it brings no picture at all. Although it was central to David's purpose and existence, David himself was such a multifaceted, bigger-than-life individual that you can study the reams of information about him for years and never think Zion to be anything more than just one of the nicknames given to David's capital, Jerusalem. There is no mention of the word "Zion" before David gave it as the name for the hill he took from the Jebusites. It is difficult to find a definition for the word "Zion." All dictionaries, both Hebrew and English, just say it is the name of David's capital city.

The word "Zion" has no etymology. It is not from the ancient Aramaic or other early languages. The reason is because it was not an earthly name. It was the name God gave to His holy hill in heaven (see Heb. 12:22). Before David, the name Zion was not known except in heaven.

Apparently, God revealed the name to David during that "significant three months" for the purpose of naming the place where He would establish His worship on earth as it was in heaven. The worship on God's holy hill in heaven that we saw in Revelation was going to be established on a hill by the same name on earth. Psalm

78:69 says that God built His sanctuary on Mount Zion "like the heights." God patterned the sanctuary on David's Mount Zion after the one on His own holy mountain in heaven. David's hill had been sanctified by Melchizedek generations before and then left as fallow ground until David came to redeem it for God's purposes.

Moriah

Early on, Jerusalem was a city of two hills, Zion and Moriah. "Jerusalem" itself is a dual word that *Strong's Concordance* suggests is in allusion to these two hills (*Strong's* OT3389). Both of these hills were significant in God's plan. Both of their destinies were launched in the days of Abraham.

Moriah is where God led Abraham to present his son Isaac as a sacrifice to God (see Gen. 22:2-3). "Moriah" means "seen of God." What God saw on Moriah was Abraham's faith. God then provided His own lamb for the sacrifice, and Isaac was saved. Abraham called the place Jehovah-jirah, God provides (see Gen. 22:14).

A thousand years later, a Jebusite named Ornan, who had stayed in the city after its fall to David, set up his threshing floor on the same high place that Abraham had offered Isaac on—Moriah. The high bare rock was probably a good place to toss the threshed wheat in the air to let the wind blow away the chaff. It was there that David saw the Angel of the Lord standing to bring destruction on Jerusalem. David made a sacrifice on Moriah, which thwarted the city's destruction.

Moriah would later be the site where Solomon built the temple (see 2 Chron. 3:1-2). Moriah was therefore associated with a saying that went, "In the mount of the LORD it will be provided" (Gen. 22:14, *NASB*). This was the foreshadowing of the sacrifice of Jesus, the Lamb of God, who was God's provision to reconcile His people unto Himself.

The Other Hill

The other hill in Jerusalem, Zion, had a different significance. It was the place God would choose as His dwelling place forever. In

Psalm 132:13-14, we see Zion's purpose: "For the LORD has *chosen* Zion; He has *desired* it for His habitation. '*This is My resting place forever*; Here I will dwell, for *I have desired it*'" (*NASB*, emphasis added). God specifically chose Zion. He desired it. It would be His habitation: He would dwell there. He wanted it for His resting place, and all this would be forever, not just for the 40 years David would have his tabernacle there.

Why this place? Only God knows, but it was His choice. No other place would do. It was Zion's hill that God would not only dwell on but also rule from. God said this hill could not be moved and would abide forever (see Ps. 125:1). God said He loved its gates more than any others (see Ps. 87:2). God said anyone who hated this chosen hill would surely be put to shame (see Ps. 129:5). God was serious.

Salem

Zion's hill, the place where David's tabernacle was to be erected, was first known as Salem (see Ps. 76:1-2). There was a king/priest there named Melchizedek. This king/priest had no father, no mother, no beginning or end (see Heb. 7:1-3); nobody knew where he came from or where he went.

Abraham recognized Melchizedek by tithing to him from the spoils he gained at the slaughter of the kings that had carried off his nephew, Lot (see Gen. 14:20-21). So we see that God sent His priest, Melchizedek, to abide in this place that would one day be His chosen dwelling place. Melchizedek's presence suggests that God was sanctifying Salem for the purpose it would later serve.

Generations later the Levitical priests and Levites would minister to God there, but first it was consecrated by a higher priesthood than theirs. Melchizedek's priesthood was a king/priest order to which Jesus belonged. Jesus was from the tribe of Judah, not the priestly tribe of Levi. But the writer of Hebrews tells us that the Levites, who lived off the tithe, paid their tithe to Melchizedek's higher priesthood through their father Abraham (see Heb. 7:9-10).

Jerusalem

When Joshua came to Canaan, the name "Salem" had been expanded to "Jerusalem" and was ruled by an Amorite king named Adoni-zedek (see Josh. 10:1). Melchizedek's effect was still there somehow. The city's name had been expanded instead of done away with. Whereas "Salem" means "peace," "Jerusalem" means "a flow of peace." And whereas Melchizedek's name meant King of Righteousness, this current king's name meant Lord of Righteousness: a very godly name for an Amorite king.

Nevertheless, this Amorite king opposed Joshua and was destroyed. But the Israelites did not occupy Jerusalem, so in Joshua 15, we see that the Jebusites moved into it and the sons of Judah could not drive them out. The Jebusites renamed the city "Jebus" (see Judg. 19:10), which means "trodden." The place that God had chosen to be His dwelling place—a place where there was a flow of peace—was now trodden down by the enemy.

Jebus

After Joshua's death, Judah mounted another campaign against Jebus. This time they captured it but, again, did not occupy the city (see Judg. 1:8). Jesus said in Revelation 2:25 to hold on tight to what you have until He comes again. We need to occupy the territory we have gained. When we don't, the devil always comes to steal it back and often reinforces his stronghold there.

The Jebusites, at some point, came back and probably refortified the city so that when the Benjaminites tried later to drive them out they were unsuccessful (see Judg. 1:21-22). This was the last attempt Israel made to dislodge the Jebusites, until David came on the scene. By that time, they were so confident in their invincibility that David was told that the blind and lame of the city could keep him out (see 2 Sam. 5:6-7). So strong was the devil's hold on this important location that it remained "trodden" for hundreds of years.

Although Satan probably did not know what God intended for this place, he knew that God had marked it by the presence of

Melchizedek. It's like a child who cares nothing about a certain toy until he sees another child take an interest in it.

There was nothing special about the site that Jerusalem occupied. It had no harbor, no river frontage and was not on either of the major trade routes that ran between Egypt and Mesopotamia. The "King's Highway" trade route ran along the plains on the other side of the Jordan, and the Via Maris (Way of the Sea) ran along the Mediterranean coast. Jebus was served only by a dogleg from the Via Maris called the Ridge Route that went through Hebron and Shechem as well. The Jebusites could have moved 15 miles to the east and located on the fertile banks of the Jordan River. Or they could have moved 30 miles or so to the west and located on the Mediterranean Sea. But the only place the Jebusites would have was the place that Melchizedek had sanctified. I believe the Jebusites were demonically driven and demonically empowered to hold their little plot of ground.

The tribes of Judah and Benjamin, as well as the whole nation under Joshua, had not been able to liberate Jerusalem for any significant length of time. These Jebusites were a thorn in Israel's side.

On the Border

The border between Judah and Benjamin ran along the southern slope of Jerusalem (see Josh. 15:8). In fact, except for Mount Zion and Mount Moriah, most of Jerusalem eventually lay in the territory of Benjamin. But neither tribe had any great desire to possess the city. Judah probably said, "Let Benjamin deal with them." Benjamin replied, "Let Judah handle them." And so it went for years. Although Jerusalem was destined to be God's holy city, and Zion's hill was to be the place of God's habitation, no one in Israel walked in this revelation and they were content to let the Jebusites have it. It is noted that both the tribe of Judah and the tribe of Benjamin learned, instead, to "live with" the Jebusites (see Josh. 15:63; Judg. 1:21-22). No Israelite leader ever wanted Jerusalem for a capital. Even Saul, the nation's first king—a Benjaminite—had no desire to possess the city.

Then came David. David knew that he had to have this city; no other city would do. He already had Hebron. God had led him to Hebron, and it was there that he was made king over Judah and eventually all of Israel (see 2 Sam. 2:1-4). As a capital, Hebron was fine. But God's plans were for more than a capital city. God was going to bring the worship of heaven into the earth and He had prepared the ground and sanctified it through His king/priest, Melchizedek.

We don't know what revelation David had about the site during this part of his reign. All we know is that David was a man after God's own heart (see 1 Sam. 13:14), and God's heart was set on the old city of Salem. Any city in Israel would have welcomed David to make his capital there, but David was determined to have the Jebusite-infested hill; it would be where he would build his house, rule his kingdom, set up his tabernacle and inaugurate a paradigm of worship that God would resurrect in the last days.

True Beauty

Why was this hill so precious to the Lord? What did He find about it that made it so beautiful and desirable to Him? Zion's hill is not on today's list of luxury resort locations in the travel guides, and there are countless places that I would consider more beautiful and desirable. Why not Hawaii or Victoria Falls? Surely a more desirable place could be found than that dusty little hill in Jerusalem.

Even though the Sons of Korah proclaimed that Mount Zion was beautiful in elevation (see Ps. 48: 2), I believe the thing that caused the Lord to desire it was not its aesthetic beauty but instead what went on there. Remember, David himself was not chosen for his physical appearance. Samuel had been impressed with Eliab, David's oldest brother, because of his impressive stature. When Samuel saw Eliab, he said, " 'Surely the LORD's anointed is before Him!' But the LORD said to Samuel, 'Do not look at his appearance or at his physical stature, because I have refused him. For the LORD does not see as man sees; for man looks at the outward appearance, but the LORD looks at the heart' " (1 Sam. 16:6-8).

When God looked at Zion, He saw not the dusty hill but the prophetic, passionate, energetic, radical, anointed, face-to-face, heaven-like worship that He desires to dwell in and enthrone Himself on.

Hermon

If God were looking for a beautiful majestic peak, Hermon would have been the best choice. Hermon was the "Eliab" of the mountain peaks, but David points out:

> Is Mount Bashan the high mountain of summits, Mount Bashan [east of the Jordan] the mount of God? Why do you look with grudging and envy, you many-peaked mountains, at the mountain [of the city called Zion] which God has desired for His dwelling place? Yes, the Lord will dwell in it forever (Ps. 68:15-16, *AMP*).

Bashan was not actually a mountain, but a mountainous region east of the northern run of the Jordan. The prominent peak of this region was the majestic Mount Hermon, rising more than 9,000 feet above sea level. Covered year round with snow, Hermon was and is a magnificent sight that can be seen as far away as the shores of the Dead Sea, 120 miles to the south. Its melting snows provide the main source of water for the headwaters of the Jordan River. In the heat of summer, when the surrounding countryside is parched from the heat, these snows condense the vapors in the high mountain air causing light clouds to hover round the summit and heavy dews to fall on its slopes.

In Psalm 133, David uses the picture of these dews—if they could be imagined coming down on Zion's hill—as an illustration of how good and pleasant brotherly unity is. But, just like David's brother Eliab, God did not choose Mount Hermon, even though it was taller and more majestic than Zion. In fact, it was those very qualities that caused the Baal worshipers to choose Hermon as their sacred high place and it was even called Baal-Hermon at times (see 1 Chron. 5:23).

Mount Hermon is actually comprised of three summits, which were probably what David was referring to in Psalm 68:15 when he said, "A mountain of many peaks is the mountain of Bashan." David knew that God was not after the highest or grandest place for His dwelling, but the place where He would be amidst the continual praises of His people. So it was only with grudging envy that the high, majestic peaks of Bashan were able to look down on the humble hill that God chose for His dwelling place. But it was on this humble hill that God established the manner of worship that He would raise up in the last days to enthrone Himself for His end-time purposes.

Location, Location, Location

David set up his tabernacle on Zion's hill: the hill the Jebusites reluctantly gave up when God decided He was ready to make use of it. As I pointed out earlier, the name "Zion" had never been used on earth until David used it to name the hill he had secured. God had given David the name because David's hill was going to be patterned after God's hill in heaven. The worship on God's holy hill in heaven that we saw in Revelation was going to be established on a hill by the same name on earth. Again, Psalm 78:69 says that God built His sanctuary on Mount Zion "like the heights." God patterned the sanctuary on David's Mount Zion after the one on His own holy mountain in heaven.

David's hill had been sanctified by Melchizedek generations before and then left as fallow ground until David came to redeem it for God's purposes. I believe that David—from his limited understanding in his first attempt to bring in the Ark—came to fully comprehend the significance of this hill God had given him to establish. He also came to understand the hill's founder, Melchizedek. After Abraham's encounter with Melchizedek, recorded in Genesis, no one in the entire Old Testament even makes reference to the old king/priest. But David, in Psalm 110, showed his understanding that the coming Messiah would be a priest according to the order of Melchizedek.

Now David understood the significance of the hill—its name, its founder and God's purpose there. "I have found David son of Jesse a man after My own heart, who will do all My will and carry out My program fully" (Acts 13:22, *AMP*).

What Happened to David's Tabernacle?

For about 40 years, David led his people in extravagant, fervent, passionate, prophetic, intercessory, face-to-face worship, with dancing and rejoicing. He had worship leaders, he had gatekeepers and he had priests—all to minister before the Lord. They enthroned the Lord on their praises, and from that throne God ruled, He roared, He dealt recompense on His enemies and He brought blessings upon His people. But when that brief season was over, we have to wonder what became of the tent that was so significant to David's purpose on earth.

Was it captured and carried off by the Amalekites? Did Solomon fold it up and put it in a venerated place in the temple like he did with Moses' tabernacle? Did a tabernacle cult whisk it off and worship it on some high place like they did the golden snakes that Moses raised up on a pole in the wilderness (see 2 Kings 18:4)? Was it burned, buried, ripped apart or stolen? No! Nor was it sold or recycled or bulldozed. Neither did raiders of the lost tabernacle set out in our time to find its secret hiding place and plunder its secret powers. I believe it was left there on Mount Zion until it just . . . fell down.

The Season Changes

The days of David's tabernacle were glorious but numbered. God had used David to demonstrate worship as it was in heaven and give a prototype of the face-to-face worship that would be possible for New Testament saints through Jesus. But this was the Old Testament, and when the season for David's tabernacle was finished, this New Testament manner of worship had to be put to rest. It was illegal in the Old Testament paradigm. The veil had to be reestablished for another thousand years until Jesus Christ came to remove it and bring us face to face with the Father, by His blood, to worship.

When Mount Zion's time on earth was done, it would be completely denuded of its glory, grandeur, notoriety and fame: the Ark would be removed, and the tabernacle that crowned it would be abandoned and forgotten. This was all part of God's plan. David would not pass on this new order of worship to his son or to the successive generations of Old Testament Israel.

Solomon

When David died, Solomon did not seek the Lord in the tabernacle on Zion's hill. Solomon never had. First Kings 3:3 tells us that Solomon walked in all of David's statutes, except in his manner of worship. Solomon sought the Lord at the Tabernacle of Moses, which was at the high place of Gibeon. Solomon's one recorded visit to David's tabernacle, recorded in 1 Kings 3:15, was not to offer sacrifices of praise but burnt offerings prescribed by the law. David was dead and the keys of David, which had opened up the worship of heaven in that tabernacle, were now going to go back to their original owner, Jesus Christ (see Rev. 3:7), and that which had been opened by those keys was shut tight for another thousand years.

Solomon's charge was to lead Israel back into the Old Testament paradigm of worship. You would think this would be a pretty hard sell after Israel had tasted the glory of worship in the manifested presence of God, face to face, for most of a generation. Now they would be expected to put the Ark of God's presence back behind its veil. No more would they sing and dance before the unveiled presence of God and bask in its glory. The Ark would be hid from Israel's eyes from that day forward, except for the high priests who entered beyond the veil once a year. It was therefore necessary for Solomon to seek the Lord, not at David's tabernacle, but at the tabernacle of Moses, and not with sacrifices of praise like David, but with the old prescribed animal sacrifices: a thousand of them (see 2 Chron. 1:2-6). Solomon was seeking the Lord according to the Old Testament pattern, and God was pleased with him and met him in a dream that very night, giving Solomon wisdom, the likes of which the world had never seen.

The New Temple

Solomon was a phenomenal success! The desire to see the temple built had been planted deeply in the hearts of all the people. Israel had longed for it for years. David's original plan had been for a temple to house the Ark, not a tabernacle. Although the tabernacle was glorious, David always longed for a more magnificent dwelling place for the Ark, a glorious temple. Through the years of his success, David had been setting aside his spoils of war for the temple that would one day be built. David's captains had done the same. All the heads of Israel's households had given as well. Even David's old nemesis, King Saul, and Saul's commander, Abner, had dedicated funds to the house of the Lord, which eventually went toward the building of the temple (see 1 Chron. 26:27-28). Samuel had also been a contributor. All Israel, from the great to the small, had given toward the temple.

Great stores of gold, silver, bronze, iron, building stones, jewels and quality cuts of wood (see 1 Chron. 29:1-9) awaited the day that the temple would be built. So much treasure was amassed that even Solomon, in all his extravagance, was not able to use it all up. The excess was brought in and placed in a special room of the temple as a memorial (see 2 Chron. 5:1). When David's days were done, Israel's thoughts turned to their long-awaited temple that Solomon was commissioned to build. When the temple was finally completed, all eyes quickly turned away from Zion to Jerusalem's other hill, Moriah.

The Ark Is Moved

"Solomon assembled to Jerusalem the elders of Israel and all the heads of the tribes, the leaders of the fathers' households of the sons of Israel, to bring up the ark of the covenant of the LORD *out of* the city of David, *which is Zion*" (2 Chron. 5:2-3, *NASB,* emphasis added).

The Ark, which had seemed so at home in its humble tent, was about to be moved to the last home it would ever see. There were no protesters to meet the assembly as they approached the tent on Zion's hill. No one locked arms around the tabernacle and chanted. No police had to be called and no tear gas had to be used to disperse an unruly throng. Israel was in one heart and one accord. There were no dissenters. As united as they had been behind David when they brought the Ark in, they were just as united behind Solomon to take the Ark out. The transition was complete. Along with the Ark, Solomon's crowd went and got the tabernacle of Moses and brought it into a special place prepared for it in the new temple (see 2 Chron. 5:4-5). No such place was reserved for David's tabernacle; the heart of the nation had effectively been turned away from it. No one stayed behind to mourn its old glory days. No one even bothered to take it down. Nothing was left to mark the site. No memorial or historical marker was ever erected.

Today we only know the general location of the tabernacle. The small plot of Jebusite ground that David took, against all odds, eventually became an unnoticed piece of real estate in a larger city. The latter walls that were built around Jerusalem did not even encompass the old City of David, Zion's hill. Today it is just an Arab neighborhood in a larger city that continually draws the attention of the whole world.

Holy Sites

It is staggering how God erased this precious site from the hearts and minds of Israel and the world. Today, Jerusalem is peppered with "holy sites," all of which are adorned with monuments, synagogues, mosques and cathedrals—all except for Mount Zion. The city of two hills now effectively has only one.

For the last 3,000 years, Moriah has held the focus of Jews, Christians and Muslims, while Zion has drifted further and further into obscurity. The Babylonians rose up against Jerusalem, plundering and ruining the temple, but the Jews, upon their return from captivity, rebuilt the temple on Mount Moriah. After hundreds of years it was rebuilt once again by Herod the Great but was never moved away from its sacred site, Moriah. The Romans tore it down stone by stone in A.D. 70 and deported the Jews all over the world.

For centuries, Moriah lay bare until a new religion, Islam, claimed it as their holy site, building upon it the Dome of the Rock, which stands there today. The Jews, in the ages since, have been left with a section of what had been the retaining wall of the temple on the southwest corner of the Temple Mount, called the Western Wall or Wailing Wall. The Crusaders captured Jerusalem for Christendom and held it for about 100 years; but when the Crusaders rebuilt the walls around Jerusalem they did not even include Zion's hill. Mount Zion was now outside the gates of the city. Later, when the Ottoman Empire took Jerusalem, the Turkish engineers who planned the restoration of the Old City walls in 1538 also failed to include Mount Zion within the walls.

Even the name, Mount Zion, was assigned to a different hill when Byzantine pilgrims to Jerusalem mistook the larger, flatter Western Hill for their quest and called it Mount Zion. Although they were mistaken, the name stuck, and today that western hill is still named Mount Zion. Although the hill of David's tabernacle steadily slipped into oblivion, Moriah was being sought by Judaism, Islam and Christianity. Today pilgrims, tourists and worshipers from these three religions, and more, come by the millions each year to see, to pray or to pay homage in some way to the mosque and the Wailing Wall, which now occupy Moriah. But the place where David once built his tabernacle cannot even be accurately identified.

Where Is Zion's Hill?

On my first trip to Jerusalem, I wanted more than anything to see David's Mount Zion. I was part of a group of prayer warriors who went to intercede in various parts of the city. The first thing that struck me was how mountainous the area was. Everywhere, we trudged up some slope or skidded down another. For two days I was not even able to get a glimpse of David's old city as we traveled to different parts of the city to pray. Mount Moriah, Mount Scopus, the Western Hill and the Mount of Olives continually blocked my view.

Finally, when I caught sight of the old City of David, I was taken aback. It is the smallest hill of them all. I immediately thought of David's phrase, "As the mountains surround Jerusalem" (Ps. 125:2). David's Zion was truly a humble hill in the midst of giants. David was surrounded by Eliabs. As I walked on the ground that Melchizedek once tread, in the area that once contained the tabernacle of David, I was amazed to see what it had become. It is now a humble Arab neighborhood outside the walls of old Jerusalem. Dogs bark and people bustle through the small dusty streets. It does not attract tourists like Temple Mound/Dome of the Rock, which towers over it to its north, or the Mount of Olives and Garden of Gethsemane to its northeast, or the modern-day Mount Zion (the Western Hill) where the Upper Room is located. I had the opportunity to spend the night in a small home only a block away from where David's tabernacle was probably pitched. At 3:00 A.M. in the morning the Muslim call to prayer blared out over the loud speakers in a minaret on David's old hill. I thought, *Lord, this hill is a long way from where it was in David's day.*

Better Days Ahead

What designs God may have for the original hill in Jerusalem that was once called Zion, I do not know. God spoke through the prophet Isaiah about a day coming when Zion's hill, "My holy mountain" (Isa. 11:9), would be a paradise on earth. In Revelation 14:1-5, where Jesus is pictured standing on Mount Zion with the 144,000, they are all worshiping—singing a "new song" to the Lord.

I have friends who are involved in 24-hour-a-day prayer and worship watches near the area that David once raised his tent. The presence of the Lord is mighty in their midst. God might use the prayers and praise from that place to bring forth the raised-up tabernacle of David in the worldwide Body of Christ, or God might have something new planned for the neglected hill that once

housed His presence. God could reinstate Mount Zion to its former glory in an instant. It does not matter who the present occu-
pants are or what zone restrictions have been put on it. The
physical and the spiritual could once again be as it was in David's
day. I am excited to see what God might do.

It's Time

When God was ready to launch Jerusalem into her destiny, nothing could stand in His way. It didn't matter that His city had been
in the hands of the enemy for hundreds of years. It didn't matter
that the many attempts throughout those hundreds of years had
failed to secure this ground. God's time had come. He raised up
His servant, David, to secure the place He had sanctified for His
own purposes, and the Jebusites were powerless to resist. In God's
kingdom, even if a plan or a vision falls into the ground and dies,
like a grain of wheat it will be raised up stronger than before and
bear much fruit (see John 12:24).

Today we see the city of Jerusalem with its holy places occupied by the enemy. A Muslim edifice is built on Mount Moriah,
and Mount Zion is a dusty Arab neighborhood. When we look at
these frustrating things, we must remember the state of these two
hills the few years just before God brought them into their places
of prominence. When God was ready to launch His designs on His
holy city, Jerusalem, there was no power on earth that could hold
Him back. The invincible city fell quickly to God's servant, David.
With God's chosen hill secured, it was time to bring in the Ark.

The Tabernacle of God Is with Man

Zion, itself, is timeless. Before the earth was, Zion was—God's holy
hill in heaven where He is enthroned on the timeless worship of
His creation. On earth, Zion was the name given to the hill where
David erected his tabernacle—where God enthroned Himself on
the praises of His people. Although the physical location, Mount
Zion, lost its place of prominence, the term "Zion" continued to

represent the place where God dwelled, enthroned on the praises of His people. In the days of Solomon's temple, "Zion" came to refer to the city of Jerusalem as a whole instead of just the hill where David had his tabernacle, Melchizedek's Salem. As the years passed, the temple Solomon built became only one of many places of worship in Jerusalem. Solomon's many foreign wives pressured him to set up places to honor their gods as well. Over the centuries that followed, Jerusalem declined dramatically as a worship center. Although revivals occurred under various kings, Zion, as a place where God is enthroned on the praises of His people, ceased to exist in the earth. The temple itself was destroyed and the people were removed into captivity.

But God's purposes for Zion were not dead, only sleeping. At the right time He intended to raise up Zion (see Ps. 102:16-18) and rebuild David's tabernacle and repair it to be used for its new purpose: to bring in the fullness of the Gentiles.

Zion, therefore, is not limited to a geographic location, and David's tabernacle is no longer a physical structure. What God intended to raise up in the last day was not a cloth tent on a physical hill, but a kingdom/priesthood of worshiping warriors. Where they came together in worship would be the Zion where He would never cease to dwell. The Son of David, Jesus Christ, now sits on David's throne, and He wants to seat that throne on the praises of these worship warriors. This is God's dwelling place forever, the place that cannot be moved, and the place of God's desire: This is Zion, the place where God is raising up the tabernacle of David and repairing its breaches. It is "us" when we enter into the purposes God has for us. Revelation 21:3 says, "And I heard a loud voice from the throne, saying, 'Behold, the tabernacle of God is among men, and He will dwell among them, and they shall be His people, and God Himself will be among them'" (*NASB*).

The Rebuilding Begins

As the leaders of the fledgling church gathered in Jerusalem, as recorded in Acts 15, the apostle James was listening to Paul's report that Gentiles were being saved when the Holy Spirit quickened the prophecy of Amos: Gentiles would come into the kingdom when God began to rebuild the fallen tent of David. James was reminded of Simon Peter's earlier accounts of Gentile conversions and addressed the council:

> Men and brethren, listen to me: Simon has declared how God at the first visited the Gentiles to take out of them a people for His name. And with this the words of the prophets agree, just as it is written: "After this I will return and will rebuild the tabernacle of David, which has fallen down; I will rebuild its ruins, and I will set it up; so that the rest of mankind may seek the LORD, even all the Gentiles who are called by My name, says the LORD who does all these things" (Acts 15:13-17).

James didn't explain how the Gentiles related to David's tabernacle, nor do I believe he understood it himself. I believe it was the Holy Spirit proclaiming through James the beginning of a new era on the earth. Joseph Garlington says:

> James was publicly announcing "that day" had come, and the baptism of the Holy Spirit among the Gentiles marked the beginning of the fulfillment of the prophecy of Amos.[1]

That which God had instituted 1,000 years earlier and then let fall into the dust, He was now going to "build it as it used to be." This was the beginning. The New Testament-style face-to-face worship that had been modeled in David's tabernacle would now be built again in the New Testament Church. The end result would be that "all the Gentiles who are called by My name" would be brought into the kingdom. The rebuilding of Zion and David's tabernacle that crowned it would be a process that unfolded over the next centuries, but James, by the Holy Spirit, proclaimed that the process had begun.

RESTORE AND REVEAL THE GLORY
CHUCK D. PIERCE

As you read this chapter, perhaps you saw something that you never understood before. *The real war in your life is over the glory of God manifesting.* His glory is in you and can be released through you. There is a glory in you that came when God created you in His image. This glory can be displayed individually and then manifest at a greater dimension corporately when we are fully integrated into the Body of Christ. Psalm 16:9 says, "Therefore my heart is glad, and my glory rejoices; my flesh also will rest in hope."

There is something deeply woven into each one of us that seeks a greater connection with Someone greater than what we have known. When God knit each of us in our mother's womb, He knit the desire to see His glory revealed in our life. Some seek the 15 seconds of fame that seem to satisfy this need. Others find a temporary satisfaction by serving as leaders in major corporations. Some find an earthly relationship in life that satisfies their need until that relationship ends. Then there are those who divert this need to the pursuit of money for their security and self-worth. However, the greatest satisfaction that a person can gain is to seek, find and get to know the One who made them.

When you divinely connect with the "Father of spirits" (Heb. 12:9), you see *His* glory, but you also realize that you have a *glory* in you. Hebrews 1:1-4 tells us:

God, who at various times and in various ways spoke in time past to the fathers by the prophets, has in these last days spoken to us by His Son, whom He has appointed heir of all things, through whom also He made the worlds; who being the brightness of His glory and the express image of His person, and upholding all things by the word of His power, when He had by Himself purged our sins, sat down at the right hand of the Majesty on high, having become so much better than the angels, as He has by inheritance obtained a more excellent name than they.

Hebrews 12:9 says, "Moreover, we have had earthly fathers who disciplined us and we yielded [to them] and respected [them for training us]. Shall we not much more cheerfully submit to the Father of spirits and so [truly] live?" (*AMP*). Because Father God is glory, and because He is Father of our spirits, then through our trials, tribulations and disciplines we can experience and see His glory!

The name of our ministry is Glory of Zion International Ministries, Inc. When I was seeking the Lord in January 1992 for the identity of what He was calling me to, I heard the Spirit of God speak the words, "*Glory of Zion*"! June Rana, my long-time assistant, came in and said, "I was reading today in the book of Isaiah, and one of the captions in my Bible in chapter 35 is 'The Future—Glory of Zion!'" I was amazed. Zion was a place. This place was where God would come and create a city—a people for His use. This place can be filled with His glory!

What is this glory? Glory is our future. When we think of glory, our most prominent ideas are of beauty, majesty and splendor. Glory belongs to men, and especially to men of prominence, such as a king. This glory may manifest in power. Glory can be seen in our portion or how much wealth we obtain. Glory can be seen when a person experiences and is known for his or her integrity and character. God's glory may mean the honor and audible praise His creatures give to Him.

Glory is the possession and characteristic of Yahweh! When His people praise Him and give homage to Him through worship, the atmosphere is filled with His presence. The Lord promises to fill His house with glory! The word "glory" means to experience "weight" or "heaviness." *Kabhodh* expresses majesty. Jacob experienced a glory because of the flocks and herds that he acquired! In Haggai 2, God shakes loose everything linked with the loss of time in rebuilding His house. He shakes everything until a greater glory is seen. Through all of your shakings, you can see God's glory manifest. Psalm 16:11 says, "You will show me the path of life; in Your presence is fullness of joy; at Your right hand are pleasures forevermore."

Let Him shake your place. Your shaking will produce new joy for your path ahead. Let Him renew your call to building His purpose. See His glory manifest!

For Study and Reflection
Read Psalm 132. Meditate on Revelation 5:12-13
and memorize Psalm 115:1.

7

Rebuilding the Tabernacle

*"In that day I will restore David's fallen tent. I will repair its
broken places, restore its ruins, and build it as it used to be, so that they
may possess the remnant of Edom and all the nations that bear my name,"
declares the* LORD, *who will do these things.*

AMOS 9:11-12, *NIV*

Preparing the Way

Two Hundred and Fifty Years
Some 250 years after David's reign, God spoke to Amos, a sheepherder in the hills of Tekoa, five miles south of Bethlehem. Israel
was divided now into two kingdoms, and though the sheepherder
lived in the southern kingdom of Judah, he was sent to the northern kingdom of Israel with a message of rebuke and a prophecy of
certain destruction upon the land.

Amos was not the first prophet from Judah that God had sent
north to Israel, and Israel had never had much love for the fiery
messengers from the south. Even worse, in the midst of God's sear-
ing words against Israel, He chooses to announce His plan to bring
in all the nations called by His name. This was a shock! God was
going to bring the nations into His commonwealth, which had always been reserved for the Jews alone. And if that wasn't shock
enough, the method He was going to use was the restored tabernacle of David. The worship of heaven that God had released on
earth for 40 years in David's reign was going to be reestablished
just "as it used to be." Zion, which had fallen into the dust, was
going to be resurrected.

While the southern kingdom of Judah had not been walking in the fullness of the inheritance of David, the northern kingdom of Israel had specifically rejected it. Such a division had arisen between the two kingdoms that Israel didn't want anything to do with the blessings promised to Judah through the house of David. They had adamantly cried out, "What portion do we have in David? We have no inheritance in the son of Jesse" (2 Chron. 10:16, *NASB*). Jeroboam, the first king of that northern kingdom, immediately set up places for his people to worship in the northern kingdom so they would not be drawn into the influence of the southern kingdom by their visits to its holy city, Jerusalem. For the most part, Jeroboam's people were well satisfied with their new religious system with its new feasts and paraphernalia.

Centuries later, when Jesus passed through this region, the woman at the well made the argument that her fathers worshiped "in this mountain" (John 4:20, *NASB*). Her mountain was just as good as the Jew's place of worship, Jerusalem. Jeroboam had done his work well. His religious system was a success. Then Amos comes and proclaims that Israel will be swept away and their "religion" would not save them, but God would raise up instead the fallen tent of David—which these people had proclaimed no part in—and would bring in the fullness of the nations under its covering.

Eight Hundred and Fifty Years

As the days of the New Testament dawned, the king that occupied David's throne was not of the house of Judah. This king was not even an Israelite, but was instead from Edom, a kingdom that Israel had suffered much bad blood with over the centuries. Herod the Great had clawed his way to power through years of political maneuvering among the giants of the quickly changing Roman Empire. Greats such as Pompey, Julius Caesar, Mark Anthony, Cleopatra and Augustus Caesar all played their parts in Herod's rise over the years to his present position as king of the Jews. But even though Herod had gained the throne, he was still no son of David, a fact that caused him great consternation when the Magi showed up looking for the newborn King of the Jews. All the same it was in these troubled times that God began to fulfill the prophecy given by His prophet of old, Amos.

About A.D. 50, Paul and Barnabas traveled to Jerusalem to meet with the leaders there. Upon hearing Paul's report about the Gentiles being saved, James, the brother of Jesus, remembered the 850-year-old prophecy out of Amos that mentioned the Gentiles coming into the kingdom of God:

> "AFTER THESE THINGS I will return, AND I WILL REBUILD THE TABERNACLE OF DAVID WHICH HAS FALLEN, AND I WILL REBUILD ITS RUINS, AND I WILL RESTORE IT, SO THAT THE REST OF MANKIND MAY SEEK THE LORD, AND ALL THE GENTILES WHO ARE CALLED BY MY NAME," SAYS THE LORD, WHO MAKES THESE THINGS KNOWN FROM LONG AGO (Acts 15:16-18, *NASB*).

James probably had no idea what the fullness of the prophecy meant, but he did know that the "rest of mankind" was beginning to seek the Lord, and all the Gentiles who were called by God's name were coming into the Kingdom. God, however, did know all that the prophecy meant and used James in an official meeting of church leaders to announce the resurrection of something that He had allowed to lie dormant for 1,000 years.

God was not going to set up a new system of worship for His new church. His New Testament Church was going to worship like they did in heaven. No more types and shadows but the fullness of face-to-face worship. This manner of worship had already been modeled for the Church in the tabernacle of David. God proclaimed through James that He would now reinstate what He had established in the tabernacle. He would raise it back up and put it back in operation. God was going to rebuild it "as it used to be." The worship of heaven that was released in the old tabernacle would be released again on His New Testament Church. There would be singing and dancing and prophecy and spontaneous songs, now from His new emerging Church, which He had poured out His

Spirit upon. These worshipers would be of the new order of king/priests like David. These would worship Him face to face, now by the blood of Jesus. There would be warring worship and He would enthrone Himself on it and rule and reign and bring in the fullness of the Gentiles. This New Testament Church formulated the foundation on which the tabernacle of David would be raised up over the next centuries.

The Throne of David

In restoring the tabernacle of David, God was not only bringing to His new Church the worship of heaven, but also the kingly authority associated with David's throne. In Isaiah we read about this throne: "In mercy the throne will be established; and One will sit on it in truth, in the tabernacle of David, judging and seeking justice and hastening righteousness" (Isa. 16:5). It is interesting that this throne is mentioned as being "in" the tabernacle of David. As I noted in previous chapters, the tabernacle was set up for praise. God enthroned Himself on that praise. Isaiah tells us that the Messiah will sit on David's throne, which will be on the praises of His people in the restored tabernacle. Kevin J. Conner, in his study of this subject, wrote:

> The immediate context of Isaiah 16:1-5 mentions Zion, a throne, a judge and thus kinship is inferred in which justice will be manifested resulting in righteousness. The person alluded to is the Messiah who will sit in David's tent as ruler, Messiah being of the line or house of David. Isaiah 9:6-9 is very similar and speaks of government, a throne, justice and judgment on David's throne. All of this is Messianic indeed.[1]

Isaiah 9:6-9, which Mr. Conner mentioned, is the famed Scripture we sing at Christmas from Handel's *Messiah*: "For unto us a Child is born, unto us a Son is given; and the government will be upon His shoulder. And His name will be called Wonderful, Counselor, Mighty God, Everlasting Father, Prince of Peace. Of the increase of His government and peace there will be no end, upon the throne of David and over His kingdom" (Isa. 9:6-7). Jesus was the rightful heir to the throne of David, and when He rose from the dead and ascended to the Father, He took His place on that throne on the praises of His people in the restored tabernacle of David, to rule for eternity. Herod's sons were left with a temple that would be razed to the ground and a nation that would be destroyed and scattered over the face of the earth, while God's kingdom would be ever increasing.

David's throne was truly different in that its ultimate occupant would not only be a king but a priest. Jesus is both the King of kings and our High Priest. David, as we have seen, took up both of these offices, but it was not something that was allowed for any of the other kings of Israel before or after David. The offices of king and of priest were separated. Kings, from David on, would be from the tribe of Judah. In Jacob's final blessings to his sons, he had prophesied, "The scepter shall not depart from Judah, nor the ruler's staff from between his feet, until Shiloh comes" (Gen. 49:10, NASB).

Priests, on the other hand, came from the tribe of Levi and from the household of Aaron. Kings were kings and priests were priests, and never the twain met. When King Saul stepped over into the priestly office by sacrificing burnt offerings at Gilgal, God tore Saul's kingdom from him as well as the dynasty that would have followed (see 1 Sam. 13:8-15).

David then followed Saul and acted freely as a priest, with God's great approval. David sacrificed burnt offerings at the dedication of his tabernacle, and God was well pleased (see 1 Chron. 16:2-3). Later David built an altar on the threshing floor of Ornan, where Solomon's temple would one day be built, and again offered the burnt offerings to the Lord. This time God showed His approval by sending down fire to consume David's sacrifice and holding back the destruction upon Jerusalem (see 1 Chron. 21:25-27). David even got away with entering the house of God and unlawfully eating the consecrated bread reserved for the priests (see 1 Sam. 21:1-6; Matt. 12:3-4) and dared to wear a priest's ephod under his kingly robes (see 1 Chron. 15:27).

But after David, the prohibition of kings to cross over into a priestly role was reinstated. When King Uzziah performed the priestly function of burning incense before the Lord in the temple, God struck him with leprosy (see 2 Chron. 26:16-19).

Why Did David Get Away with Everything?

What was different about David? Why did he get special treatment? It seemed as if God winked at David's behavior, but this is not true. David was held responsible for his sins and indeed received harsher discipline than the common man did. David's sin with Bathsheba earned him the crushing loss of his child by that union. When David numbered his people, against God's will, he suffered the visit of the death angel upon his people.

There is only one area that David seemed to "get away with" noncompliance to God's rules. This was when he entered into priestly activity. In order to manifest the worship of heaven on Zion's hill and offer a prototype of that worship for the New Testament saints, David had to function in the priesthood that operated in heaven and that the New Testament saints would be under. This is the priesthood of Melchizedek, which the Old Testament saints had no truck with because they were under the Levitical priesthood.

But David understood the king/priest role and operated competently in it. When he brought the Ark into Zion to his tabernacle, he dressed as both priest and king. He wore the stately robes of a king, but underneath he wore an ephod (see 1 Chron. 15:27), which was the garment worn by the priests when they ministered to the Lord. God had accepted David as a priest as well as a king.

As king, David sat on a throne that would never fail—a throne that would one day be occupied by the King of kings, Jesus Christ. As priest, David inaugurated a new order of worship patterned after heaven itself. Both of these offices, the king and the priest, would be raised up together in latter times when God rebuilt the tabernacle. Zechariah prophesied that the Messiah would sit on His throne as priest and that He would bring together the two offices of king and priest (see Zech. 6:12-14).

David also prophesied that the Messiah would operate in this king/priest role: "You are a priest forever according to the order of Melchizedek" (Ps. 110:4, *NASB*). Jesus is that "priest forever" in Melchizedek's order (see Heb. 5:10): our King of kings and our High Priest before God.

The apostle Peter says that *we* are now a "royal priesthood" (1 Pet. 2:9). That means that we are not only priests but also royal priests, king/priests. This means more than just going to church and tithing. This means that all of us are priests (ministers to God) and that He has given us His kingly authority. The book of Revelation reminds us again that we are a kingdom of priests (see Rev. 1:6; 5:10; 20:6). Jesus Christ is the one who actually sits on the throne, but we are the many parts of the Body of Christ (see 1 Cor. 12:27), each with our own aspect of His authority. This was originally God's plan for the whole nation of Israel. He wanted them to be His holy, set-apart nation: His "kingdom of priests" mentioned in Exodus 19:6. But when Israel chose to worship the golden calf instead, Moses stood at the gate and cried out, "Whoever is for the LORD, come to me!" (Exod. 32:26, *NASB*). The tribe of Levi answered that call, and because of their obedience, they were set apart to be God's tribe ministers. The kingdom of priests would have to wait.

Out with the Old and in with the New

The Levitical priesthood continued on, century after century, until one day the priests entered the temple at the feast of Passover and the great veil before the Holy of Holies split in two from top to bottom right in front of their eyes. God's own Passover Lamb was hanging on a cross outside the city gates, uttering His last words, "It is finished" (Matt. 27:51; John 19:30). The true sacrifice had been offered. The Lamb of God was slain. The priesthood of Aaron was concluded. No more animal sacrifices were required.

And now with the veil gone the priests could plainly see what they had known all along: there was no Ark in the holy of holies. There had never been in this particular temple. When Herod built his beautiful temple, the Ark had long since been lost, and now the veil was torn to show that the way into God's presence was open to all through Jesus (see Heb. 10:19-22). The new temple was being put in place. Its cornerstone, Jesus, was laid in Zion (see 1 Pet. 2:6), the place where God is continually worshiped and enthroned on the praises of His people. Its building blocks were the newly emerging members of the Body of Christ (see Eph. 2:19-22). The apostle Paul proclaimed, "For we are the temple of the living God; just as God said, 'I WILL DWELL IN THEM' " (2 Cor. 6:16, *NASB*).

In the book of Hebrews, we see that because the Law of Moses, administered by the priesthood of Aaron, was not able to bring us into a perfect fellowship with God, it was necessary that a new and different kind of priesthood arise, the king/priests of Melchizedek, to accomplish that through Jesus Christ, our high priest (see Heb. 7:11-17).

David was our model of the king/priest when he set up his tabernacle on the site that Melchizedek sanctified hundreds of years before. During the short season that David operated in this capacity, God allowed His worshipers to approach the Ark of His presence with no veil or covering. Up to this point no one was permitted to even see the Ark except the high priest once each year as he entered on the Day of Atonement to sprinkle blood on the mercy seat. Even then, according to tradition, a rope was tied to the priest's ankle and bells were sewn to his robe. As the high priest ministered in the holy of holies behind the veil, the other priests listened to hear the bells on the robe. If the bells kept sounding it meant the priest was still moving—he was alive. But if the bells were to stop it might mean that he had been struck down, and no one wanted the job of going in after him. That's why they tied the rope to the high priest's ankle: if he was dead, they could just pull him out. Even when the Ark was being transported, it had to be covered with the veil. No one was allowed to even look upon it.

In David's tabernacle, they approached the Ark unafraid, and not just the priests. Only in the tabernacle of David was it permissible to approach the unveiled Ark. When the Ark was removed from the tabernacle, that time of grace ended, and it once again became a deadly offense to approach the unveiled Ark.

In Spirit and in Truth

The Church Worshiped in Spirit and Truth

What had come together in David's tabernacle with the unveiled Ark was the heavenly combination of spirit and truth. In heaven there had been no separation between the two. On earth there had been, but in the fourth chapter of John, Jesus told the woman at the well that the hour was at hand for these two essentials to come together on earth permanently: "An hour is coming, and now is, when the true worshipers will worship the Father in spirit and truth; for such people the Father seeks to be His worshipers. God is spirit, and those who worship Him must worship in spirit and truth" (John 4:23-25, *NASB*).

You can sense the air of excitement in Jesus' words. For centuries God had limited mankind to worshiping Him in truth alone—according to the Old Testament Law. But the forms and rituals that embodied the truth were just a shadow of the true worship that would be possible when the Holy Spirit fell on the Church at Pentecost and breathed the life of the Spirit into the truths of the Old Testament Law. God was spirit, and after the Holy Spirit fell, He could be worshiped in both spirit and in truth, like He had been in heaven for ages past, and like He had been for the short season of David's tabernacle. When that season ended, worship was once again centered on the formal procedures prescribed by the Law. So when Jesus met with the woman at the well, the Samaritans had been worshiping at their mountain, the Jews at their temple; but now worship would transcend any earthly locations or rituals. A transformation was coming, and God was looking for worshipers that would make that transition.

The apostle Paul picked up this theme of worship in spirit and in truth. First, of the Spirit, he says, "Be filled with the Spirit, speaking to one another in psalms and hymns and spiritual songs, singing and making melody with your heart to the Lord" (Eph. 5:18-19, *NASB*). Of the truth, he says, "Let the word of Christ richly dwell within you, with all wisdom teaching and admonishing one another with psalms and hymns and spiritual songs, singing with thankfulness in your hearts to God" (Col. 3:16-17, *NASB*). Paul mentions no form or ritual that we should follow, only the two re-quirements of being filled with the Spirit and letting the truth of the Word richly dwell in us.

What does it mean to worship in spirit and in truth? The key is in Ephesians 6:17. Paul tells us to take up the sword of the Spirit, which is the Word of God, the truth. The thing to remember here is that it is the Spirit's sword, not ours. As we pick up the Spirit's sword, we must allow Him to wield it. Without the guidance of the Holy Spirit, men turn the powerful Word of God into a set of rules and regulations. The Pharisees were experts at this. No one knew the Scriptures better than the Pharisees, but without the Holy Spirit, the Scriptures were used to bring people under bondage. Un-der the direction of the Holy Spirit, the Word of God becomes "liv-ing and active and sharper than any two-edged sword, and piercing as far as the division of soul and spirit" (Heb. 4:12, *NASB*).

We can, by the law, conform our soul to many of the tenets of the Word of God, but the Holy Spirit can quicken our spirit to come alive to the truth of the Word. This is the key with New Tes-tament worship. We can no longer follow the rituals of worship, even with reverence and devotion. Although this was acceptable and good for the Old Testament saints, we have been given the Holy Spirit and are expected to allow Him to direct us in our wor-ship. Just worshiping in the truth that the rituals portrayed is no longer enough. God, being spirit, now wants us to worship Him in spirit and in truth, "for we are the true circumcision, who worship in the Spirit of God and glory in Christ Jesus and put no confi-dence in the flesh" (Phil. 3:3, *NASB*).

Pentecost

It is interesting to note the day that God chose to send His Holy Spirit down on the New Testament saints. We all know it as the day of Pentecost. In the second chapter of Acts we see the Spirit descending like a mighty rushing wind with tongues of fire. Those gathered were all filled with the Holy Spirit and spoke in tongues. For the past 2,000 years the Church has celebrated this event as Pentecost Sunday. But for the 2,000 years before the Spirit fell, the

Jews had celebrated this day as the Feast of Pentecost, the day the Truth came down—God's Word, the Law.

This was the day, 50 days after the feast of Passover, that God appeared to Moses on Sinai and carved out the Ten Commandments in stone. The Jewish people sometimes refer to the Feast of Pentecost as "the feast of the giving of the Law." My pastor, Robert Heidler, says that they would celebrate this day by staying up the night before reading the Word, the Torah. Consequently, on the night before the Spirit was poured out on the Church, the disciples were most probably engaged in this traditional activity, studying God's Word. After an evening of being immersed in the Truth, God poured out His Spirit on the saints. God joined together the two aspects by which we, as New Testament saints, were to worship: in spirit and in truth.

Worship in the New Testament Church

In Spirit and in Truth

Now in spirit and in truth, the first-century Church began to enter into a new and living way of worship. Slowly freeing themselves from forms and rituals, the Church began to expand into heaven's manner of worship as the apostles equipped them to do so. Ernest B. Gentile says, "Early Christians quickly developed a unique system of worship that was fluid and flexible, easily adapting their format to Psalmic worship form that provided the best format for spontaneous, joyful worship."[2]

The similarities we saw between the worship in heaven and the worship in David's tabernacle began to be evident in the worship of the New Testament Church:

- It was face to face.
- It was spontaneous and dynamic.
- It was prophetic.
- It was intercessory.
- It was warring.
- It was continual.
- God interacted with it.

The Church Worshiped God Face to Face

One of the most distinguishing characteristics of New Testament worship is that the worshipers—legally for the first time, because of the blood of Jesus—were able to come before God to worship him face to face. The veil was now removed. The saints were now invited to come boldly before the throne (see Heb. 4:16). This was how they worshiped in heaven, but on earth it had not been permissible except for the brief season of David's tabernacle. That which was characteristic about the worship in heaven, and later in David's tabernacle, was now to become the norm for all saints.

In Christ's death the veil of the temple was rent, and His blood forever after gave us boldness and power to enter into the Holiest of all and live there day by day in the immediate presence of God. It is by the Holy Spirit—who issued forth from that Holiest of all where Christ had entered to bring its life to us and make us one with it—that we have the power to live and walk always with the consciousness of God's presence in us.[3]

The Church's Worship Was Spontaneous and Dynamic

They worshiped in the temple, they worshiped in their homes and they worshiped in the open areas of the city. They ate together. The book of Acts says that they met from house to house, breaking bread together (see Acts 5:42). Jesus had given them the example in the upper room. Now the meal was a part of their times together. They eventually called it the *agape*, the love feast, as mentioned in Jude 12.

They danced before the Lord as they had in David's tabernacle and apparently developed quite a reputation because of it. "The Persians called the earliest Christians *tarsa*, or shakers," says Gordon Rattray Taylor.[4] The writings of several Early Church fathers make mention of their dancing before the Lord. Clement of Alexandria, in the late second and early third century said, "So also we raise the head and lift the hands to heaven, and set the feet in motion at the closing utterance of the prayer."[5] Gregory Thaumaturgus (A.D. 210-260), bishop of Pontus, wrote, "The ring-dance of the angels encircles him, singing his glory in Heaven and proclaiming peace on earth.[6] Also, Basileios (A.D. 344-407), bishop of Caesarea, wrote concerning a recently deceased Christian brother, "We remember those who now, together with the Angels, dance the dance of the Angels around God, just as in the flesh they performed a spiritual dance of life and, here on earth."[7] And in another letter, "Could there be anything more blessed than to imitate on earth the ring-dance of the angels and at dawn to raise our voices in prayer and by hymns and songs glorify the rising creator."[8]

The Church also *halaled*. Paul, writing to the Christians in Rome (see Rom. 15:7-11), quoted the psalms and Deuteronomy to exhort the Gentiles to praise. In doing this he used the Hebrew word for praise, *halal*. Paul wanted the Church to praise God in the most vibrant way the Hebrews knew how, the *halal*: just like they did in David's tabernacle and just like they did in heaven. We can see that their worship was not in a rut. It had many aspects to it that kept it fresh and alive, springing from their hearts instead of from rituals.

The Church Worshiped Prophetically

Another hallmark of David's tabernacle had been its prophetic worship. When God poured His Spirit out on the Church, He was giving the saints the gifts of the Spirit mentioned in Romans 12, 1 Corinthians 12 and 14, and Ephesians 4, as well as other places in the Scripture. As the gift of prophecy began to operate in the Early Church, it came out in their worship. Paul encouraged the saints to not only sing psalms and hymns, but also to sing spiritual songs. Spiritual songs are just what the term indicates. They are songs of the spirit, not the intellect. Songs that require the intellect are psalms and hymns. Spiritual songs deal with things beyond our intellect, like prophecy and tongues. Paul wrote, "I will sing with my spirit [by the Holy Spirit that is within me], but I will sing [intelligently] with my mind and understanding also" (1 Cor. 14:15, *AMP*). Bob Sorge describes this phenomenon of spiritual song:

> They begin to have a new song rise up from within, begging for expression. We appreciate the lyrics that songwriters give us, but when we're in the river, our worship surges

over the banks of pre-written lyrics and published hymns.
Suddenly we find ourselves wanting to express a song of
the moment, a song that comes directly from the heart of
a lovesick worshipper . . . it is a "now" song that expresses
our immediate heart cry. And it is powerful![9]

These spiritual songs were prophetic, and it was this prophetic
nature of the New Testament Church that allowed them to tap
into heaven's worship just like they had in David's tabernacle.
God's heart and purposes were released from heaven into the worship of His Church on earth.

The Church Worshiped with Intercession
When God's heart and purposes are released into the worship on
earth through prophecy, the natural progression is then toward
intercession. As the Church is made aware of the gap between what
God desires and what is happening in the earth realm, it is com-
pelled to press into prayer to bridge that gap. The New Testament
saints "were continually devoting themselves to prayer" (Acts 1:14,
NASB). The Church is admonished throughout the New Testament to keep pressing into that place of prayer:

- "Pray at all times" (Eph. 6:18, *NASB*)
- "Always offering prayer with joy" (Phil. 1:4, *NASB*)
- "In everything by prayer and supplication" (Phil. 4:6, *NASB*)
- "We have not ceased to pray" (Col. 1:9, *NASB*)
- "Devote yourselves to prayer" (Col. 4:2, *NASB*)
- "Pray without ceasing" (1 Thess. 5:17, *NASB*)
- "We pray for you always" (2 Thess. 1:11, *NASB*)
- "Therefore I want the men in every place to pray" (1 Tim.
  2:8, *NASB*)

That which is foundational in a person or group comes out in
everything they do. The church I am a part of is strong in intercession. By the time Sunday comes around many of us have met several
times during the week to pray and intercede—early mornings, late

nights, middays, and more. Our worship on Sunday morning has become an out-product of those times of intercession. Many who attend our services do not realize how intercessory our worship is because we usually don't conduct ourselves on Sunday mornings as intensely as we do in our Tuesday morning prayer meeting; yet by the Spirit, we tap into the things that were brought forth in the throes of intercession of the meetings held during the week.

This was certainly true with the Early Church saints who were so devoted to prayer. Their worship would have been an outflow of the prayer they immersed themselves in during the week. The psalms give us a record of the intercession that was so much a part of David's tabernacle, and Revelation shows us the integral part intercession plays in heaven's worship, but the dedication the Early Church had for prayer gives us an indicator of how intercessory their worship must have been.

The Church Warred in Their Worship

The natural progression that leads from prophecy to intercession invariably leads to war as we pray for God's will to be done on earth. Jesus came to destroy the works of the devil (see 1 John 3:8) and proclaimed to His Church that He had not come to bring peace but a sword (see Matt. 10:34). Paul took up this theme and exhorted the Church to take up the sword of the Spirit and put on their spiritual armor in order to make war against the forces of evil (see Eph. 6:10-17), and to tear down everything that raises itself up against the knowledge of God (see 2 Cor. 10 15). Paul told Timothy to take up the prophecies that had been spoken over him and war with them (see 1 Tim. 1:18-10).

The Early Church was in a war not of its own choosing, but a war all the same. The enemy of their souls was determined to wipe them out or at least undermine their effectiveness as God's representatives in the earth. As David's tabernacle had been important to his military commanders in their physical battles, the reforming tabernacle of David became an essential element to the new Church's spiritual battles. Their everyday life was a battleground of the soul, and they were exhorted to continually rejoice and give thanks (see 1 Tim. 5:16) and praise (see Heb. 13:15). Their attitudes of praise were the weapons they used to do the work of the Father and advance the kingdom of God.

God Interacted with Their Worship

When Paul and Silas took up their weapons of praise in the Ephesians' jail, God interacted with their praise, bringing an earthquake that freed them and brought in a harvest of Gentiles. When Peter was imprisoned, the saints gathered to come before the Lord for Peter's freedom. God interacted with their intercession and sent an angel to free Peter. The saints' prayer meeting was interrupted by someone banging on the door: it was Peter. God made it plain that He desired to interact with the worship and intercession of the Early Church. He enthroned Himself on their praises to bring forth His intentions.

The Church Entered Continual Worship

In heaven the worship never ends; it just goes on and on; it is continual. David accomplished this aspect of continual worship by incorporating a paid staff of 4,000 Levites who worshiped in shifts around the clock.

In the New Testament, the saints were infused with this same standard of continual worship. They were not organized as David's Levites or as tireless as those with heavenly bodies above, but the apostles persistently admonished them to enter a mindset of continual worship. In the last verse of the Gospel of Luke, it states that after the ascension of Jesus, the saints were "continually in the temple praising God" (Luke 24:53, *NASB*). In Hebrews the New Testament Church is admonished to "*continually* offer up a sacrifice of praise to God, that is, the fruit of lips that give thanks to His name" (Heb. 13:15-16, *NASB*, emphasis added); and Paul urged the Church to rejoice continually (see 1 Thess. 5:16; Phil. 4:4).

As the Church would grow over the centuries and spread throughout the earth, whatever they might have lacked in the tirelessness of the heavenly bodies or the organization of David's Levites they made up in the vastness of their numbers as they spread through the different time zones of the earth. Although the saints on one side of the earth slept, the ones on the other side offered up their praises. As the earth turned, some people group or another would be in worship. Today there are groups in many points on the globe that worship God 24 hours a day so that now there is not only worship going up to God from some time zone at any given time of the day, but many of those time zones never cease in their worship. If God enthrones Himself on our praises, we must make sure our praise is continual.

A Glimpse at an Early Worship Service

The Early Church was active and exuberant in their walk with God and with the worship they offered. My pastor, Robert Heidler gives a thumbnail sketch of an early worship service from his extensive study of Early Church history:

> As you walk through the door, you look across the entrance into the large open courtyard of the time. There appears to be some kind of party going on. Some of the people are playing flutes, lyres and tambourines, while others are singing, dancing and clapping their hands. You immediately look around to make sure you have come into the right house! As you listen to the words, however, you realize that this is the right place, for the words of the songs are words of praise to Jesus! These people are overflowing with joy because they have come to know the living God.
>
> What you are witnessing is the way the early Church praised God. This type of worship is foreign to much of the Church today, but from the biblical and historical records, this is what the worship in the early Church was like. It was a free and joyful celebration, with a great deal of singing and dancing.
>
> Most church services would begin with the people getting in a ring (or several concentric rings) and dancing Jewish-style ring dances (like the Hora).[10]

The First Three Centuries

For three centuries the hallmarks of David's tabernacle continued to be restored to the Church. The Church worshiped face to face in spirit and in truth. Their worship was dynamic, spontaneous, prophetic and intercessory. They warred in their worship and God interacted with their worship. They were persecuted, martyred and driven into hiding. In spite of this the Church prospered and grew and spread throughout the known world. In Acts 17, the Thessalonians proclaimed that Paul had turned the world upside down. For three centuries the saints continued to change the world. The pagan religion of the Roman Empire fell continually to the power of Christianity. But then, in the fourth century, the devil changed his tactics to, "If you can't beat 'em, join 'em."

Tabernacle Lost

The Beginning of the End

In A.D. 312, Constantine became emperor of the Roman Empire after defeating his rival in battle outside of the gates of Rome. Constantine was said to have seen a sign of a cross in the sky before the battle. Eusebius Pamphili, Constantine's biographer and historian, relates the story: "He said that about noon, when the day was already beginning to decline, he saw with his own eyes the trophy of a cross of light in the heavens, above the sun, and bearing the inscription, CONQUER BY THIS. At this sight he himself was struck with amazement, and his whole army also, which followed him on this expedition, and witnessed the miracle."[11] Constantine had his artisans fashion a cross, which his troops used as a battle standard. Under this standard they were victorious and Constantine became the undisputed emperor.

The very next year Constantine issued the Edict of Milan, which gave the persecuted Christians of the Roman Empire the freedom to worship openly. The Church, which had just suffered one of the most severe persecutions under Constantine's mentor, Diocletian, was now an accepted religion and free to worship openly in the empire. Constantine proclaimed that any property of the Church that had been confiscated during the previous emperors were to be restored to the Church, if need be at government's expense.[12] New monetary grants were given to the Church for its advancement.[13] These were great blessings to a heretofore persecuted Church, but at the same time there were other developments that were quite concerning.

The New High Priest

By A.D. 325, Constantine had made Christianity the state religion of his Empire. Roman emperors were considered the *pontifex maximus*, or high priest, of the pagan religious system of their empire. Finley Hooper, in his secular book *Roman Realities,* says that Constantine "kept his title of *pontifex maximus* and all the paraphernalia of the old state religion."[14] The religious system of the empire was now Christianity and Constantine considered himself the high priest of his newly adopted religion.

In A.D. 325, he drew together the church leaders from throughout his empire to the Council of Nicea. This was the first time all the Christian leaders had been gathered together since the council of Jerusalem in Acts 15. This time, however, they were not under the apostles of old, but under the emperor of the Roman Empire who set about to mold the scattered and sometimes disjointed leaders of Christianity into one homogeneous entity with a common doctrine and clear lines of authority leading directly to the *pontifex maximus* himself. The Nicene Council was in complete unity—except for two dissenting leaders who were summarily excommunicated.

The New Church Buildings

The historian Eusebius said that Constantine began to pour enormous amounts of money into the churches.[15] These new Church buildings were called basilicas, which means "the hall of the king." Roman emperors, over the past century, had used basilicas to hold their imperial courts. Consequently, these new Church buildings were not suited for the ring dances and worship celebrations that the Church had formerly known, but were designed so the Church could operate more like an imperial court: the "clergy" separated and elevated so they could lead the "laity" in the newly developing forms and rituals. Church historian Philip Schaff says, "Not a few pagan habits and ceremonies, concealed under new names, crept into the church."[16]

The New Rome
The Church became so patterned after the Roman government that even after the Roman Empire fell, its culture, organizational structure and law lived on through the institution of the Church. As Moses Hadas writes in his secular book *Imperial Rome,* "The organization of the Church, in turn, was constructed largely on the Roman model. . . . The hierarchy of the Church corresponded to the Roman administrative apparatus. . . . Ecclesiastical law was strongly influenced by Roman jurisprudence (the guiding principle was Roman corporate law) . . . With the decline of the Roman state, the Church became the chief repository of Latin culture."[17] The Church's new "high priest" had taken it a long way from the patterns of David's tabernacle.

Puttin' on the Ritz
Worship now had to make the grade in the sophisticated Roman world. Schaff observed that Christian worship had to "adapt itself to the higher classes and to the great mass of the people, who had been bred in the traditions of heathenism."[18] Worship began to take on a new splendor in its outward appearance, to which Schaff observes, "While the senses and the imagination were entertained and charmed, the heart not rarely returned cold and hungry."[19] More and more the common everyday Christians, the "laity," accepted their place as spectators while the clergy became a privileged class under Constantine.

Stand Up and Shut Up
Finally, the privilege of singing was taken away from the laity altogether. In A.D. 364, the church leaders met again at the council of Laodicea. Canon XV of that council reads: "No others shall sing in the Church, save only the canonical singers, who go up into the

ambo (*raised platform*) and sing from a book." That was it. Worship was now in the hands of professionals, and the common man was to stand in worship and keep his mouth shut.

In the fifth century, the Huns and Barbarians besieged the Roman Empire (and thus the Catholic Church). The long-feared Huns ended up turning back before completing their expected sack of Rome and the churches of the civilized world, but the Germanic tribes they had driven out of their homelands poured over into the western Roman empire, bringing it to its final end.

As the Roman Empire fell, the Latin language slowly fell out of use as well. But as the Church was the "chief repository of Latin culture," Latin was still the official language of the formal services of the Church. Common people no longer spoke Latin, so now they couldn't even understand the words of the songs that were sung in church by the professionals. Beautiful songs were written over the next several centuries: the Gregorian chants, which were also known as plainsongs. One of my favorite hymns, "O the Deep, Deep Love of Jesus," was originally a plainsong. The plainsongs were majestic and beautiful but only the monks or other male clerics were allowed to sing them. They were out of the reach of the common person, who could not sing along or even understand the words.

Gone were the days of spontaneous and dynamic worship. Gone were intercessory and prophetic worship, replaced now with merely "excellent" music sung by professionals. No longer was God enthroned on the praises of His people. The authority of the Church was now by its political might and not by God's Spirit. The Church was as far away from David's tabernacle as it could be, and this would be its lot for more than a thousand years to come. It is no wonder that the next era of history would be called the Dark Ages.

Unless a Grain of Wheat Falls

God, however, was not finished with the tabernacle of David. He had only allowed it to fall into the ground once more in order to raise it up again, this time with even more fruit.

The Sound of Heaven Will Lead Us Forth
Chuck D. Pierce

The restoration of David's Tabernacle *is* advancing in the earth realm. Notice the present tense of the preceding sentence. Every generation is called to build a Tabernacle of Praise. David built a new model in the earth. Amos prophesied that this model would be built again. In the book of Acts, the apostles said, "This is that which Amos prophesied!" In the book of Revelation, John is brought into a heavenly dimension and sees this tabernacle filled with a worshiping army. In latter days, the same army on earth will express triumph because they have won the war in the heavens. We, God's army in the earth, will co-labor with the host of heaven to express a holy God's overcoming power throughout the nations of the earth. This level of worship will unlock a global harvest.

David was a warrior. He knew the reality of an Almighty God, and he praised Him violently. He was a shepherd and a king. He had a heart after God, and his heart had to release praise. Your violent praise is preparing a storehouse for Kingdom harvest. Worship is the key issue at this time in the history of the Church. I believe worship will dethrone any throne that the enemy has built in this world. Let us stand together to put a canopy of protection around the nations as we worship, intercede and believe that God will move on our behalf.

The other key issue that breaks us forth in times of crisis and change is the anointing. David was anointed. His anointing was progressive. As a lad, the youngest of eight brothers from the house of Jesse, he was anointed by Samuel. He was anointed as king of all of Israel. However, this anointing led him through many dangers. He was anointed by Judah after winning a great battle at Ziklag. He was eventually anointed by all of Israel to the hill that no one had ever taken, a hill that David would name Zion.

To do this, he had to battle. To restore, recover all and fulfill God's ultimate plan, he had to war. The Lord's troops were led for-

ward by sound. The goal of His company of saints was to establish
His glory. David's ultimate goal as king was to get the Ark of His
Covenant to the resting place on Zion's Hill. To do that, he and
his mighty army had to "take the hill" first. Once the hill was
taken, they had to hear clearly how to advance. But the enemy also
heard that this anointing and glory were on the move. The
Philistines, David's long-time enemy, heard of his new anointing
and how David had taken the Jebusites' stronghold and secured
the Hill for the Lord. They were determined to stop the Ark from
getting to the place that God had ordained. David had to maneu-
ver his way past this enemy force, but to do so he would have to
hear the right sound!

The sound that he was to listen for was "the wind in the mulberry trees." In 2 Samuel 5, David had experienced a major breakthrough in his own life. What had been prophesied over him 29
years prior had actually come into fulfillment. He then had to lead
the armies forth into battle. When the Philistines heard that David
had been anointed as king, they rose up against him. David defeated the Philistines and drove them out of his jurisdictional authority. However, they regrouped and came back at him again. He
asked the Lord if he was to pursue them. In 2 Samuel 5:24, the
Lord answers, "When you hear the sound of the marching in the
tops of the mulberry trees, then you shall advance quickly." The
sound of marching was not just the wind blowing the tops of the
trees, but the hosts of heaven and the armies of God rustling the
leaves and signifying they were present to help David in victory.

Now is a time to recognize the angels and hosts of heaven
among us! If we will keep our spirits active and in communion
with the Holy Spirit, we will begin to see the presence of God and
His hosts of heaven that are contending on our behalf. In the book
of Revelation, we find the real issue is the relationship between the
sounds of heaven and the demonstration of God on earth. Sound
leads us forth. Be willing to allow the sounds of heaven to order
your actions today. Ask the Lord for a new anointing. Do not be
afraid to take "your hill." Not only take the hill, but be willing to
establish a new form of worship in the place that God has called

you to dwell. Let His glory and anointing in you shine outward.
Dwell with Him and watch Him tabernacle with you.

For Study and Reflection
Read 1 Samuel 30 and 2 Samuel 5. Meditate on Psalm 92
and memorize 1 John 1:21.

Rebuilding the Tabernacle Again

*Truly, truly, I say to you, unless a grain of wheat falls into the earth
and dies, it remains alone; but if it dies, it bears much fruit.*
JOHN 12:24, NASB

Dawn's Early Light

The Reformation

Finally, the sixteenth century dawned with the light of the Protestant Reformation. After centuries of darkness, the reformers began to put worship back into the hands of the people again. Repair work, however, is not always quick. Sometimes it takes longer to repair something than to build it in the first place. God only took three months to give David the pattern for his tabernacle. He has been repairing it for centuries.

Sometimes the first part of the repair process doesn't seem too impressive. One tent pole doesn't look like much, but unless that tent pole is standing strong, there is nothing on which to hang the rest of the tent. First, they just had to sing, and that's what the new churches of the Reformation did. They just sang. Their songs were not intimate in worship or prophetic or spontaneous songs of the Spirit. The reformers gave their people the new doctrines of the Reformation to sing: their new revelation of God and His attributes.

LaMar Boshman writes, "The [Reformation] songs were doctrine heavy in content. . . . That caused many of the songs to have a horizontal focus; their purpose was to testify, reason, and proclaim principle. It was in essence singing the sermon. The song service did not focus on a greater agenda than that of singing songs. There was no need to lengthen it or wait on the Holy Spirit. There was little demonstration of the charismata."[1]

Through Martin Luther (1483–1546) and others, the common saints began to find their voice again. The Protestant hymn writers put their songs in the language of the people and often to well-known folk tune melodies that everyone was familiar with. They were singable and enjoyable for the masses. Martin Luther played a great role in the development of hymnology. Not only was he a radical theologian, but he was also a fine musician with a deep knowledge of German folksong, an influence that can still be heard in his famous hymn *Ein' feste Burg* ("A Mighty Fortress").

After a darkness that had lasted more than 1,000 years, God's people could once again express their hearts to God in song. The Protestant hymns breathed life into God's people. They were new and exciting. Collections of these new hymns were brought together in hymnbooks. Guttenberg's invention, the printing press, launched these hymnbooks into wide circulation, exploding their popularity and use. The Church was worshiping again.

Repairing the breaches of David's tabernacle was a long process that involved bringing God's people step by step into the freedom of worship that David had once experienced. The Church was still far away from spontaneous prophetic songs or dancing or many of the other things that were common in David's tabernacle. For quite a few years the battle was just to get God's people to sing. This involved bringing songs down from the lofty places into which they had been lodged—out of the reach of the common people—during the Dark Ages. Then as revivals and renewals erupted through the centuries following the Reformation, the breaches of the tabernacle of David began to be repaired, slowly but steadily.

Lining Out

Not all of the Reformers were ready for such boisterous worship as Luther was bringing to his people through the hymns. John Calvin in Geneva considered folk songs inappropriate for worship and instead introduced metrical versions of the psalms. The psalms were given a rhyme, a rhythm and a verse structure and translated into the language of the people so they could be sung or recited by a congregation.

The Anglican Church also adopted this practice. Ernest B. Gentile notes that the Church of England eventually grew "more and more strict, allowing only rhyming versions of the Psalms to be sung. And even these were sung in the most distressing way. A church clerk read aloud one line at a time, and the people would follow by singing that line."[2] This is what was called "lining out" because they read or sung the psalms one line at a time in seldom more than two or three notes. Not the most exciting way to release the power that resides in the psalms.

One young man complained to his father about the songs he had to sing at church, to which His father replied, "Then write some better ones." He did. Although this sounds like someone from today's generation breaking from the hymns of old, it was not. It was Isaac Watts, 300 years ago, complaining about the "lining out" of the metric psalms in church. Isaac ended up writing more than 600 hymns. Hymnbooks today still carry many of his hymns, like "When I Survey the Wondrous Cross" and "Joy to the World." With Isaac's hymns we see a slight move away from the "doctrine heavy" songs of the early Reformation into expressions of personal feelings of love and joy toward our God. Watts empowered God's people to express a little bit of their emotions as they touched the heart of God with their worship.

These hymns caused quite a stir in England in the early eighteenth century. Hymns were maligned as irrational music sung by mobs of extremists. Pastors who dabbled in them were brought up on charges before denominational hierarchies. Bitter infighting over these hymns ravaged congregations, and many churches split over the issue. It was a controversy that raged in England for almost 100 years. (Remember, we are talking about songs like "When I Survey the Wondrous Cross" and "Joy to the World.") Isaac himself was not allowed to attend Oxford University because he was considered a "dissenter." Madeleine Forell Marshall, in an article in *Christianity Today*, notes:

> We easily forget that hymns were written and sung by men and women who lived their lives and practiced their faith on the margins of conventional English Christianity. Anglicans resented, even hated, Dissenters [those who separated from the established Church of England] and Methodists. Thus, hymn singing, which Dissenters and Methodists practiced, came to stand for all that was wrong with non-orthodox faith.[3]

It is amazing to see the fight that Satan put up to keep God's people from entering into effective praise and worship. For more than a thousand years Christendom was kept from singing, much less worshiping. Although the clergy sang their beautiful songs to the laity, they sang in Latin, which the commoner could not understand.

Now, more than 200 years into the Reformation, Satan was still frustrating the development of worship in the Church. He persecuted those who tried to bring their churches into the vibrancy the hymns were fetching. Satan's intention was to keep the Church from that on which God desired to enthrone Himself.

The Great Awakening

Still Lining Out

The hymns of Isaac Watts, however, would soon play a large role in a move of God that fell on America, England, Scotland and Germany. In early eighteenth century America, most churches followed the practice of "lining out" the metrical psalms, which had driven Isaac Watts to improve upon this method with his hymns. The lining out practice, for the Americans, had become frustrating as they bogged down in repeating the line or two of psalms that had been recited to them. One of the exasperated pastors of that day was Thomas Symmes, who is quoted as saying:

Hence you may remember, that in our Congregation we us'd frequently to have some People Singing a Note or Two, after the rest had done. And you commonly strike the Notes not together, but one after another; One being half way thro' the second Note, before his Nei'bour has done with the First.[4]

The Singing Schools

To remedy this, a group of ministers in New England started singing schools in which worshipers were taught how to read music so that they could improve the quality of congregational singing. These schools were the forerunners of the "shaped note" musical notation in which the notes of the scale were represented by different shapes that the singer could easily recognize.

This made music reading easy and brought a fresh impetus to worship even though at the time they were still only "lining out" the metrical psalms. The detonation for worship came when the Great Awakening burst onto the scene:

> The Great Awakening in America that began in 1734 under the ministry of Jonathan Edwards in Northampton, Massachusetts, and brought into prominence the itinerate ministries of such men as George Whitefield and John Wesley. Wesley's ministry was centered primarily in Britain, where this great outpouring of God's Spirit was known as the Evangelical Awakening.[5]

As Jonathan Edwards' church came alive in the Great Awakening, they began to bring in the radical new hymns of Isaac Watts, and with their increased musical prowess from the music schools the congregation began to soar in worship.

Revivalists thought music was important. New ways of singing, by note and in parts, contributed to the emotionalism of eighteenth-century revivals. Many evangelicals noticed the power of music to stir religious feeling and promote revival. In his account of the Northampton revival, Edwards wrote, "No part of the public worship has commonly had such an effect on [the people of Northampton] as singing God's praises."[6] Edwards concluded that singing should be frequent in worship services because of music's power to arouse religious affections.

In England, the "Evangelical Awakening," as it was called there, was fueled not only by the hymns of Isaac Watts but also by "the Poet of Methodism," Charles Wesley. Charles was a firebrand who preached—alongside his brother John Wesley—on the streets of England, at coal mines and other places where the common and poor people were found. In addition to his preaching, Charles touched their hearts with his music, writing some 6,500 hymns, many of which still dominated the hymnbooks of the twentieth century. Such hymns as "O For a Thousand Tongues" and "Jesus, Lover of My Soul" and "Hark the Herald Angels Sing" are tributes to Charles Wesley's abilities in music. Charles, even more than Isaac Watts, filled his hymns with flowing tributes of love and gratitude toward God. This was one more step in enabling worshipers to express the fullness of their hearts to God, which proved very successful, as Rev. Dr. Alan C. Clifford relates:

> A selection of Charles Wesley's hymns was first published in 1739, and these became instantly popular, judging by Joseph William's account: "Never did I hear such praying or such singing. Their singing was not only the most harmonious and delightful I ever heard, but they sang 'lustily and with a good courage. . . . If there be such a thing as heavenly music upon earth I heard it there."[7]

The Second Great Awakening

The Tunesmiths

As the generation of Isaac Watts and Charles Wesley passed, new flame tenders in the late eighteenth century picked up their mantles. One of these was William Billings, a Boston tanner, who took the American singing schools to new heights of success and popularity. Billings and others like him were called "tunesmiths." The tunesmiths progressively brought worship music out of the formal European modes, composing hymns that were more emotion-filled and familiar in their styles to the common people of the time. In a magazine article in 1895, Lydia Bolles Newcomb said that William Billings "spurned the rules of art, such as there were, and sung out of the abundance of his heart," quoting Billings as saying, "I have often heard of a poetical license; I don't see why with the same propriety there may not be a musical license."[8]

Edward James Kilsdonk, in his study of the American middle class, said, "The old New England choirs . . . commonly sang tunes by William Billings and the other New England tunesmiths, as well as some secular tunes rewritten to accompany sacred lyrics."[9] Here again was the practice of putting Christian lyrics to well-known secular tunes. In this fashion people could sing the familiar melodies of the day to express their heart of worship toward their God. Another important tunesmith was Oliver Holden, who was most well known for his melody "Coronation," to which Edward Perronet's lyrics to "All Hail the Power of Jesus' Name" were added in 1793. This hymn is said to be the earliest American hymn tune still in general use today.

As the Second Great Awakening swept across America and eventually to other parts of the world in the early nineteenth century, the hymns of these tunesmiths came into great use by the new movement's worshipers. On the American frontier, thousands of people would flock to camp meetings, traveling from as far away as 100 miles. Men and women, old and young, blacks and whites joined together to worship. The "black spirituals" of the slaves mixed with the folk songs and hymns of the whites. Edward James Kilsdonk comments on this as well:

> Also common in the South and West were the musical practices that had grown out of the revivals and spiritual meetings that we now refer to as the Second Great Awakening, practices that often showed strong African influences. These include the spiritual ballad, a narrative song telling of doubt and salvation, often following the narrative structure of the folk ballad it was based on.[10]

Their music was simple, repetitive and catchy and greatly appealed to the less-educated frontier folks who sang them and spread them. Although the worship of the Second Great Awakening was criticized as being too emotional, I like what Bob Sorge has to say:

> A study of the Old Testament, especially the Psalms, clearly reveals that the Hebrew people were very emotional and vocal in their expressions of praise and adoration before their God. May it not be testified of us that we were too modern or too sophisticated to rival their enthusiasm about God.[11]

The apostle Paul said that we should be making the Jews jealous. Instead we find ourselves jealous of the enthusiasm the ancient Jews expressed in their worship. But not the frontier worshipers of the early nineteenth century; their new way of worship demonstrated their passion for God, and their songs became testimonials of what God had done in their life. Even the more structured hymns of Charles Wesley, Isaac Watts and others were often modified with a new melody or rhythm. In some cases an extra chorus was added, such as the one added to Robinson's timeless hymn "Come, Thou Fount of Every Blessing":

> I am bound for the kingdom,
> will you go to glory with me?
> Hallelujah, praise the Lord.

Edward James Kilsdonk adds, "Another popular musical form took scraps of lyric or portions of the Methodist Hymnbook and combined verses to make new songs. Choruses, simple verses that contained one or two words that could easily be altered . . . were one of the many places where African influences shaped American hymnody."[12]

Like David Danced

One of the breaches of David's tabernacle that was repaired during this season was worship in dance. The camp meetings of the

Second Great Awakening "inspired the dancing, shouting and singing associated with these events."[13] At the revival at Cane Ridge, Kentucky, led by Barton W. Stone, "there was dancing, running and singing—all of which Stone said were manifestations of God's presence."[14] Lucinda Coleman, in her studies of Christian dance through the ages, sums up her findings like this:

> Dance within the Christian context, having sprung from the Jewish tradition, was embraced by the early church as an integral part of celebrations and of worship. During the Middle Ages various influences affected the development of Christian dance and despite increasing proscriptions concerning its value and use, it survived as a sacred dance form. However, with the commencement of the Reformation, the dance was forced out of its place in the liturgical celebrations of the Christian church, and with few exceptions flourished instead in the secular realm.[15]

Although the Reformation had put worship music back in the hands of the people, it had finished off what was left of the dance as a form of worship. Interestingly, this is when the secular world, through the Renaissance, began to take what the Church had cast off and refined it for its own purposes. Ballet and the court dances of the European nobles emerged to capture the wonder of the people. It is startling to realize what the world has done with the arts that the Church discarded.

Charles Grandison Finney

The Second Great Awakening was said to have been at its peak in the 1830s when Charles Finney burst on the scene with his fiery sermons and calls for salvation. Referring to Finney's revivals, Edward James Kilsdonk wrote:

> These revivals used new forms of music. The most popular tunebook in upstate New York during the middle part of Finney's revivals was Charles Leavitt's *The Christian Lyre*,

released in 1830. Leavitt took melodies from popular tunes and attached them to new lyrics, as Luther had done during the early days of the Reformation.[16]

Leavitt was criticized for "using tunes whose secular associations destroyed the religious effect of the hymns," but once again the common people were enabled in their worship.[17]

Visitors to the United States during this time were struck with the atmosphere of the nation caused by these "awakening" revivals. French author Alexis de Tocqueville commented in his book *Democracy In America*, "the religious atmosphere of the country was the first thing that struck me on arrival in the United States."[18] Frances Trollope, an English novelist, wrote a condescending account of the domestic manners she encountered in America after her visit in the late 1820s:

> We had not been many months in Cincinnati when our curiosity was excited by hearing the "revival" talked of by every one we met throughout the town. "The revival will be very full"—"We shall be constantly engaged during the revival"— were the phrases we constantly heard repeated, and for a long time, without in the least comprehending what was meant; but at length I learnt that the un-national church of America required to be roused, at regular intervals, to greater energy and exertion. At these seasons the most enthusiastic of the clergy travel the country, and enter the cities and towns by scores, or by hundreds, as the accommodation of the place may admit, and for a week or fortnight, or, if the population be large, for a month; they preach and pray all day, and often for a considerable portion of the night, in the various churches and chapels of the place. This is called a Revival.[19]

The "This I Know" People
Around this same time, Sunday Schools sprang up in England and America, generating another form of easy, singable songs for the children. One of the most famous of these Sunday School songs was written by Anna Bartlett Warner in 1860 and has been sung the

world over for the past century and a half. The universal familiarity that this little song had was made use of by the underground Church within China operating in secret under the oppressive Communist regime there.

When Mao Tse Tung founded the People's Republic of China in 1949, the Christian Church was severely persecuted, with little information coming to the outside world. In 1972, some Americans received an unusual message from China—that the "This I know" people were well! The Chinese authorities thought the message nonsensical, so they let it through. The Americans clearly understood the reference to Anna Warner's simple hymn: "Jesus Loves Me."[20]

The Third Great Awakening

D. L. Moody's Chief Musician

The last half of the nineteenth century saw what some call the Third Great Awakening, which started in Canada and spread around the world. This awakening saw the coming of great revivalists such as D. L. Moody, William and Catherine Booth (founders of the Salvation Army), Charles Spurgeon and, later on, Billy Sunday in North America and Andrew Murray in South Africa. Some of the worship that came out of these revival meetings was the newly developing "gospel hymn," which had a little bit of the old hymns, a little bit of the Sunday School songs, camp meeting songs, negro spirituals and the folk hymns, along with "popular American secular vocal and instrumental music, particularly 'parlor songs' and concert band music like that of John Philip Sousa and his predecessors."[21]

Dwight L. Moody is remembered for his evangelistic preaching, but he also began the repair of one of the breaches David's tabernacle had suffered. Moody had traveled to London in 1872, on business, but had been asked during his visit to preach as a substitute in a London pulpit. When he gave his invitation at the end, more than 400 people responded.

Moody returned the following year to resume his evangelistic endeavors. This time he brought with him a song leader, Ira Sankey. Others had led songs in church before, but Ira brought something new to the table. He had the ability to draw the congregation into the praise and worship in an exciting way. He made use of the powerful, newly emerging gospel hymns and he empowered the people to sing. It was as if he were "anointed" to lead the worship. He was.

I believe that in Ira Sankey we can see an aspect of David's tabernacle that had been dormant for 2,883 years. I believe Ira was the first fruits of the chief musicians (worship leaders) of old, the "glimmering lights" of David's tabernacle that served as beacons to direct God's people into the presence of the Lord in worship. The combination of Ira's song leading and Dwight's preaching was explosive. What started out as a small preaching tour turned into a major two-year evangelistic campaign throughout England, Scotland and Ireland. Thousands packed the churches and meetinghouses to hear the evangelist from America and his song leader.

Fanny Crosby

When Moody and Sankey returned home to the United States, they were immensely popular and embarked immediately on an American preaching crusade. Sankey began to make use of the hymns of a famous blind secular poet turned hymn writer, Fanny Crosby. Fanny was a prolific hymn writer and surpassed Isaac Watts and Charles Wesley together in the sheer number of hymns she produced: some 9,000 in all. The Moody/Sankey evangelistic team brought Fanny Crosby's hymns to the masses; hymns like the timeless "Blessed Assurance, Jesus Is Mine." God's people were enabled as never before since the days of David's tabernacle to sing their hearts out to the Lord with Fanny's heartfelt songs. Even as an old woman (Fanny lived to be 95), Fanny would sit at the piano and play everything from classical works to hymns to ragtime. Sometimes she even played old hymns in a jazzed-up style.[22]

The Twentieth-Century Revivals

The Welsh and Pentecostal Revivals

The dawn of the twentieth century brought a powerful revival among the Welsh people that had a worldwide effect. Soon after that, the Pentecostal revival that started at Azusa Street in California also swept around the world. The Spirit once again fell on God's Church. This put a new power in the accompanying music that sprang forth. As the hymns of Isaac Watts, Charles Wesley and Fanny Crosby had energized the revivals of the past centuries, a new style of hymn emerged to do the same for the unfolding twentieth century.

Early Pentecostal patriarch Howard Goss recognized that Pentecostals were doing something very different with their music and that this fact was key to the movement's growth. Looking back in the 1950s, he noted that Pentecostals "were the first . . . to introduce this accelerated tempo into gospel singing" and contended that without the new musical style "the Pentecostal Movement could never have made the rapid inroads into the hearts of men and women as it did."[23] Another leader noted that the "joy of the Lord was so built up on our young people that when they got a chance to sing, they exploded."[24] "Dancing" was also a significant aspect of the Pentecostal revival.[25] Aimee Semple McPherson (1890-1944) founded the Foursquare Pentecostal Churches and incorporated the "jazzy" music into her elaborate church services. Robert Bahr, a contemporary of Aimee, made the following analysis of her success: "She threw out the dirges . . . replacing them with jazz hymns and promises of Glory."[26]

The "upbeat" music, the "jazzy" songs, these were the things that enabled God's people to praise Him with everything that was within them. The Reformation got people singing. The Great Awakenings helped people to express the emotions within them toward God and got them dancing again. Now the Pentecostal Revival brought it all up a level. Even though no "jazzy" hymns were probably ever sung in David's tabernacle, the upbeat music of the Pentecostal revival was doing the same things for the twentieth century saints that David's lively, passionate music did for the tabernacle worshipers.

Billy Sunday, the former baseball player for the Chicago White Stockings, had a winning personality and an exciting style of evangelism. He had sawdust thrown down on the aisles of the meeting halls to muffle the noise of the people's shoes on the floor. We all know the term "sawdust trail," which immediately brings to mind the revival meetings of the first half of the twentieth century. Billy, like Moody, saw the advantage of a dynamic song leader and added Homer Rodeheaver to his team. Rodeheaver was invigorating as a song leader and trumpet player. I doubt that Dwight L. Moody, Ira Sankey, Billy Sunday or Homer Rodeheaver had a vision for restoring David's tabernacle, yet I believe God was using them to reestablish the place of David's chief musicians. These song leaders were the forerunners of the modern-day worship leaders. Rodeheaver, in time, started a music company that eventually became the well-known Word Music that has produced many contemporary Christian music artists of the last few decades.

The Mid-Century Revivals

In the late 1940s, the Church saw the great revivals of the Healing Movement and the Latter Rain Movement, with fresh outpourings of the New Testament gifts. Healings and miracles and prophecy were prominent in these movements. Leaders such as Oral Roberts who started Oral Roberts University, and Gordon Lindsey, who started Christ for the Nations Institute, were born out of these outpourings. Worship in prophetic dance came forth in the Latter Rain Movement. Bill Hamon tells of the outbreak of dance that came at a meeting held by the Latter Rain Movement in 1954:

> Suddenly a sister began to prophesy, "The King is coming, the King is coming—go ye out to meet Him with dances and rejoicing." She started taking ferns out of the flower basket and waving them in the air and laying some of them as if before the Lord as she praised the Lord in the dance across the auditorium in front of the platform. The head of the conference started to stop her but the Holy Spirit told him not to, for it was of God. Within a few minutes most of the audience was praising God with legs swinging and bodies moving in rhythmic praise to God.[27]

The Charismatic Movement

In the 1960s, the Spirit began to fall on denominational Christians that would never darken the doors of a Pentecostal church. Episcopalians and Baptists began to speak in tongues, prophesy, cast out demons, heal the sick and many more things that were not permitted in their church bylaws. A Dutch Reformed Church pastor named Harold Bredeson described all this as a "great charismatic movement," using the New Testament Greek word *charismata*, which means "gift." God's gifts were falling on His people, empowering them to do the work of the ministry mentioned in Ephesians 4.

During the late 1960s and early 1970s, the charismatics had a great desire to worship God, but what they experienced in their denominational churches on Sunday mornings was not satisfying them. They wanted more. They began to gather in homes during the week to worship and pray together. The songs they sang were folksy and simple, just like Fanny Crosby's hymns were to her generation. They were different from the songs they considered so dull at church, just like Isaac Watts's hymns in his generation were different from the music they experienced in church. The charismatics took popular songs of the day and put Christian lyrics to them just like Martin Luther had done. They sang the Jesus Music that was springing forth from the Jesus Movement. They often had someone leading the songs on guitar, piano or some other handy instrument. These music leaders eventually began to be known as worship leaders. I was one of them. It was during these years that the giftings of these worship leaders began to develop and their anointing to lead worship grew. None of us made any connections of what we were doing to what the chief musicians of David's tabernacle had done so many centuries before.

For years I was troubled, because I didn't see worship leaders in the New Testament. I knew that what I experienced when I led worship was more than just a natural talent. I knew that the Spirit of God operated within me to lead God's people in worship, but I just couldn't find "worship leader" listed in Romans 12, 1 Corinthians 12 or in Ephesians 4. The term "worship leader" didn't even appear in the world's vernacular until 35 or 40 years ago. I asked the Lord, "Where is my gift seen in the Bible?" My answer came as I studied the Scriptures on David's chief musicians. I realized that what David was doing was creating a prototype of New Testament worship, and worship leaders were a part of that. As God rebuilt David's fallen tent, worship leaders would be a part of the restoration. Now, 3,000 years after Asaph, Heman and Ethan, God was repairing this breach. Worship leaders were being raised up again.

An Oddball No More

Several years ago, Dr. C. Peter Wagner wrote a book on spiritual gifts. More recently he told me that he was rewriting this book because of what he had observed over the past few years. This new rewrite would include the gift of worship leading. I was delighted. Christian leaders were verifying the validity of worship leading as a gift. I was excited when Dr. Wagner's book *Discovering Your Spiritual Gifts* finally came out and I read on page 22:

> I have now observed something which was not on my radar screen when I did my previous books on spiritual gifts, and that is that there is a spiritual gift of leading worship. It is more than musical skills. It is a God-given ability to usher others into the very presence of God in an extraordinary way.[28]

Many of the small groups of the late 1960s and early 1970s developed into the Charismatic churches of the late 1970s and 1980s. Worship became a major part of the ministry of these churches. Some people called them "praise churches" or "charismatic churches," and they all had one of the newly developed worship leaders. By the 1980s, the contemporary Christian music that had made its way forth in the 1960s and 1970s had become an established music form. Christian music groups began to flourish and Christian music companies were springing up to facilitate them. Praise and worship tapes began to abound. I owned a Christian bookstore from 1974 until 1982 and watched the tremendous development and expansion of Christian music during that period.

Also during that season the Church began to come into an understanding of David's tabernacle. The term "Davidic worship" began to be heard. Leaving the rituals and traditions of formal church worship behind, saints began to worship with Davidic-style celebration: with dance, banners, flags, tambourines, and more. Prophetic worship began to develop, as well as warfare worship. The Church began to see that worship was more than singing a few songs before the message on Sunday morning. They began to come boldly before God's throne in their worship. Christians experienced a deeper intimacy in their worship. God was bringing out more and more of the aspects of David's tabernacle as His people pursued Him more and more in worship.

In the 1990s, the music that had been exclusive to the charismatic or Spirit-filled churches began to trickle into the mainline denominational churches. In 1994, *Charisma* magazine made this observation: "Today, praise music has entered the mainstream. Songs that were only sung in charismatic churches a few years ago are now heard throughout mainline and non-charismatic churches."[29]

I remember when someone commented to me that they were singing charismatic choruses down the street at the large denominational church. Their inference to me was, "See, you're not so special. They're doing that stuff everywhere now." I had been one of the oddballs in the city for so many years, singing the charismatic choruses. Now I was practically mainline. Well, not really, but I wasn't quite an oddball anymore.

The Explosion of New Songs

Before David's time, the Israelites had written a few songs; but during the days of the tabernacle, there was an explosion of songs. The same thing is happening in our day. The expansion of church music is ever increasing. Now more and more people are writing worship songs. Many churches have at least one songwriter in their midst. C. Peter Wagner told me that not many years ago he knew most of the songs sung in the different churches he was asked to speak in. More recently, though, each church he visited sang a completely different set of songs, most of which he had never heard. "What's happening in church music?" he asked. The answer is that over the last few years there has been an explosion of song-writing in the Church. Numerous churches now sing at least some songs written by their own church members. Some churches sing almost exclusively their own songs.

Since emerging from the Dark Ages, we have seen one then another songwriter top their predecessor's record: Martin Luther was topped by Isaac Watts's 300 hymns, who was topped by William Williams in the early Welsh revival with 800 hymns, who was topped by Charles Wesley's 6,500 hymns, who was topped by Fanny Crosby's 9,000 hymns. Today it is not just one songwriter, but thousands of them writing tens of thousands of songs.

Worship is once again becoming dynamic and spontaneous. We are seeing prophetic worship again. Many are bringing intercession and warfare into their worship, and God is interacting with His worshipers in a whole new way. Numerous ministries are conducting continuous 24-hour-a-day worship and intercession. David's tabernacle is being rebuilt. Its breaches are being repaired, and Zion is being reestablished in the earth. God is once more using the praises of His people to enthrone Himself on and ruling and reigning from the midst of His Church.

We stand now at the opening of a new day in worship. I believe the Lord has been positioning His worshipers to lead the Body of Christ. It has been His intention to do so for centuries. Judah (praise) is to go first (see Num. 10:14; Judg. 1:2; 20:18). God is raising up His apostles to establish the government of God in the Church, and they are sending forth the praise teams as Jehoshaphat did against the Moabites and Ammonites (see 2 Chron. 20:21). We, as worship warriors, must therefore come into a new comprehension of our relationship with our God, availing ourselves to Him for His governmental purposes in the earth. This is the season to pursue the Bridegroom into His kingdom work.

Your Transition to the New
Chuck D. Pierce

Change can be good or devastating. The evolution (used in the right sense) of one structure to another is very important to understand. When we read the history of change in a field, any field, we are amazed at how God chose gifted, submitted people with creative ability to lead us through changes and then end up with a product of greater quality than the one that began the process. The transition that occurs in that reforming process is amazing. Transition has three key phases: an ending or death, confusion in development of the new process and, finally, a new and better display of the original. Another way of saying this is: *A hard death causes a germination process that results in a new thing*.

As time has progressed, the original Ford Model T car has now transitioned to many different forms of much greater quality. That prototype has now been used by many throughout the world to bring change in how we reach our destination. To build or rebuild is to create something with a new look or of a better quality than the original. To build means to add "sons and daughters" to what is being built. God's intent in every generation is to find someone or a group who would build a new David's Tabernacle—the best prototype that had ever been built for His Presence to dwell within. This prototype would be used for worship.

New, or *neos*, can mean something that has never been before. Usually, new is better reflected in the word *kainos*, which means something from the original that is now of much better quality and more efficient for the time. The only place that we find both these words working together is in Matthew 9, when our Lord is helping the next generation of disciples prepare to build the future prototype for the Church to come.

I want you to read this passage that we often use to justify change. Jesus made a famous statement about a new wineskin. Matthew recorded the statement for us to understand for the centuries of time that would follow. He said, "Neither is new [Greek *neos*] wine put in old wineskins; for if it is, the skins burst and are torn in pieces, and the wine is spilled and the skins are ruined. But new wine is put into fresh [Greek *kainos*] wineskins, and so both are preserved" (AMP). *Neos* means "new" in respect to time, implying immaturity or lack of development. *Kainos* means "new" or "renewed or rebuilt," in respect to quality. This statement contrasted the "old" or "not renewed" and implied superiority; however, I want you to read this statement in full context.

The first issue in changing and moving into the next structure for a new season is: How teachable are you? Matthew 9:12-13 says:

> But when Jesus heard it, He replied, "Those who are strong and well (healthy) have no need of a physician, but those who are weak and sick. Go and learn what this means: I desire mercy [that is, readiness to help those in trouble] and not sacrifice and sacrificial victims. For I came not to call and invite [to repentance] the righteous (those who are upright and in right standing with God), but sinners (the erring ones and all those not free from sin) (AMP).

Jesus had changed His approach from the way John the Baptist evangelized (calling many out to the desert for repentance) to actually going where the sinners were. Jesus knew that there was such a need for grace with prostitutes, thieves and others of low reputation whose sins were blatant and obvious. Established religion did not give these types the opportunity to change. The religious structure had rules and laws that they themselves had grown blind to because of their "righteous" understanding, and pretexts could cover their conscience. Jesus was teaching that those who said that they were "righteous" were actually worse and resisted any new teaching.

The next issue in shifting is how your worship and authority develop as you enter a new season.

> Then the disciples of John came to Jesus, inquiring, "Why is it that we and the Pharisees fast often, [that is, abstain from

food and drink as a religious exercise], but Your disciples do not fast?" And Jesus replied to them, "Can the wedding guests mourn while the bridegroom is still with them? The days will come when the bridegroom is taken away from them, and then they will fast. And no one puts a piece of cloth that has not been shrunk on an old garment, for such a patch tears away from the garment and a worse rent (tear) is made" (Matt. 9:14-16, *AMP*).

In an attempt to validate Jesus' discipleship method, John's disciples brought up how John had trained them to fast and wear certain garments. Notice, John's disciples had actually gone backward to align with the Pharisees' form of worship and teaching. Jesus was warning that the last season's spiritual methods, such as fasting, would not be the real key to unlocking the season that they were presently forming and building. Actually, He was showing them that the old structure of religion and Judaism could not be patched by the Messiah-infiltrated Kingdom plan. Old teaching without a new *mashach*, or anointing, is not enough to produce spiritual life. A new anointing without a foundation can be disastrous. Therefore, a shrinking of the original garment and the new piece must occur. This is important as the two fit together. This becomes one of the most difficult lessons as you approach the new. One must determine how to align the new with the old. One must worship in *spirit* and *truth* to find *reality!*

There has to be an adjustment as you move into the new. However, the adjustment must occur without compromise.

Neither is new wine put in old wineskins; for if it is, the skins burst and are torn in pieces, and the wine is spilled and the skins are ruined. But new wine is put into fresh wineskins, and so both are preserved (Matt. 9:17, *AMP*).

Old wineskins have lost their strength and elasticity so that they cannot withstand the pressure of new wine still fermenting, although an old wineskin can be restored to service if it's useful qualities are renewed. Here it is Judaism that must be adjusted to messianic faith. If one tries to put new wine (messianic faith) into old wineskins (traditional Judaism), the faith is lost and Judaism ruined. But if Judaism is freshly prepared and reconditioned so that it can accommodate trust in Yeshua the Messiah, both the faith and the *renewed* Judaism, messianic Judaism, are preserved.

The new wine of Kingdom living cannot be poured into an old religious form that continues to remain rigid from the past way of learning and doing. If these old religious forms will become "fresh," they can accommodate Yeshua, the Messiah, the Anointed One. When *kainos* is rendered "new," the wineskin or structure becomes a vessel that can hold the new wine of messianic life in a Jewish setting. The renewed, restored, reconditioned and refreshed form of worship can now suffice for adding sons and daughters into for the future.

The key to any new season is either to press through and come out of the last administration, or to be resurrected into the new administration.

> While He was talking this way to them, behold, a ruler entered and, kneeling down, worshiped Him, saying, "My daughter has just now died; but come and lay Your hand on her, and she will come to life." And Jesus got up and accompanied him, with His disciples. And behold, a woman who had suffered from a flow of blood for twelve years came up behind Him and touched the fringe of His garment; for she kept saying to herself, "If I only touch His garment, I shall be restored to health" (Matt. 9:18-21, *AMP*).

The number 12 means new administration. One woman confined and diseased for 12 years pressed out of the old diseased prison of life and touched the new structure. She pressed past her gender, her impure state and the legal bondage that held her. A young girl who was 12 years of age fell asleep and died but was resurrected and awakened into the new administrative structure. This proved that if you were held captive in a legal structure or past season, you could get out through faith or be raised by faith with no effort into the new that was waiting.

Are you ready to go again into the new? We must be willing to press through each season to become part of the new that is being birthed and the structure that houses the future. If we do so, we can both be poured out again and change the world around us! Your transition to the new may have been difficult. You may have needed to die in many areas and are confused from all you have gone through. However, to press through for the new is worth the difficulties!

For Study and Reflection
Read Matthew 9. Meditate on Acts 15 and
memorize Matthew 9:17.

Pursuing the Bridegroom

Come, my beloved, let us go out into the country,
Let us spend the night in the villages.
Let us rise early and go to the vineyards;
Let us see whether the vine has budded.
SONG OF SOLOMON 7:11-12, NASB

Pursuing the Bridegroom

The Song of Solomon gives us a beautiful picture of the relation-ship the Lord wants to have with us. Here the bride and the Bride-groom express their love for each other. They are each smitten by the other and are utterly lovesick. Each of them wants to spend every waking moment with the other and they are unabashed in their praise of the other's attributes. The bride gives the perfect ex-ample of how we, as the bride of Christ, should boast about our Bridegroom. "His hands are rods of gold set with beryl. His body is carved ivory inlaid with sapphires. His legs are pillars of marble set on bases of fine gold. His countenance is like Lebanon, excellent as the cedars. His mouth is most sweet, yes, he is altogether lovely" (Song of Sol. 5:14-16). She extols His manly characteristics.

The apostle Peter exhorts us to do that very thing: "But you are a chosen generation, a royal priesthood, a holy nation, His own special people, that you may proclaim the praises of Him who called you out of darkness into His marvelous light" (1 Pet. 2:9). A fellow worship leader, Greg Otis, shared some insights on the word "praises" as it is used in 1 Peter:

This word "praises" that this Scripture exhorts us to show forth comes from the Greek word *arête* (ar-et'-ay), which means virtue, valor and excellence, but in its root form means simply, "manliness."[1]

Peter is exhorting us to praise our God like the bride praising the manliness of her bridegroom. As we show forth the praises of our God, we are extolling the "manliness" of the Bridegroom. He is altogether lovely. Likewise, the Bridegroom extols the lovely qualities of the bride that make her so desirable to Him. God brags on us in heavenly places: "Have you considered my servant Job? For there is no one like him on the earth" (Job 2:3, *NASB*). When Gabriel came to Mary, he had just come from the presence of God and apparently heard such good things about her that when he saw the girl he said, "Rejoice, highly favored one" (Luke 1:28).

Passionate Worship

The Church today has come into a love relationship with Jesus that can only be compared to the bride in the Song of Solomon. The passion and intimacy we see in today's worship are on a level, I believe, that has not been seen since the days of David. Not many decades ago the word "passion" was nowhere in our worship vernacular. This new generation of worshipers has introduced it to us. I have been in worship ministry since the early 1970s and have watched the Body of Christ, in general, dramatically increase in its intensity in worship.

It has blessed my heart to see the zeal with which our younger generation presses into the Lord in worship. The Church is more intimate and passionate in its worship today than it ever has been, and we owe this younger generation a debt of gratitude for the radical place they have led us in their worship. No generation has better exhibited the heart of worship that the bride had in the Song of Solomon than this present one: unashamed, expressive, genuine and vibrant. This passionate, intimate worship is our foundation.

His Larger World

But another thing we see in the Song of Solomon is how much larger the Bridegroom's world is than the bride's. The Bridegroom loved being out in His kingdom, leaping on the mountains, skipping on the hills, checking on His flock, tending His garden, making sorties into the wilderness with His warriors.

The bride—at least in the first part of the book—was focused on the Bridegroom, but not necessarily on His domain. We see her venture out asking where He pastured His sheep so she could go out to be with Him, but for the most part, the Bridegroom skipped on the hills by Himself; she watched. Although she went out into His kingdom at times, her primary objective seemed to be to get Him back into the chamber. The Bridegroom represents the apostolic gifting, the government of God. His larger world is where He operated in His kingly, apostolic anointing. This is where He wanted to be enthroned on the praises of His people, His bride. He wanted His bride to be aware of His larger world and enter into a corporate worship that He might come to dwell in and enthrone Himself upon. The Bridegroom had brought her to His chamber in the first chapter, and she liked it. She loved Him and He loved her. They were unashamed in their love for each other. As far as the bride was concerned, what could be better?

What Could Be Better?

The apostle Paul, in Ephesians 3:18, said his desire for all of us was that we would "be able to comprehend with all the saints what is the breadth and length and height" of God. In 34 or so years of walking with the Lord, I have still not comprehended it. Any time I have said, "What could be better?" God, I'm sure, just laughs.

The Bridegroom in the Song of Solomon probably laughed. It was He who had brought her into His chamber and He loved their companionship there, but His world was bigger than that, as was His concept of intimacy. The Bridegroom—though He cherishes the tenderness of their private moments—wanted to bring the bride into a broader aspect of that intimacy: not just in the secret place but also out in His kingdom. He wanted to enjoy her company and fellowship in every aspect of His life. He wanted her with Him when He tended His garden or looked to His flocks. He wanted her to leap on the mountains and skip on the hills with Him. He wanted her close to Him when He went out into the wilderness. Chuck Pierce says this:

> Many people confuse the church with the kingdom of God. However, they are not the same. The Kingdom is the overall divine purpose that includes the church. The church exists to see the Kingdom established and operating on the earth. The church facilitates the Kingdom. . . . The Greek word for church is *ekklesia*, which means gathered to accomplish something, or a group of people called out.[2]

She Is Not His Whole Life

If the Church, then, is a group of people called out and gathered to accomplish something, we can understand why the Bridegroom is continually saying, "Come away, my beloved." He is calling His Church out and gathering us to accomplish something, to affect the world around us. Dr. Jonathan David, a Malaysian apostle, says:

> Our quest is to understand the fundamental kingdom dynamics behind apostolic churches in the New Testament writings. These churches lived and grew in their environments only to influence and impact their communities. They had within them the dynamics to prevail over their limitations and create dramatic changes to the spiritual, political and economical landscapes of their cities.[3]

Jesus wants His Church, His bride, to, as Chuck says, "see the Kingdom established." That Kingdom is the Bridegroom's overall divine purpose. In the Gospel of Luke, the crowds tried to keep Jesus from leaving them. He had healed them and they had fallen in love with Him. They didn't want Him to go on, but Jesus said, "I must preach the kingdom of God to the other cities also, for I was sent for this purpose" (Luke 4:43, *NASB*). Dr. C. Peter Wagner says:

When Jesus said, "I will build My church," He immediately
connected it with the kingdom of God. He then went on to
say, "The Gates of Hades shall not prevail against it [because
I am giving] you the keys of the kingdom of heaven" (Matt.
16:18-19). Whenever He sent His disciples out, He instructed them to "preach the kingdom of God" (Luke 9:2).
After His resurrection, during His last 40 days here on
Earth, Jesus taught His apostles about the kingdom of God
(see Acts 1:3). And He concluded their final training session
by telling them that, after He left, the Holy Spirit would
come and give them power to be witnesses for Him (see Acts
1:8), presumably witnesses of the kingdom of God, which
Jesus brought to Earth.[4]

If you search the Gospels you will find that Jesus mentioned
His kingdom close to 100 times, but the Church less than a handful. It's not that Jesus doesn't love His bride; it's that His responsibility extends to the larger sphere of the kingdom of God. LaMar
Boschman speaks to this in his book *Future Worship*:

> I believe the church is the bride of Christ. But I also agree
> with Charles Simpson who said, "The Church is Christ's
> Bride, but she's not His whole life!" Godly men cherish,
> honor and enjoy their wives. We would die for them. How-
> ever, a quick survey of a man's life will reveal that a relatively
> small portion of his work and pursuits are concentrated
> on his wife. The Church's collision course with reality is a
> reflection of her illusion that she is His whole life. The
> Kingdom of God is His life. She's His wife. The church is
> a part of His kingdom. But it is not synonymous with the
> Kingdom![5]

Have You Seen My Beloved?

I believe the Bridegroom wants us to be in "His whole life." It is only
us who balk at the idea. The bride had a hard time understanding

the Bridegroom in the perspective of His larger world, the kingdom. He was always calling her out to join Him in His endeavors there. Once it was past bedtime, the bride had already put her hair up in rollers and smeared her face with Noxzema. She had her fuzzy house robe on and her bunny slippers and did not want to get up. The Bridegroom goes on without her but the bride knows that she can't live without Him, so she wipes off the Noxzema and kicks off her bunny slippers and runs off to find Him. Unable to find Him, she tells the daughters of Jerusalem, "If you see Him, tell Him I love Him." When I read this recently my heart stopped. I thought, *We are the Church, the bride of Christ. The last thing the world should hear us saying is "Where's Jesus?"* And this is not the first time the bride had run around the streets saying, "Have you seen my beloved?" But if we continue to resist the Bridegroom's invitation to His larger world, we will all eventually find ourselves one day left behind while He tends to His kingdom. He will come back, of course, but the fullness of the relationship that we could have enjoyed with Him will not be realized. He wants us out with Him in His kingdom, and if we decline the invitation, we will find ourselves saying, "Where's Jesus?"

Sex Begins in the Kitchen

In trying to be a better husband, I have read several books over the years on the subject of the husband/wife relationship. Dr. Kevin Leman, Christian author and former consulting psychologist for *Good Morning America*, wrote a book entitled *SEX BEGINS IN THE KITCHEN Because Love Is an All-Day Affair*. In his book, Dr. Leman was not referring to where to have sex but to how a husband and wife should treat each other. How you treat your spouse in the kitchen will affect how he or she responds to you in the bedroom. Intimacy means to be very close and personal. Certainly this describes the relationship of a married couple in the bedroom, but the bedroom should not be the only place they are close or personal. My wife and I are very close in the kitchen as we discuss our day and the things that are on our hearts. We are very close in our care for our family, our outreach into our community and in our ministry to the Body of Christ. We are also very close in our private times together in the bedroom. The Bridegroom wants to be very close to us in every part of His life, as well as in the chamber.

Who Is This Coming up from the Wilderness?

As the Song of Solomon progresses, we see the bride coming to a new understanding of intimacy. Although she didn't want to go out into His larger world, she was lovesick. She couldn't stand it without the Bridegroom, so she allowed Him to draw her out and change her very nature. And change she did. By the end of the book we see the bride, not the Bridegroom, saying, "Come, my beloved, let us go forth to the field; let us lodge in the villages. Let us get up early to the vineyards; let us see if the vine has budded, whether the grape blossoms are open, and the pomegranates are in bloom" (Song of Sol. 7:11-12). All the areas she had not been interested in earlier, she was now taking the initiative to venture into. Watchman Nee says of the bride in this Scripture:

> She is no longer interested in "my meetings," "my work," "my church," "my community," but in the vast total field of the Lord's interests in the world. . . . The whole field of the Lord's interests has become her scope of service, and she is one with Him in all of it.[6]

Finally in the last chapter of Song of Solomon, we find someone saying, "Who is this coming up from the wilderness, leaning upon her beloved?" (Song of Sol. 8:5). It was the bride! Every place the Bridegroom had invited her to earlier in the book she had now joined Him in, even the wilderness. The Bridegroom had drawn her completely into His larger world.

God's Fullback

As our concept of intimacy in worship is expanded, worship takes on a new aspect. The Bridegroom has brought us to His chamber, but He has also called us out into His kingdom. He has desired our communion in the inner court, but He has also determined that it would be through our praise and worship that He would bring about things in His kingdom. Although our personalities might be better suited to worship in the chamber, we must be willing to allow the Bridegroom to draw us out for His purposes in His kingdom.

The apostle John is known in Scripture as the one who laid his head upon the Lord's breast, John the beloved. But John did not remain in the upper room with his head laid upon the Lord's breast. When the Lord moved out into His kingdom through the newly formed Church, John's prowess in the kingdom became as greatly known as his intimacy in the chamber. Yale historian Ramsey Mac-Mullen says that John walked into the temple of Diana in the city of Ephesus and boldly prayed, "O God . . . at whose name every idol takes flight and every demon and every unclean power: now let the demon that is here [in this temple] take flight in thy name."[7]

The temple fell and much evangelism immediately occurred. John's intimacy with the Lord was just as powerful out in the kingdom as it was in the chamber. Now he was "John the beloved, shaker of the Roman Empire." John the beloved caused such a furor in the Roman Empire that they tried to execute him. When he did not die, they banished him to the Isle of Patmos for the rest of his days. From there he was chosen by God to be brought up to heaven and write the Revelation. But first he was the one who laid his head upon the Lord's breast.

As for me, I am by nature an easygoing, happy-go-lucky, come-what-may friendly fellow. I am a loner who, if given the choice, would rather be cooped up in my back bedroom with my guitar, singing my little love songs to Jesus. I am the quintessential "bride" in the chamber. I enjoy the intimacy of the secret place and have no natural desire to see the Bridegroom's larger world. I am a teddy bear.

My reputation, however, is that of a wild, loud, aggressive worship warrior: ever pressing forward, doing whatever it takes to break the Church through into victory. Robert Stearns, of Eagle Wings Ministry, calls me "God's fullback."

Why is my reputation so different from my natural character? It is because, after 15 years of seclusion in His chamber, the Bridegroom called me out into His larger world. I didn't want to come. I was comfortable in the secret place. But when the Bridegroom left the secret place to go out into His kingdom, I couldn't resist going with Him. I was lovesick. I had to follow Him. To do this I had to overcome the passivity in my character and move in a realm outside my own nature. In his book *God's Unfolding Battle Plan*, Chuck Pierce says:

> Passivity and peacefulness are two different things. Passivity causes us to pass up the God-appointed opportunity to declare Him victorious over the enemy. Ultimately, it renders us ineffective to war against the enemies of God—which we are called to do! The opposite of being passive is praising violently.[8]

I recently attended a personality seminar in which you answer a long list of questions by which your personality type can be determined. My personality type was called "phlegmatic," which the *Merriam-Webster Dictionary* defines as "having or showing a slow and stolid temperament."[9] At this seminar my personality was further described as low-key, easygoing, peaceful, unenthusiastic, relaxed, quiet, shy, reticent, compromising, uninvolved and indifferent; we phlegmatics avoid conflict, are not exciting, are not self-motivators, often resist change and always try to find the easy way. My wife can testify to every one of these qualities in me. If anyone could say to the Bridegroom, "Lord, I don't want to go out of the chamber . . . that's just not my personality," it would be me. In order to follow the call of the Bridegroom to "come away, my beloved," I have to overcome every single personality trait mentioned above . . . daily! But I'm lovesick, so I do it.

As I began to move out of that secret place, anointing began to fall on me to accomplish what God desired of me. I found, then, that I could not sit still. I had to get up and move. I had to leap: leap out of my own personality and inclinations and into the arms of God. Will Rogers once said, "Even if you're on the right track, you'll get run over if you just sit there."

Apostolic Worship

What we see in the Song of Solomon is a transition from personal worship as well as pastoral corporate worship in the chamber to apostolic worship, which is out in God's kingdom. Should we now abandon the chamber? No, it was the Bridegroom who brought us there, and He does not intend for us to abandon what He has established with us in that place. Our personal times of worship are not only the foundation of our relationship with God, but they are also the groundwork from which we launch our corporate worship before Him.

The word "enthroned" that we looked at in the first chapter also means, by implication, to "dwell." Since God has come to enthrone Himself on our praises, the implication in the Hebrew is that God has come to stay or to dwell: even to marry. Where most translations of the Bible use the word "enthroned," the *King James Version* says that God "inhabits" our praises. The different translations are not at odds with each other; they just express two dimensions of the same Hebrew word. As we have seen, God has chosen Zion—that place of continual praise—as His dwelling place; His resting place forever (see Ps. 132:13). David, by establishing continual praise in the tabernacle on Zion, provided a dwelling place for the Lord.

Today, God is rebuilding the tabernacle and rebuilding Zion in us, His people. We are His dwelling place, His throne room. In us and in our praises God comes to dwell and to enthrone Himself. From that dwelling place, that chamber, God is drawing us out into apostolic worship in His larger world, to effect the issues in His kingdom and bring in the harvest of the earth.

What Do We Do Now?

We must now examine where we stand in our corporate worship. What are we accomplishing? Are we just entertaining the crowd?

Are we more concerned about the "wow" factor in our worship than the anointing? Are we using the corporate worship times as our own personal "chamber" times, because we don't have one outside of our gathering times . . . or worse, are we using the wonderful anointing of our corporate worship times as an escape from reality rather than a time to truly enter into the presence of God? Jim Hodges explains one of the problems the Church today has in its corporate worship:

> It seems the Church today struggles with the corporate dimension of worship. We tend to be individualistic in our worship services. We sing, "Lord, love me: Lord, don't leave me." The emphasis is upon "me," not Him. Suddenly, worship is about me and my needs rather than Him and His Kingdom purposes. While it is true the Lord loves each one of us individually and is certainly concerned about the needs of His children, worship is not ministry to you and me; it is ministry to Him![10]

If heaven is our pattern for corporate worship, we must consider where we fall short of that pattern. Is our worship prophetic or has our modern-day doctrine written that aspect off? Is our worship intercessory? Is it dynamic, spontaneous and warring? Does God interact with it, or do we leave Him any space to squeeze into our program?

We came back into "face-to-face" worship when Martin Luther and the other Reformers put worship back in the hands of the common people of the Church. The other aspects of heaven's worship that were demonstrated in David's tabernacle have been in the process of steadily being restored to the Church over the last centuries and especially over the last few decades. We must therefore make sure that we are entering into all the things that God has chosen to restore to us.

THE BRIDEGROOM'S KINGDOM RESTORATION
CHUCK D. PIERCE

In the last chapter, you read how Jesus alluded to Himself as the Bridegroom (see Matt. 9). God is not a God who distinguishes our gifts and callings based upon gender! Therefore, all males in the kingdom of God must pursue the Bridegroom. All males and females together in the kingdom make up what is called "His Bride." Husbands learn how to love the Church by the way they love their bride. I actually think married men learn how to love themselves based upon their understanding of their bride. To "pursue the Bridegroom" must be a phrase that is understood by male and female alike.

A man who has recently been married or is about to be married is known as the bridegroom. This is a term that represents the maturity of a relationship and implies timing. John the Baptist also called Jesus the Bridegroom. I do think John the Baptist had a revelation of Jesus as Bridegroom, but I do not feel he ever really understood the role of the bride that would pursue the Bridegroom. If he did, he would have violently pursued the Lord! A couple of his disciples (Andrew and Phillip) did pursue, but at the end of John's life he was questioning, "Are you the One that we are looking for?" So the bride pursues the Bridegroom.

The bride, of course, is the Church! The Church is a pure virgin that will pursue (see 2 Cor. 11:1-2). These are those, who by faith through grace, have pursued Him to form a relationship and go with Him throughout the earth. This can be to people, nations, highways and byways, based upon us following Him, the One we love. My whole testimony revolves around two statements: "I will restore what you have *lost*" and "Follow *Me* and you will see revival and restoration!" These two statements have built my life's pursuit of our Lord!

In Revelation 21:9, the Church is called "the Bride, the Lamb's wife." In the Old Testament, Jehovah and the Jewish nation were Husband and Bride. He was betrothed and married to His nation.

The prophet Hosea best revealed the relationship of a husband and his unfaithful bride. As a whole, the nation of Israel rejected and was unfaithful to the One who formed them and developed His relationship with them, the people and the land. As the Church pursues the Bridegroom and matures in this relationship, Israel will be restored by grace, and will be forgiven and reinstated as a nation to the firstborn, first-wife status that God intended. This will give Israel a unique status among nations as God's elect nation (see Rom. 11). This will bring them back to their call as "bride." All nations will then reconcile around this call and restored status.

We, the Church, the Body, the bride of Christ, must pursue our Lover as He sends us to gather His inheritance among the nations (see Ps. 2). We are being fragranced as a bride through the baptizing work of the Holy Spirit. The Bridegroom rejoices over the bride! We must not hesitate in our comfortable beds to open the door and leave our bedroom chamber to frolic after our Lord as He leaps from mountain to mountain into the cultures of our society.

In 1 Samuel 30, David is a picture of the pursuit of the Bridegroom as he pursued his wife (Abigail), family and belongings that had been taken by the Amalekites. He inquired of Jehovah, "Shall I pursue?" The answer was: "*Pursue, overtake* and *recover all*" (see v. 8). We must pursue the Bridegroom as He pursues the restoration of all things to make the earth and the fullness thereof His own. Pursue as He pursues!

For Study and Reflection
Read John 3 and 1 Samuel 30. Meditate on Matthew 11 and memorize Ephesians 5:20-30.

How Must We Then Worship?

But the hour is coming, and now is, when the true worshipers will worship the Father in spirit and truth; for the Father is seeking such to worship Him.
JOHN 4:23

Our Worship Must Become Intercessory

Apostolic Worship and Intercession

Chuck Pierce wrote a book called *Interpreting the Times* in which he laid out the importance of understanding the times we are living in and adjusting our lives accordingly. Of worship he said:

> This will be a season of a different type of worship than you've ever known. Worship patterns are changing in the earth. One generation worshiped in one way, and now a new generation will lead us in worshiping in new ways. The tabernacle of David is being established. Individual worship will turn into corporate worship. Corporate worship is a key to the transformation of our regions.[1]

We must enter into apostolic worship because we have entered into a new apostolic age. This means giving up our own agenda in worship. Because apostles represent the government of God, apostolic worship moves us from a place where we might or might not have our personal desires fulfilled in our worship, but God's agenda will always be accomplished. "But seek first the kingdom of God and His righteousness, and all these things shall be added to you" (Matt. 6:33). If we put God's purposes first, His blessings will always come back on us. This is apostolic worship. Our needs will be met as we seek His purposes first and enter the call into the Bridegroom's larger world.

The first step I had to take in coming into the apostolic worship of the Bridegroom's larger world was into intercession. As we have seen, intercession plays a large part of the worship in heaven and in the worship that was in David's tabernacle. We must therefore look to see how we might incorporate intercession into our own worship.

Intercession is prayer, but it's a particular genre of prayer. God presents us a picture in the Bible of a wall that has a broken-down section. It is into this broken-down area—the breach—that He expects His intercessors to go as repairers of the breach. We see this in Ezekiel as God reproves His people: "You have not gone up into the breaches, nor did you build the wall around the house of Israel to stand in the battle on the day of the LORD" (Ezek. 13:5, NASB). The world today has broken-down parts—breaches—and as long as we stay in the "chamber," which the Bridegroom has drawn us into, we don't have to worry about those breaches. But just as the Bridegroom drew us into the chamber, He also comes to draw us into His larger world: "Come, my beloved, let us go forth to the field; let us lodge in the villages. Let us get up early to the vineyards" (Song of Sol. 7:11-12). If there is something broken down in the vineyard, then He desires to press us into that breach to stand in prayer until it is built up again.

Let me explain how this came about in our church. Back in 1987, our pastor asked Chuck Pierce to teach a series in our church on intercession. I was the worship leader and had to go lead worship for the meetings each Thursday night, which I dreaded. How boring was this going to be? But after a few weeks of teaching, we began to actually enter into intercession. Chuck introduced us to the heart of God that was longing for His children to enter into the long-neglected work of intercession. "And He saw that there was no man, and was astonished that there was no one to intercede" (Isa. 59:16, NASB).

We began to answer the call of God's heart to intercede for His purposes. Instead of a time of worship, then a time of prayer, we began to mix the worship and the intercession like they had done in Revelation 5:8, with the harp and the bowls. Then as we prayed, the Lord began to show us areas in our city where He wanted us to intercede: the education system, the government system, the financial system and others. As we answered God's call, He put us into the "gap" to build up the breach in the wall: "I looked for a man among them who would build up the wall and stand before me in the gap on behalf of the land so I would not have to destroy it" (Ezek. 22:30, *NIV*).

Our church worship began to have its foundation in intercession. Our Sunday morning services began to take on the flavor of what we had engaged in during our intercessory times. Our congregation was brought into the process of "repairing the breach." They were "restorers of the streets" as Isaiah proclaimed: "You will be called the repairer of the breach, the restorer of the streets in which to dwell" (Isa. 58:12, *NASB*). Most of the time they didn't even know they had entered the ranks of those "flaky intercessors" (sometimes they had a pretty good idea though). But through worship, we were able to bring to bear the power of agreement God gives us when we come together as the Body of Christ.

The key is for us as worshipers to become involved in the intercession of our church or at least to be aware of what our intercessors are experiencing in their intercession. What gap has God put them into and how are they standing in it? Has a spirit of fear or unbelief come in to distract God's people? Are there issues in our church or community that God wants us to cover in prayer? My favorite church meeting of the week is our early morning prayer every Tuesday. Chuck Pierce leads it, and it is always alive and engaging. Often we are able to see what direction our Sunday morning worship is to take during these meetings. But I also check with the leaders of our other intercession watches during the week to get perspective. Our Sunday morning worship then takes on the flavor of what our intercession had experienced during that week.

Our Worship Must Enter the Fight

The Inevitable Product of Intercession

One thing our church found out was that intercession unavoidably led to war. God's Spirit led us into the gap to intercede for the lost, for the wounded, for those held in bondage, for the school system that He had been removed from. We cried out for the endangered unborn children, for the injustices in our nation and the earth. We interceded for the things that belonged to God, but had been stolen. And we found that the devil did not want to give them back. So what do you do? The magic words "please" and "thank you" were not as effective as we had hoped. We found that the inevitable product of intercession was war.

Our church wanted to live in peace, but peace at what price? Some think that if we show ourselves to be peace-loving we will obtain peace, but a quick survey of the history of mankind will show that to be anything but successful. It is not our predisposition for war that invites war; it is our possession of something that someone else wants. Passivity does not bring peace, never has. And pretending that our adversary is not there does not make it so, as C. Peter Wagner observes:

> There are some who believe that Satan and demons are real, but that we should ignore them as much as possible. Their attitude is "If we don't bother them they won't bother us."[2]

History has shown us that as long as we are willing to hand over what is ours, we will not have to face war: slavery maybe, or even death, but not war. If we give up what God has given us, war can be averted. If we give up our rights, war can be averted. If we give our children as slaves, war can be averted. Wait a second, how far are we willing to go here? That's a good question for the Church today. We've given up prayer in our schools. We've given up the rights of the unborn. We've allowed a small minority to determine what is acceptable in society: same-sex marriages and the adoption of innocent children into those marriages. We have allowed that same minority to rewrite our children's textbooks concerning our founding fathers' determination to make this a nation of Christian values. We've allowed ourselves to be ridiculed for taking any kind of stand for righteousness and learned to keep our mouths shut in public about anything concerning our Lord and Savior, Jesus Christ.

Thomas Jefferson said, "The price for liberty is eternal vigilance." We haven't been vigilant, and much has been lost. Now God wants His stuff back and He is looking to us to go get it. "But we are the bride of Christ. We are lovers, not warriors. And what kind of man would send his bride out to get his stuff back?" What are we to do? After we have answered the Bridegroom's call to His kingdom, we can't be satisfied with just the chamber: we are lovesick and must be with Him wherever He goes. When He calls us to His chamber, we go; when He calls us to His kingdom, we go. We want our worship to be apostolic, to facilitate His government on earth as it is in heaven. If He sends us into the gap to intercede, we go, and if that means war, then we will war.

If there is one thing apostles are known for it is leading the fight. Paul led the fight for the gospel into a world of Roman idolatry. When the apostles in Jerusalem were dispersed during the Roman persecutions, they turned the world upside down through their faith and their giftings. Apostolic worship is full of fight. It never backs down. It addresses powers and principalities. It takes back what the enemy has captured. It always moves the Church forward.

Robert Stearn, in his book *Prepare the Way*, says that our warfare is, in the end, about God's lordship:

> We must understand that spiritual warfare is ultimately about lordship. All authority belongs to Christ. There is no domain free from the imposition of His sovereign will. . . . So when we talk about warfare, the goal of our warfare is not the battle, but the lordship of Christ we seek to bring to every domain. . . . This begins with the revelation that all domains—companies, armies, universities, even nations—are run by mere people. . . . We cannot—

must not—we dare not see these people as the enemy. We are not wrestling against them. They are the precious lives for whom Christ died.[3]

Although these forces of darkness influence people to do their bidding, we must always keep in mind that our war is not against the people. Even in times when we have to confront people in love, we keep our perspective clear. Our enemies are the spiritual forces of wickedness in the heavenly places. Therefore, we can be as wise as serpents in the spirit but gentle as doves in the natural (see Matt. 10:16): in other words, militant in the spiritual realm, but full of the fruit of the Spirit in the natural realm.

> Giving no cause for offense in anything, so that the ministry will not be discredited, but in everything commending ourselves as servants of God, in much endurance, in afflictions, in hardships, in distresses, in beatings, in imprisonments, in tumults, in labors, in sleeplessness, in hunger, in purity, in knowledge, in patience, in kindness, in the Holy Spirit, in genuine love, in the word of truth, in the power of God; *by the weapons of righteousness* for the right hand and the left (2 Cor. 6:3-7, *NASB,* emphasis added).

Our weapons are righteous. Our weapons give no cause for offence in the natural but employ the elements of endurance, patience, genuine love, truth and the power of God, which, in the spiritual realm, are mighty.

> For the weapons of our warfare are not carnal but mighty in God for pulling down strongholds, casting down arguments and every high thing that exalts itself against the knowledge of God, bringing every thought into captivity to the obedience of Christ (2 Cor. 10:4-5).

In our worship, we are bringing the lordship of Jesus Christ over areas that have exalted themselves against the knowledge of God.

With the high praises of God in our mouth and the sword of the Spirit in our hands, we are executing the judgment written against the enemy of our faith (see Ps. 149). The earth and all that is on it is God's, and He wants to possess it: "Behold, all souls are Mine; the soul of the father as well as the soul of the son is Mine" (Ezek. 18:4, *NASB*).

Our Worship Must Become Prophetic

Becoming Prophetic

Early in our walk with the Lord, my wife, Violet, and I operated in two very different spiritual gifts. She had a prophetic gift, and I had teaching. These two gifts complemented each other well when they didn't fight. She could discern things in the spirit and speak a word into people, and I could teach them the principles in the Word to walk by.

This worked well for a while until I began to notice that certain people were not able to put into action the principles I taught them. What was wrong with them? I had given them good advice and clear instructions. I had spent years devouring the Word and digging out its principles of life; the *ABC*s of walking before Him; the *123*s of overcoming in this world. But more and more, I saw people who couldn't get the 2 before the 3, or put the C in front of the A. *It's simple!* I thought, *123! ABC!* It was as if there was an evil force preventing them from seeing the simple pathway to take to victory—some wicked power that kept them from taking the counsel I gave. And indeed there was! Satan's forces were at work to bind them up and keep them from doing the very things they so wanted to do to get free and be victorious. I had no idea how to fight these forces. I was a teacher and a worship leader, but I did not understand the schemes the devil used against people or against the Church when it came together. I loved Jesus, and could lead people in pouring their hearts out in adoration of Him, but I did not know how to bring the Body against the powers that strove to keep people locked in their oppression.

Week after week, we would come home from church, and Violet would ask, "Didn't you see what was going on in the Spirit?" "Uh . . .

no." Indeed, much was going on in a realm I did not perceive. The enemy was at work, and God was at work, but I was just having a good time in worship. And believe me, God can accomplish much through our simple worship and praise, but He wants to bring us up to a level of co-laboring with Him to accomplish His purposes.

Violet said, "We've got to pray for you to get some discernment and start moving in the prophetic." I said, "Can we do that? Is that kosher? Can you ask for another gift?" She said, "I don't know, but we've got to do something!" So we began to pray. And God began to answer. Over time, I began to see what God was doing in people's lives from a pastoral standpoint so that I could better pastor them in the things of God. And I began to sense the moving of the Spirit in worship services; to pause when God wanted to speak to His people; to feel the mood of God's Spirit when He wanted to bring us into war or celebration or intimacy. This was the beginning of apostolic worship for me, though I barely knew the word "apostle" at the time. I began to enter into the government of God in my worship, not just what I wanted, but what He wanted in my worship.

That Thing You Do
My private time with the Lord began to change. I began to open up the Word and sing it, chapter after chapter: first the psalms, then the prophets, then the epistles and the Gospels. I could sense the mood of the Spirit in the Scriptures that I sang: passion, love, anger, concern, joy, excitement. I began to prophesy and to preach and to war—all in my private times with God. Paul said, "I will sing with my understanding and I will sing with my spirit" (see 1 Cor. 14:15). So I began to sing with my spirit as well. I sang in tongues, and not just simple little songs, but beautiful, sweeping melodies: sometimes warlike and forceful, sometimes more like a love song or ballad, and sometimes even operatic aria. I sang over my household. I sang over my sleeping children. I sang when I gathered with small groups of friends to pray. My friends began to call my prophetic singing "that thing you do." "Hey, John, do that thing you do."

For eight years I flowed like this in my private times with God. Then one evening, at an all-night prayer meeting at our church, I sang forth a song in the Spirit before the congregation. Whoa! Can you do this stuff in church? I had not thought about that; it had just come out. I do not think that everyone has to develop in their private times for eight years before they bring it into the corporate worship of the church, but I do believe that what you do in church should be an overflow of what you are doing alone with God, not the other way around.

Chuck Pierce had brought an understanding of intercession into our church and into our worship. Now he began to bring us into an understanding of prophecy; and under his strong prophetic gift, we began to move into prophetic worship.

The Endless Aspects of Prophetic Song

Prophetic songs can come out in an endless variety of expression. They can be the innermost gushings of our heart toward our Father as we allow His creativity to flow out of us in song. They can be spontaneous songs interlaced with the voice of God. Here they become *prophetic*. And they can be a specific word from the Lord. Then they become *prophecy*. The apostle Peter says, "For no prophecy was ever made by an act of human will, but men moved by the Holy Spirit spoke from God" (2 Pet. 1:21, *NASB*). As the Spirit stirs in us, we are moved by Him to sing from God. Cindy Jacobs, in her book *The Voice of God*, gives an instance of these songs:

> A beautiful expression of the prophetic is when the Lord gives the songs of the Lord or prophetic songs to the singers or instrumentalists. This is not a rehearsed song, in the same manner that a prophecy is not rehearsed. Rather, it is spontaneous. Those on the instruments, led by one of the musicians, may play a set pattern of three chords or so while the prophetic song is released. I have been in churches where the whole congregation started singing the words as they were repeated again and again. It is as if the Lord wants to give the message many times until it is indelibly printed on the pages of our hearts.[4]

The Father Sings Over Us

We often think of worship being one-sided: We sing to God. But the Scriptures tell us an interesting thing that occurs when God is in our midst: "The LORD your God in your midst, the Mighty One, will save; He will rejoice over you with gladness, He will quiet you with His love, He will rejoice over you *with singing*" (Zeph. 3:17, emphasis added).

The word "rejoice" here means literally to spin round under the influence of a violent emotion. God, in His violent love for us, is spinning around, rejoicing over us with singing. The word "singing" in the Hebrew means to emit a shrill shout of joy and gladness and triumph. What a picture this presents to us! It reminds us of the Hebrews' highest, most vibrant form of praise, the *halal*. Not only does God want us to *halal* before Him, He *halals* over us, singing at the top of His voice. Here is where the gift of prophecy should enter our worship. If God is singing over us, we should be able to prophetically hear what He is singing over us.

When God speaks to His Church, it is through His prophets. When He sings to His Church, it is through His prophetic singers— one aspect of the song of the Lord. Prophetically, we can hear the things God sings over us.

Different ones receive songs in different ways. When my wife, Violet, sings prophetically, it comes out like a well-fashioned song: verse one, chorus, verse two, chorus, and so on. Also it is always in first person, "Thus saith the Lord." But as different ones of us express the songs the Father sings over us, I believe they touch into other of the prophetic speaking gifts as well. For instance, the songs might come forth as a word of wisdom, a word of knowledge or the gift of exhortation. They might not be first person, and they might not have a traditional song structure. Also, these songs might include the brooding and intercession of the Holy Spirit, which we will look at later. And in as many ways as they might come to us, they are released through us in even more ways. As Chuck Pierce says in his book *The Future War of the Church*:

If we do not attempt to understand how differently each of us processes the voice of God, we can easily miss God's message of redemption, warning and salvation.[5]

Jesus Sings in the Midst of Us

There is a heaviness in these times, an anointing, a weight. The presence of God is manifested in song. The angel of the Lord told the apostle John, "For the testimony of Jesus is the spirit of prophecy" (Rev. 19:10, *NASB*). This spirit of prophecy can be released in prophetic song when we, in the Spirit, hear and sing what that spirit of prophecy is singing in the midst of the congregation. The writer of Hebrews gives us a glimpse into the spirit realm, showing us what Jesus is doing in our midst as we worship. He says Jesus is not ashamed to call us his brothers, and then he quotes from Psalm 22:22, which is a prophetic psalm in which Jesus is speaking: "I WILL PROCLAIM YOUR NAME TO MY BRETHREN, IN THE MIDST OF THE CONGREGATION I WILL SING YOUR PRAISE" (Heb. 2:12, *NASB*).

When we are together as a congregation, Jesus is not ashamed to call us His brothers; and in our midst He sings His praises to the Father. His testimony, that spirit of prophecy, that mantle, comes down on us in worship, and I believe we can prophetically hear those songs that Jesus is singing in our midst. LaMar Boschman tells of this experience he had as a young man during a powerful, anointed worship service:

> About a half hour into the worship service I began to sing spontaneous lyrics . . . as fast as it came I sang it. . . . Several minutes later I realized I was singing a song that had a structure. While I had been worshiping, a melody and chord pattern had evolved that resembled a written song. Even the lyrics were in proper meter. . . . When the worship of the congregation had quieted, I didn't hesitate to lift up my voice and sing it out. "The Lord reigneth, the Lord reigneth, blessed be the name of the Lord, for the Lord our God omnipotent reigneth in majesty."[6]

Many of you who have been around a few years recognize this song. It was a widely circulated chorus in the charismatic movement of the 1970s and 1980s. Most of us did not realize it was a prophetic song at the time or would have understood what that was back then. I think LaMar was hearing Jesus' song of praise to the Father and just began to sing it out. Many prophetic songs are directed toward the Father. Jesus is in our midst, singing and stirring up that spirit of prophecy, and we are loosing His songs.

The Holy Spirit Travails Over Us

We've seen the Father singing over us; we've seen Jesus singing in the midst of us. What about the third Person of the Trinity? Does the Holy Spirit play a part too? Of course He does. As we saw earlier, the Spirit is interceding. When we are worshiping and that spirit of intercession comes upon us, that travail often comes out in song. There is a heaviness in these songs, an intensity. We feel the brooding, the hovering; something is being "birthed" as we travail with the Spirit. Often these songs are not the beautiful, sweeping melodies of the Father singing over us, or Jesus praising God in our midst. They may range from groaning to crying out, to repetitive phrases expressing God's heart. Sometimes they are addressing the enemy, sometimes the church, sometimes quoting the Word, but always expressing the heart of God, which the Spirit is searching out.

Not Ready for Prime Time

I will say that most of these times are in our personal prayer times or in intercession prayer meetings, because the intensity of travail in song is a little more that the normal Sunday morning crowd would be ready for, and that's fine. Sunday mornings should be more evangelical and pastoral than our intercession meetings, though that spirit of intercession should be in our hearts in any worship service. Other forms of prophetic music are fine on Sunday morning, because they are evangelistic and pastoral. The apostle Paul says, "But one who prophesies speaks to men for edification and exhortation and consolation" (1 Cor. 14:3, *NASB*). This is very pastoral and appropriate for our diverse Sunday morning crowd with visitors and members of various maturity levels. Then Paul adds:

> Therefore if the whole church assembles together and all speak in tongues, and ungifted men or unbelievers enter, will they not say that you are mad? But if all prophesy, and an unbeliever or an ungifted man enters, he is convicted by all, he is called to account by all; the secrets of his heart are disclosed; and so he will fall on his face and worship God, declaring that God is certainly among you (1 Cor. 14:23-25, *NASB*).

Prophetic song can be evangelistic, and Paul recommends this type of activity for Sunday morning services, but he lets us know that some of our other activities might make folks think we are mad. Indeed, there have been times when I've wondered myself if we were mad as we have interceded in song. But we are not, we are just in travail, and that's a little different from our normal, everyday activities. I would not invite my next-door neighbors over to visit while my wife was in the travail of childbirth. Just imagine. In the same way, we should not invite Sunday morning visitors in while we are doing the work of travail in intercession. But we need to make sure we have meetings that are reserved for intercession so we are free to allow the Spirit to bring us into the travail necessary to birth God's purposes. The fruit of these times should then be released into our corporate worship services. God's heart can then permeate our services, even though our visitors and less mature members are not overpowered by the intensity of our travail. God can bring them along at their own pace as He moves in their lives.

Who Can Do This?
Although we are not all prophets, we can all participate in this prophetic phenomenon. The apostle Paul says that "to each one is given the manifestation of the Spirit for the common good" (1 Cor. 12:7, *NASB*). Paul goes on to list these manifestation gifts

of the Spirit, one of which is the gift of prophecy. LaMar Boschman explains how this comes about in our worship:

> At times the prophetic cloud may be over an entire con-
> gregation and anyone could flow in prophecy at that point
> if he exercised faith to do so. This is what happened when
> the seventy elders who assisted Moses in leading Israel all
> prophesied as the spirit of prophecy came upon them
> (Numbers 11:24-30). Saul experienced a similar anointing
> when he met a company of prophets and prophesied
> among them. He himself was not a prophet, and did not
> have the gift of prophecy, and yet he did speak the word of
> the Lord under a prophetic anointing. Most prophetic
> songs fit into the realm of the spirit of prophecy, for, rel-
> atively speaking, there are more "ordinary believers" than
> there are genuine prophets or even persons possessing the
> gift of prophecy. It stands to reason that far more people
> will prophesy by entering into this flow than by exercising
> either the office or the gift of prophecy. Yet there is no rea-
> son why someone with the office of a prophet or the gift
> of prophecy could not sing when prophesying.[7]

This "spirit of prophecy" that LaMar speaks of is like a mantle or garment that comes down on God's people in worship. We
call it a prophetic mantle. It can come down on an individual or on
a whole congregation. Cindy Jacobs explains this in her book *The
Voice of God*:

> At times, the Holy Spirit will manifest through prophecy
> in a meeting. When this occurs, many prophecies will be
> spoken and many who do not usually prophesy will be
> able to do so. It sometimes seems like a river of prophecy
> is flowing through the gathering as one person picks
> up where the last person left off. The song of the Lord
> (a spontaneous prophetic song) may take place during
> this time. One of the most moving services I've been in

was when one person started with the song of the Lord and then one person after another picked up additional verses and sang. This kind of service leaves a person with a sense of awe.[8]

Ascending in Worship

Bringing prophecy into our worship is not always an easy, overnight process. Our own church had to learn to ascend in worship and break open the oppressive resistance in the mid heavens so that the mantle of prophecy could descend. Chuck Pierce and I explain this process in our book *Worship Warrior: Ascending in Worship, Descending in War*. In a nutshell, we learned to press forward in our worship into the presence of the Lord, overcoming obstacles in the heavenly places, ascending level by level. In each level into which we ascended we were enabled to move in songs that would not have had as much power in one of the lower levels. As God would lead, we would move in warfare or praise or celebration or proclamation until there was a "breakthrough" into the heavenly realms. Here in this place we would often see a prophetic mantle come down for us to move in. Then we were able to prophesy or sing the prophetic song or just bask in the presence of the Lord.

On My Instrument?

Can instruments prophesy? Of course they can! We see it in the Scripture and we see it in the Church today. King David had a whole pantry full of prophetic musicians: "Moreover David and the captains of the army separated for the service some of the sons of Asaph, of Heman, and of Jeduthun, who should prophesy with harps, stringed instruments, and cymbals" (1 Chron. 25:1). Here we see a variety of instruments that David's musicians were expected to prophesy on. Now, the Scripture clearly teaches that it was David's worship leaders who were to play the loud-sounding cymbals (see 1 Chron. 15:19; 16: 5). But, alas, even with this preponderance of biblical evidence, my worship team will not let me anywhere near our cymbals. But that still leaves us with a variety of other instruments to prophesy on.

One of David's worship leaders, Jeduthun (also known as Ethan), was especially known as a prophetic musician. Jeduthun "prophesied with a harp to give thanks and to praise the LORD" (1 Chron. 25:3). How do you know when an instrument is prophesying? It speaks to our spirit. All of us love a good instrumental solo. It blesses our soul but our spirit could care less; it is only affected by spiritual things. When God sent an evil spirit upon King Saul, David was called in to play his harp. David had a prophetic anointing on him, as we have seen clear enough through his psalms. When David played, that prophetic anointing came out of his instrument and the evil spirit was not able to stay in that presence of the Spirit of God. It fled (see 1 Sam. 16:14-23).

When an instrument prophesies, the Spirit of God is speaking through it. It can be interpreted like a message in tongues. Our musicians prophesy on their instruments, the most prolific of which is our lead guitar player, Thom Rana. Our spirits light up within us when he prophesies. Our spirits know the difference between a good lead lick and a prophetic expression on the guitar.

Chuck Pierce often interprets what the guitar is prophesying. Sometimes our singers sing what the guitar is saying. I remember one Sunday morning as we were before the Lord in worship that Thom began to play behind me. I literally felt the power of the prophetic song hit me in the back like a blast of air. I opened my mouth and began to sing as he played. As I started each phrase of the song, I didn't even know what the end of the phrase was going to be, but it flowed freely and easily as the guitar played behind me. Several of the prophetic songs we have written down and put in our songbook are interpretations of Thom's prophesying instrument.

Many of our other musicians have experienced the anointing of God on their instrument as the spirit of prophecy has come upon us in worship. A young trumpet player on our worship team once excitedly told me, "John, during the worship I hear the things I am supposed to play and I just play them." It is as easy as that. We just have to be bold and step out and try.

We see all these representations of the exercise of prophecy in the different ways prophetic song comes forth, bubbling out of us at times, raining down on us at other times. Sometimes a weight comes upon us, as Cindy Jacobs relates:

> The worship service itself can amount to a prophetic message that God is expressing to the church. When this happens, a powerful anointing will come upon the music. The worship will quicken within the hearts of the people. For instance, if the Lord is saying to His people "Fear not," and a song is sung that proclaims those words, life will spring up in those who are singing. It will give them special faith. They are not to fear, for God is with them through their trials.[9]

The List Goes On

The three persons of the Trinity are not idle during our worship. Some people don't care much for worship, but the Father, the Son and the Holy Spirit love it. They get right in there with us. I have only scratched the surface of the ways the Trinity moves in us prophetically in song. I have seen God bring forth His message in song through the many different personalities of His churches and ministries across the land. There is no one right way. God didn't make us all to have one personality, but one Spirit. I love seeing the diversity of the prophetic gift.

Some places use one style of music, some another. In some places the river runs like rapids through a narrow gorge; in other places it is wide and meandering. God uses singers and dancers and musicians. He uses prophetic actions and travail. He uses the old and the young, the great and the small, the gifted and the ungifted, the willing and sometimes the unwilling. And what more shall I say? For time would fail me if I tell of songs coming forth on the streets, in staff meetings, in cars, at dinner parties or while the preacher is in the middle of his message; songs sung as personal words over people in a worship service, during the ministry time, in the foyer after the meeting; songs of comfort, songs of war, love songs and lullabies. God is limitless in the creative ways He looses His prophetic songs in us.

What Are Our Boundaries?

The boundaries are simple: We are people under authority. This is what gives us the authority and faith to move in the prophetic anointing. Cindy Jacobs tells of an important exhortation she received from the Lord early in her ministry:

> When I received my call to ministry from the Lord, the subject of authority was heavy on my heart. One day in prayer, the Holy Spirit cautioned me, "Cindy, if you want to move in great authority, you must be subject to others in authority. Your anointing will grow in proportion to your understanding of spiritual submission."[10]

We can see this truth modeled for us in David's tabernacle. David's worship leaders submitted themselves to David, and because they did, it brought them up under the anointing that was in David. The worship team, then, submitted to David's worship leaders and came up under the anointing in the worship leaders, and so on. David's three worship leaders, Asaph, Heman and Ethan (Jeduthun), had sons who were appointed to prophesy in the tabernacle. But they were not just turned loose to do anything they pleased. They were being trained and given direction in their prophesying: "The sons of Asaph were under the direction of Asaph, who prophesied under the direction of the king" (1 Chron. 25:2, *NASB*).

It goes on to say the same thing about the other two worship leaders and their sons. The sons prophesied under the direction of their fathers, the worship leaders, who prophesied under the direction of David, the king. As they came under the authority of the one over them, they had faith to step out in their gift and know that the one over them would back them up. Being under authority did not hinder them; it enabled them.

Inevitably, I get the question, "What if God gives me a song and there is no avenue for me to give it?" This is not uncommon. We have to understand that there are many spiritual things going on during a worship service. We have to trust God to work through the authority structure He has put in place. If we feel that we have a song, but we are not able to give it, then we can stay in our place and pray through the message of the song. Perhaps God wants that song to be a burden of intercession in you for a season, and when that season is completed, He will make a way for you to release it. I always place myself under those God puts over me. There are times when I will have a song from the Spirit but it turns out that someone else is able to bring forth that message in a different way in a higher anointing than I have. Sometimes the opportunity for the song I have passes as the service moves on to another direction. Any number of things might happen in an active service. Sometimes we just miss God. As humans, we sometimes do, but you would be surprised how many times I have seen God tell the leader when I have had a song.

Once I was leading worship at one of Barbara Wentroble's conferences. She was speaking on the roar of the Lion of Judah. Toward the end of her message, God dropped a song in my spirit. I said, "Lord, there is no way for me to give this song; we are about to be released to lunch." But in the process of dismissing the congregation, Barbara stopped abruptly, turned to me and said, "John, do you have a song?" I said, "Yes!" and got up and released a powerful song called "Raise Up a Roar," which we later recorded on our CD entitled *Let the Lion of Judah Roar.*

Another time, while we were in worship, the Lord began to stir a song in me. But before it had become strong enough for me to release, the worship time had come to an end. When the speaker came to the platform, he said, "The Lord says we are not finished worshiping." We entered back into a powerful time of worship, and the song that had been stirring in me came bubbling back up and I released it in power.

The Lord is well able to make a way for His song. At times we have to be patient and trust in His timing. Once the Lord gave my wife a song in a service, but there was no opportunity to give it. She didn't get upset or try to push her way in to give it. When we got home from church that day she said, "Hey, John, listen to this song the Lord gave me!" It was awesome and powerful and one of those first person "thus saith the Lord" type of songs that she gets.

I later wrote the song down and we started singing it in our church services. Eventually we recorded it on one of our CDs and it has gone out all over the world.

Do We Judge It?

If it is prophecy, we are obliged to judge. The apostle Paul said, "Do not despise prophetic utterances. But examine everything carefully; hold fast to that which is good" (1 Thess. 5:20-21, *NASB*). This is another aspect of the apostolic in our worship. Judgment is a governmental attribute. As God's government comes to bear in our worship through the emergence of the apostolic gifting, we must properly judge what comes forth in our prophetic singing.

As I mentioned earlier, these songs can be anything from the gushings of our heart toward God, to spontaneous songs interlaced with prophecy, to specific prophetic words. If someone is singing out his or her love to God, there is not much judging needed. Generally, we just look to see whether the song is edifying the whole congregation or if it would be better if the person would just keep the song in personal worship.

As the voice of God becomes evident in a song, it becomes necessary to "examine everything carefully" and to "hold fast to that which is good." A leader can do this by repeating or emphasizing that which he could discern to be the voice of God in the song and, if necessary, completing that which was lacking in the message of the song. We exercise much grace in this type of song, always affirming "that which is good." As noted earlier, we all process the voice of God in different ways. Barbara Wentroble says, "The nature of our hearing is imperfect. We don't even hear others clearly."[11] Knowing this, we just want to make sure the song fulfills the purpose of prophecy by edifying, exhorting and consoling (see 1 Cor. 14:3).

It is always good to encourage people who participate regularly in prophetic song to be strong in the Word. Cindy Jacobs gives this advice to people who would be prophetic singers:

> One critical factor for anyone who is going to be used by the Lord to prophesy is to make sure his or her prayer life

and time in the Scripture stays in balance. You can always tell a prophetic person who spends time steeped in God's Word. There is a richness to a person's prophetic gift when it is liberally enhanced with Scripture. This is also a great safeguard against deception.[12]

The more we hide the Word in our hearts, the more the Spirit can bring to remembrance the things Jesus has spoken (see John 14:26). When a song becomes a specific prophetic word, it needs to be judged like any other prophetic word. This is done by those with a prophetic gift who can discern the voice of God as Paul exhorts us: "Let two or three prophets speak, and let the others pass judgment" (1 Cor. 14:29, *NASB*). In our judging we again try to "hold to that which is good" instead of giving a detailed critique of the prophecy in front of the whole congregation. Those judging can bring attention to the "good" of what was sung and, if need be, add that which was lacking in the message God was bringing to His people.

Open Our Eyes, Lord
There are many things going on when we come together and worship. God is singing, Jesus is singing, the Holy Spirit is interceding and we are looking at our watches, wondering when this is going to be over so that we can go home and eat. Paul prayed that "the eyes of your heart may be enlightened" (Eph. 1:18, *NASB*). We, as the Church, need to let God open the eyes of our heart so that we can be enlightened. Just imagine, God in three persons, the Trinity, is very much a part of our times of worship. I have used the majority of this chapter to explain prophetic worship because it is the area in which I receive the most questions.

Our Worship Must Become Dynamic and Spontaneous

The Flow
Many charismatics like myself like to point out how predictable are the liturgical churches in their worship when all the time our

own "Spirit-led" services have too often drifted into our own little "three fast songs, three slow songs, then a time 'in the spirit.'" Bob Sorge draws from the vision of God's river in Ezekiel 47 in which Ezekiel is drawn deeper into its flow until he can no longer touch the bottom and must swim. He says:

> There is a flow to be found in corporate worship that is so deep and compelling that the waters cannot be crossed. . . . "God, give us such a depth in the river of God in worship that people are swept off their feet in the glory of this lifegiving flow! Give us worship services that can't be crossed!"[13]

We must do more than sing our three fast songs and three slow songs and have our little time before the Lord. We must press into the dynamic flow of God's river. We can't guess its flow. It is dynamic: moving. It is spontaneous: the unplanned springing forth of God's life in new songs or prophetic song I explained earlier. Bob Sorge describes how this kind of service might come about:

> In congregational worship, worship leaders are constantly reaching out in their spirits to discern when the meeting touches the river of God. They'll throw out a song—and then search with their toes (in a metaphorical sense) to see if their feet have found water. . . . And so worship leaders will tend to go through their song list, one song after another, hoping that at some point in the worship service we will somehow find the river of God. They strain to find the thing God's Spirit is wanting to breathe upon as we have gathered in Christ's name. When the river of God catches up a worship service, we find ourselves carried along by a divine impetus. God Himself is energizing our worship. Trying to sustain a worship service with musical means and human strength is one of the most wearisome chores a leader will ever attempt. But oh, when God takes the meeting! When that happens, leading worship is one of the most exhilarating joys God can give to His leaders.[14]

We Must Allow God to Interact with Our Worship

Enthroning Him

When we enthrone God on our praises, we facilitate the interaction between heaven and earth. What we saw in Revelation—God enthroned on the praises coming forth on His holy hill, Zion—becomes a reality on earth, God enthroned on the praises coming forth from the earthly Zion, us. In heaven they knew they were enthroning God on their praises and they knew what would happen when God was enthroned. Today we know that God is enthroned on our praises, but I don't believe we always understand what that means. Perhaps we have understood that we are enthroning God as the Lord of our own life, but we need to understand that God is taking up His authority over the world from His throne on our praises. This is apostolic worship, when we enter into God's governmental perspective in our praise.

With this understanding we can come into a more informed attitude toward our corporate worship. It's not just a time for us to get warmed up or mellowed out. It is a time for each of us to bring the strength of our own personal worship into the corporate setting and gain the synergism of our corporate worship (one can put a thousand to flight, two can . . .), the power of corporate agreement (when two or more agree) and the promise of Jesus' presence when we gather (when two or more are gathered, Jesus is in their midst). We can come out of our escapes, our narcissism or our personal needs in worship to throw ourselves by faith into the Bridegroom's larger world, enthroning Him on our worship and seeing Him interact with us to launch His purposes in the earth.

Face to Face

We have such a great privilege to enter into the presence of God by the blood of Jesus and worship Him face to face. It is important that we exercise this privilege in our worship and "come *boldly* to the throne of grace" (Heb. 4:16, emphasis added). In his book *Possessing Your Inheritance*, Chuck Pierce says:

Praise is that element of celebration that can transport us into the throne room of God. Once we are in the throne room at His feet, we need to worship and adore Him. As we worship Him in that intimate place, He begins to reveal His glory to us.[15]

There is nothing more breathtaking than God's Church worshiping face to face with Him. God desires to interact with us, breaking the chains over us, giving us strategies for victory in our lives.

Continual Worship

Slowly over the centuries our worship has been becoming more and more continual. In one way it has been through spreading Christianity throughout all the time zones of the earth. Any hour of the day God is being worshiped in some location or another in the earth. More recently prayer ministries have sprung up in more and more places whose purpose is to maintain worship and intercession 24 hours a day, 7 days a week, 52 weeks a year. Why is it important to have continual worship? If anyone has gained anything from this book I hope it is the knowledge that God is enthroned on our worship, and what happens when we enthrone Him. If we understand the importance of enthroning God on our praises, then we can understand, like David did, how important it is to have Him enthroned continually. As the worldwide Church, we can, together, make sure God is continually worshiped from our many ethnos groups, from our many styles, from our variety of expressions.

The Tabernacle in 1000 B.C.

When David set up his tabernacle, Israel entered into the greatest period of expansion in its history. David extended the borders of Israel to the north, south, east and west. He amassed riches that would one day enable his people to enter their golden age under Solomon. Solomon did not have to expand the kingdom or amass plunder; his father, David, had done it all for him. And it is no coincidence that—during those years David was bringing in the fullness of territory and plunder—God was being enthroned on Israel's praises in the tabernacle. From that throne God ruled; He waged war; He pronounced judgments on David's enemies; and He aided David's commanders in their fight to expand Israel's boarders. David was then able to possess the fullness of territory that had been promised to Abraham in Genesis 15:18: "To your descendants I have given this land, from the river of Egypt as far as the great river, the river Euphrates" (*NASB*). David could not have accomplished all of this without the tabernacle, and when the time of war and expansion was ended, so was David's tabernacle.

The Tabernacle in A.D. 2000

Today God's goal is not land acquisition; it is souls. God's stated purpose of restoring the tabernacle of David is to bring in the fullness of the nations called by His name; the very thing James saw in the beginning of Acts 15. It is no coincidence today that David's tabernacle is being rebuilt so that God might enthrone Himself on our praises and from that throne rule, wage war, pronounce judgment on our enemies and aid our leaders in their fight to open up the way "so that the rest of mankind may seek the LORD, even all the Gentiles who are called by My name" (Acts 15:17). The tabernacle of David represents the government of God, because the tabernacle is where God has chosen to rule and reign from. The worship in this governmental place is, by nature, apostolic as we enthrone Him to rule and reign.

Israel tried for almost 500 years to conquer the land they had crossed the Jordan to possess under Joshua, but it was not until David came and set up his tabernacle that they were able to finish the job. We have labored for 2,000 years to bring in the fullness of the Gentiles, but we will not see it happen until David's tabernacle has been fully built again. David did not trust in "the strength of his arm" to bring him military prowess, but instead he put worship first.

As we seek to bring in the harvest of the earth, we must move in the same apostolic principles that David did to bring in the territory. If we seek first to enthrone God on our praises, He will from that throne bring in the fullness of the nations. We can't say, "Worship is fine, but we have work to do to in the Kingdom." Instead we must come to an understanding of the part our worship plays in fulfilling God's plan in the earth. If God is rebuilding Zion and restoring David's tabernacle for His desired end, we must allow the aspects of that restoration to become a reality in our worship. God is restoring worship "as in the days of old" (Amos 9:11). If the worship in David's tabernacle was intercessory and prophetic and warring, then we must have those characteristics as our goal. If it was dynamic and spontaneous and continual, then we must strive for ours to be the same. God longs to interact with our worship to bring in the fullness of His harvest on the earth.

Finally, as we enter into the fullness of our call to worship, God wants to reinstate to us many of the weapons of our warfare that the enemy has incapacitated over the centuries. This is a day of restoration, and we need to be attentive to everything God puts His finger on to reinstate for His purposes.

MAKING WORSHIP A REALITY IN ALL THE EARTH
CHUCK D. PIERCE

We must worship in truth. Once God's chosen nation left Egypt, they journeyed through several wildernesses as they followed Moses toward a land called Promised. Before they could enter this land, they had to stop and receive heaven's instructions for their life. At Mount Sinai, Moses went up and the people stayed below and waited. Truth—the Torah, the Tablets of Covenant laws—was given by the One they followed. Truth would become part of their worship.

We must worship in Spirit. Joel prophesied that there would come a time when God would send His Spirit on all flesh (see Joel 2:28-29). This outpouring would cause our sons and daughters to prophesy, meaning from generation to generation there would be a remnant who worshiped. Old men would dream. Young men and women would have visions, or prophetic revelation, that would keep the Kingdom fresh and advancing. Menservants and maidservants would not be restricted by slavery, but would have spiritual insights and be free to worship the God who created them. The Spirit would be the key to Kingdom life. For the Kingdom within us to manifest and be seen on the earth, we would worship in Spirit.

We must worship in Spirit and truth to experience the reality of life in our time and space. In the midst of our Lord's trials, He had a need to visit Samaria. Samaria was a nation that was hated by the Jewish people.

I love the woman at the well (see John 4). She had a desperate need for change. Her questions and Jesus' answers changed the course of life for all nations. He asked for a drink of water and offered her water that would quench her thirst for eternity. If she gave Him the water she had access to, He would exchange that with what He had and she would never thirst again. The whole context of this exchange was within the differences of nationalistic worship between Jew and Samaritan. This interchange of communication in John 4:19-26 around worship is revealing for all generations:

> The woman said to Him . . . "Our forefathers worshiped on this mountain, but you [Jews] say that Jerusalem is the place where it is necessary and proper to worship."
>
> Jesus said to her, "Woman, believe Me, a time is coming when you will worship the Father neither [merely] in this mountain nor [merely] in Jerusalem. You [Samaritans] do not know what you are worshiping [you worship what you do not comprehend]. We do know what we are worshiping [we worship what we have knowledge of and understand], for [after all] salvation comes from [among] the Jews. A time will come, however, indeed it is already here, when the true (genuine) worshipers will worship the Father in spirit and in truth (reality); for the Father is seeking just such people as these as His worshipers. God is a Spirit (a spiritual Being) and those who worship Him must worship *Him* in spirit and in truth (reality)."
>
> The woman said to Him, "I know that Messiah is coming, He Who is called the Christ (the Anointed One); and

when He arrives, He will tell us everything we need to know and make it clear to us."

Jesus said to her, "I Who now speak with you am He" (*AMP*).

The understanding of this type of worship changed her forever. She did not let her past failures keep her from intimately worshiping and turning outward toward those around her. This woman tore down her prejudices, overcame her past, experienced a new reality of the Lord and left her mundane daily exercise of getting water to run and evangelize her entire city.

The disciples could not understand why the Lord would go to Samaria and visit with the woman at the well. They did not yet understand the type of worship that would produce reality in the earth. However, because of His love and boldness to break a religious standard, an entire city was saved. Thank God that Jesus talked to this person with a past, who was a Samaritan, and a woman. He was not afraid of His reputation being marred. He pressed through the mores of society to explain worship for a Kingdom that was forming. The woman became part of this Kingdom. She then led many others into this reality that she had found.

For Study and Reflection
Read Exodus 19–20. Meditate on John 4 and
memorize John 4:24.

The Apostolic Perspective

*The creation waits in eager expectation for the sons of God to be
revealed. For the creation was subjected to frustration, not by its own choice,
but by the will of the one who subjected it, in hope that the
creation itself will be liberated from its bondage to decay and
brought into the glorious freedom of the children of God.*
ROMANS 8:19-21, NIV

Missing the Purpose

The $20,000 Plant Stand

The world that the Bridegroom is drawing us out into has been
waiting for us. It is a world that has been subjected to frustration.
This world hasn't been able to live up to its potential, and feels, as
the Hebrew puts it in Genesis 1:2, "transient and empty." This
world has missed its purpose.

Civilization has missed its purpose.

The world governments have missed their purpose.

Science has missed its purpose.

Education has missed its purpose.

Art has missed its purpose.

Music, which came forth "out from the presence of God," has
missed its purpose.

God's frustrated creation is like a $20,000 grand piano that
has been relegated to use as a plant stand. Make no mistake, a
grand piano would be a beautiful plant stand, but that's not the
purpose for which it was created. Oh, people might rave about
what a fine-looking plant stand the piano is, but the piano itself
waits in hope for the day someone will rescue it from its bondage

as a plant stand and release it into its true purpose.

Although music is a multibillion-dollar business that has made musicians and singers into rock stars and demigods, it has not been liberated completely into its true purpose and still waits in eager expectation for the sons of God to be revealed.

Music was to facilitate our worship in the earth as it had done for the inhabitants of heaven for millions of years, but we have instead seen its evil potential realized more than its good. We have seen music accompanying every wicked activity imaginable: even glorifying the devil himself. This has caused many in the Church to limit or abandon music altogether, which I am sure has delighted the devil. That medium, which is used in heaven to facilitate worship, has been diminished or nullified altogether on earth. We have seen churches over the centuries shun various musical styles and instruments because they were first used by God's frustrated creation, the world. Instead of redeeming these musical instruments and styles from their frustrated state, we have condemned them to their fate. They were waiting for God's redeemers to show up; but instead of being redeemers we were condemners.

This is the exact opposite of the model set before us in the Word of God through Miriam's redemption of the Egyptian tambourine at the Red Sea and even more so at David's redemption of the world's instruments in his tabernacle. Jimmy Dunn, in his study of ancient musical instruments, says:

> The musical instruments that we find coming into use in Israel from the time of Joshua until David had all been established instruments of the Egyptian culture for generations before, most notably the trumpet, the harp, the flute, the lyre, the pipe and more. Some of these instruments were indigenous to Egypt and others had been introduced to Egypt from Babylon, southern Palestine and other near eastern locations.[1]

David had no qualms about redeeming these musical instruments for their true purpose of glorifying God. And after redeeming the worldly trumpets, harps and flutes, David went a step further. The worship of heaven that God released into David's tabernacle could not be completely brought about by the musical instruments of the day. David had to invent new instruments that could facilitate the heavenly music (see 1 Chron. 23:5). As for us, we have not even tried to use all the instruments available to us. A good portion of them have just been left for the devil to make use of as he pleases. He has. Now we need to take them back.

As we saw earlier, Jubal, who was the father of all who played musical instruments, operated out from under the presence of God, and all that he fathered has missed God's purpose, according to Romans 8:19. Just about every musical instrument ever invented, except for David's, has missed God's purpose for it. Altogether they are part of God's creation, which waits in frustration for the revelation of the sons of God: us. As God restores David's tabernacle, we need to bring these instruments and musical styles into their true purpose, as well as the new ones we will, like David, be inventing to facilitate the worship that God brings to us. As we enthrone God on our praises, it will be to music played by instruments of His redeemed creation.

Taking Back Music

The Apostolic Perspective

Apostles look at things differently. While others might look at the corrupted things of the world and run from them to keep from being corrupted by them, apostles look at them and say, "That thing belongs to God, and I'm not going to rest until I see it reconciled back to Him." Paul, in Colossians 1:19-20, says, "For it pleased the Father that in Him all the fullness should dwell, and by Him to reconcile all things to Himself, by Him, whether things on earth or things in heaven, having made peace through the blood of His cross." Apostles believe that we are the ones through whom Jesus reconciles all things to the Father. Jesus saves, but it is us that He uses to preach the gospel. In the same way, Jesus reconciles, but it is us that He uses to wrestle the unreconciled to the Father.

The Wicked Church Organ

The problem has been that there are many things that we—God's representatives on the earth—have not wanted to see reconciled. Paul said that God will reconcile "all things" (Col. 1:20), but we are often interested in a few particular things. Over the ages, we Christians have always seemed to know which musical instruments were worthy of being reconciled and which were not: which could be sanctified enough for use in our church worship services and which were definitely beyond salvage. As the ages have changed, so have our perceptions.

The traditional church organ—which graces so many of our church worship services today—was once spurned as unfit for use in glorifying God. Church historian Philip Schaff says, "In the Greek Church the organ never came into use, but after the eighth century it became common in the Latin Church, not, however, without opposition from the side of the Monks."[2] In the sixteenth century the reformer, John Calvin, believed pipe organs were "of the devil."[3] Martin Luther said, "The organ in worship is the insignia of Baal."[4]

Eventually the hated organ found its place in Christian worship, and over the last few centuries has probably been the most common feature of Christian musical accompaniment. The denominations founded by Martin Luther and by John Calvin, as well as scores of others, have made the church organ an indispensable part of their worship services. Most Christians today would never imagine that the church organ had ever been questioned as an instrument to facilitate worship. Indignantly they would say, "Of course the church organ is a sanctified musical instrument! Who could possibly think otherwise?"

The Wicked Tambourine

The truth is, the very first instruments that were used on earth to worship God had to be wrested from the hands of the enemy and pressed into service for the Lord. After the Israelites came safely through the Red Sea, "Miriam the prophetess, the sister of Aaron, took the timbrel in her hand; and all the women went out after her with timbrels and with dances. And Miriam answered them: 'Sing to the LORD, for He has triumphed gloriously! The horse and its rider He has thrown into the sea!'" (Exod. 15:20-21).

The *timbrel*, or tambourine, is an instrument the Hebrews had picked up from the Egyptians.[5] The ancient Egyptians were the first early culture whose entire society was permeated with music and dance: private parties, larger social events, festivals, religious services and everything in between were alive with harps, lutes, drums, flutes, cymbals, clappers and tambourines.

Miriam had seen the tambourine and the dance used by the Egyptians in their celebrations and religious ceremonies. These instruments and expressions had truly come into being "out from the presence of God" and had missed their purposes and had been subjected—like the rest of creation—to futility. Not only this, but the tambourine was also actually a demonic instrument, one of two instruments that had their origin in Satan himself before the foundation of the earth. As we saw earlier, Satan was formerly the worship leader of heaven, Lucifer, and had timbrels and pipes in-laid in him like precious stones that were a part of his being (see Ezek. 28:13). When Lucifer fell, these instruments were still a part of his makeup, and as we can see from history he set about to take control of their use on earth, employing them in the worship of false gods and demons. Miriam could have refused to use such a tainted instrument in her praise to the true God, but she chose instead to redeem the tambourine to its fullest purpose and destiny: to praise the God of the universe. In the same way, the highest purpose the dance could fulfill was to glorify God. Although Miriam had seen the tambourine and the dance used in the Egyptians' false worship, she and the Hebrew women chose to bring these two art forms to their highest purpose.

Today the tambourine is received with mixed emotions (at best) in our churches, and for good reason. Satan, I'm sure, hates for it to be used in worship more than any other instrument. I believe our praise on the tambourine still rattles his timbrels. He can't get away from it. Those timbrels are a part of his being. Consequently, I believe he tries to either eliminate its use in churches or to bring it under his influence, and I will tell you how I think he tries to accomplish this.

If you are in a church that even allows tambourines, you know that tambourine players are seldom on the worship team and seldom realize their connection to the corporate worship. Instead, they are scattered and unconnected throughout the sanctuary, often at the back or the peripheries of the congregation, each doing their own thing. The problem is that the tambourine is a percussive instrument used to establish rhythm and has a loud, piercing sound to accomplish that purpose. That sound usually pierces through the sound of all other instruments in the sanctuary and can be heard distinctively over the singing of the whole congregation. Often the scattered tambourine players are lost in their personal worship and have no idea of the effect they are having on the rest of the congregation. It is said that an idle mind is the devil's playground, but in church it's an idly played tambourine that is the devil's playground. And play he does. I truly believe the devil uses those idly played tambourines to bring dissonance in a worship service. Even for those who conscientiously try to keep the beat, the properties of sound make it virtually impossible to do so.

The Pokey Nature of Sound
Here is why. Sound travels at a little over 1,100 feet per second, which is pretty pokey considering that light travels at a little over 186,000 miles during that same second. That's why at track meets you see the smoke from the starting pistol before you hear the sound of the shot. Even though a second is not very long, it's long enough to adversely affect the beat of a song.

When I was very young we played Hide-and-Seek. If you were "it" you had to hide your eyes for 10 or 20 seconds while everyone else hid. So that we wouldn't count too fast, we had to say, "Tennessee one, Tennessee two, Tennessee three," and so on, because it took about a second to say "Tennessee one." When the beat of the worship proceeds from the loud speakers at the front of the church, it takes just a little bit of time to reach the back of the church. Try saying, "Tennessee one" during a song and you can see that the beat of a song might get off just a tad by the time it gets to the tambourine players at the back. Then imagine the piercing beat of the tambourine traveling back to the worship team at the front of the church. Maybe its just a half a beat off, but that little bit throws the worship team off in its rhythm.

This frustration causes most churches to prohibit the use of tambourines altogether in their worship services. Those churches that still allow tambourines end up wishing that the same laws regulating the purchase of firearms would also apply to the purchase of tambourines (background check and three business days waiting period) and that intensive training and a license would be required to carry tambourines in public.

As a worship leader, I understand firsthand the frustrations that tambourines cause, but I believe that if we forbid them, Satan has won a victory by keeping a musical instrument from fulfilling its purpose in glorifying God. After all, it was God who created Lucifer and the timbrels that were a part of his being. So, even though we can say tambourines are truly satanic instruments because they are now a part of Satan's being, we must also realize that the tambourine is also an instrument that God Himself created. That's right, God Himself made the first tambourine. Therefore, I believe He wants it to be used in praising Him, and at the same time, rattling the devil's timbrels and driving him crazy in our worship.

In our church, I try to educate tambourine players in the dynamics of their instrument and the responsibility they bear in playing them in church. I encourage them to come to the front of the church where they can clearly hear the beat and concentrate on keeping that beat. If they just can't keep a beat, no matter how hard they try, I encourage them to find a different way to release their praise to God.

The Wicked Trumpet, Harp, Pipe

As the children of Israel traveled into the wilderness on their journey to the Holy Land, God had them make silver trumpets (see Num. 10:2) to use in their ministry to God. The Egyptians also used trumpets, but God had no reservations about having His people use them in their service of worship. It's too bad some folks from our age could not have been there to tell them, "You can't use those trumpets in church. That's what the Egyptians use in their idol worship!"

And as we just saw in the previous section, the pipe was not only used by the Egyptians, but was, along with the timbrel, built into Lucifer's being, prepared for him by God on the day he was created (see Ezek. 28:13). Lucifer also played a harp, which he held on to as he fell from heaven. Isaiah 14:11 says, "Your pomp and the music of your harps have been brought down to Sheol" (*NASB*). But as we see in the Revelation, it didn't stop the inhabitants of heaven from continuing to use their harps even though Satan had his with him down in Sheol.

The Wicked Piano and Mandolin

Although God's biblical example was to redeem the musical instruments that Satan had taken captive, somewhere along the way the Church decided that this was not the best policy. So we stopped taking the devil's musical instruments away from him and started letting him keep them. Constantine's successors even went a step further by removing musical instruments from Christian worship altogether.

During the Reformation of the 1500s and 1600s, musical instruments tried to make their entrance back into the Church even though many of the Reformers had their own misgivings about them. The church organ, as we saw, came in amidst much opposition. After that, other musical instruments began to make their way into the Church as well, but not without a fight. In 1749, a ruling was issued in one denomination that only the organ, stringed instruments and bassoons were to be allowed in worship. A strict ban, however, was still in place against "kettle-drums, horns, trombones, oboes, flutes, pianos, and mandolins."[6] Imagine a church today that banned pianos but used bassoons in their worship? How these people determined that bassoons were sanctified but mandolins were not is a mystery to me. But though we laugh at the decisions made by the saints of a few centuries ago, we fight our own present battles over electric guitars, drums, congas, keyboards, and the like. Pianos and organs are all right; even bassoons are acceptable, but don't bring that electric bass into this church. Again and again we limit the expressions of worship that could be available to us.

In the 1800s, the Salvation Army brought those drums, trombones, trumpets and other band instruments into worship as well as tambourines, which later found their way into the Holiness churches. When the Pentecostal revival erupted at the beginning of the 1900s, Larry Eskridge noted that:

> Many Pentecostals welcomed not only the brass and horns of their Holiness-influenced Salvation Army cousins, but guitars, banjos, accordions, fiddles and even drums into their Holy Ghost-charged services.[7]

The Restoration of All Things

I believe that God wants to fully restore music for His own purposes in the earth. It has, for the most part, missed its purpose. The Scripture tells us that Jesus must be held in the heavens "until the period of restoration of all things" (Acts 3:21, *NASB*). God intends to restore all things. Among these things is, of course, music, which has missed its purpose and remains in frustration until we, the children of God, are revealed to liberate it from its bondage and bring it into its freedom (see Rom. 8:19-21).

God once spoke to my spirit that He had hidden His sounds in the earth. So I began to seek how to redeem His sounds that the enemy had taken and perverted. Different sounds in music produce different effects. We should have these different effects in our arsenal instead of allowing the devil to use them for his purposes. Different styles touch different ethnos groups, and God desires to reap a harvest from all those groups. He is restoring David's tabernacle to do this very thing.

In Luke 19:10, Jesus says, "For the Son of Man has come to seek and to save *that* which was lost" (emphasis added). Notice that Jesus does not say "those." He specifically used the word "that," which encompasses more than the word "those." Jesus came to seek and to save not only people but also everything else that was lost. Remember in Revelation we saw that every created thing was worshiping

God, not just every created being. But now, here on earth, the whole creation groans, waiting for restoration. Music groans, waiting. Worship itself groans, waiting. Everything that was lost, Jesus came to seek and to save. God is rebuilding David's tabernacle, restoring everything that was established there.

Realizing the Tabernacle

The Beat Goes On

I grew up in the 1950s and 1960s. My family went to church Sunday morning, Sunday night and Wednesday night. If our church had a revival, we went to every night of it. I sang the hymns until I knew most of them by heart and still do. But though those hymns were new and exciting to Isaac Watts and Charles Wesley and Fanny Crosby, they were not new and exciting for me. Nothing in our hymnbook was newer than 50 years old, and eventually those powerful hymns grew dull and boring to me. The world, however, over the same 50 years had been continually developing and reinventing its musical styles and content.

As I approached my teenage years, a new style of music burst on the scene. It did not come from the Church. It should have, but it did not. As the be-bop rock 'n' roll of the 1950s evolved into the rock music of the 1960s, my attention was grabbed. All of a sudden music, which had been a non-issue for me for my first 12 years, now came to the very forefront of my life. Music was now influencing my thinking and my lifestyle, but it wasn't church music. The cutting edge of music was not in my church. I still went to church and dutifully sang what was put before me, but what I concluded was that church is where you go because you are supposed to, but "life" happens out in the world where the music touches my innermost being.

Pie in the Sky

While the world was "rockin' 'round the clock," we were in our pews singing about how miserable we were now, but one day, by and by, we would leave all this and fly away to heaven. It was the doctrine of "pie in the sky, by and by." Bill Click, in his look at twentieth-century Christianity, gave this observation:

> Heaven was what Christianity was all about, and their understanding of a believer's status was tantamount to being suspended animation here on Earth. Their lives were almost exclusively focused on Jesus to come for them or death to unite them with Him. Their theology was one of holding on to the end by staying pure and unstained by the world.[8]

Although many moves of the Spirit swept through the twentieth century shaking that "pie in the sky" philosophy, the late '60s brought a turn that would forever change the face of Christian music. Hippies in California began to come to the Lord in great numbers. The dropouts of society whose rally cry had been sex, drugs and rock 'n' roll were now coming into the kingdom of God. They were radical in their faith and they wanted to affect the society around them, not just wait around doing nothing until one day they died and went to heaven. They witnessed on the streets, they set up missions to feed the hungry and clothe the naked. They, for the most part, were not welcomed into the established Church. As the movement spread across the country and eventually around the world, many started their own ministries, communities, coffee houses and small groups.

The music they worshiped with was not the music of the churches that had rejected them. It was the cutting-edge music of the world they had come out of. They took the style of music that the generation of that day was drawn to and used it to preach the message of Jesus and to express their hearts in worship. It was called "Jesus music." I loved it, and when I got saved in the early '70s, it was this music that I was able to identify with. It was the music the Church had rejected, but it was music I could relate to. Jesus music gave me a way to release my heart to God in worship that was relevant to my generation, the same as Isaac Watts's music had been relevant to his day and Fanny Crosby's had been to hers.

Why Should the Devil Have All the Good Music?

Jesus music was the forerunner of today's contemporary Christian music, and one of its pioneers, Larry Norman, wrote a song entitled "Why Should the Devil Have all the Good Music?" Why, indeed? It is because the Church—since Constantine—has rejected the cutting edge of music and has allowed the devil to have it.

If David's tabernacle were in operation when I was growing up, I would surely have been draw to the anointing, the creativity, the energy and the glory of the cutting-edge music in that place. I don't believe anything in the world could have compared with it. I believe the Beatles would have never made it to *The Ed Sullivan Show*; Woodstock would only have drawn two or three dozen people; and Jimmy Hendrix, when he burned his guitar on stage, would not have had enough money from his record sales to buy a new one.

But because the Church concentrated on restricting music instead of being on the cutting edge of it, the world was quick to fill the void. In the tradition of Adam and Eve, who gave up their dominion, we gave up the cutting edge of music. Creation was waiting for us to show up and redeem it, but we turned our backs and hid inside the four walls of our churches. We are the children of God whose job it is to redeem those things that have missed their purpose, but we have, instead, let the devil have all the good music. And just imagine, if worldly music—which has swept the peoples of the earth into its influence over the years—has missed its purpose and still accomplished all this, what could it have done if the children of God had redeemed it?

The rock music that captured my heart in the early '60s can trace its roots to the old African-American spirituals that begat blues and jazz music, which folded back into the Church as gospel music. I learned of a young successful black jazz and blues artist named Thomas A. Dorsey, not to be confused with the big band leader Tommy Dorsey of that same era. Thomas A. Dorsey grew up in the Church but found success in the jazz and blues music forms that blossomed during the early years of the twentieth century. Thomas played barrelhouse piano in one of Al Capone's

Chicago speakeasys. He toured and played piano for Ma Rainey, who was considered to be the first great professional blues vocalist and "the mother of blues."

When God called Thomas back into the fold, however, he began to mix the church music of his youth with the jazz and blues rhythms from which he had gained his early success. This mixed sound was the inception of a new genre of music called "gospel." It naturally experienced stiff resistance in the black church where Dorsey introduced it, but the enthusiasm in its expression eventually took root and spread throughout America and the world through song publishing, concerts, recordings and the burgeoning radio broadcast industry.

In the '30s and '40s, gospel radio stations began to broadcast. In the 1950s, gospel music took on a wilder delivery, especially from the lead voice, with thigh slapping and screaming top notes. At this point gospel artists found they had aspiring rock 'n' roll singers in their audience looking for inspiration. Indeed, the big debt that commercial music owes to gospel starts here in earnest, influencing such figures as Elvis Presley: "Presley, for example, absorbed the sounds, the rhythms, and the stage manner (including the leg shake) that shaped his own electric performances."[9]

Many of the major soul singers of the 1960s and 1970s got their start in church choirs. Aretha Franklin, Little Richard, Wilson Pickett, Roberta Flack, Otis Redding, Al Green, and many more, all learned the fundamentals of their intense and demanding vocal forms while wearing choir robes.

But the Church at large rejected gospel music and refused the opportunity to capture the cutting edge of music in the twentieth century. Instead it chose to live in the music of the past and allowed the guardianship of creativity and innovation to pass to the world. God—who is the Creator—watched His church take their "talent" and hide it in the ground where it would not cause controversy. The Elvis Presleys and the James Browns had to take their "talents" out into the world in order to cause them to multiply. The devil had all the good music because he picked up and used what the Church threw out its back door.

Getting Them Out of the Bars

Today, Christian music is beginning to catch the attention of the world. I'm not talking about so-called crossover music, but real worship songs that make no bones about who they are worshiping. A few years ago, Chevrolet, a division of General Motors, was the title sponsor of Michael W. Smith's "Come Together and Worship" tour. They knew exactly what Michael represented, but they wanted to sponsor him anyway. More and more Christian groups are being asked to play their Christian music in secular venues.

Over the years I have led worship in many hotel ballrooms for Christian conferences. Often I have seen the people from the hotel bar peeking in the back door. I could tell they were from the bar because they still had their mixed drinks in their hands. Sometimes they slipped in and stayed, and some would always end up getting caught up in the worship. One night after the meeting was over, I left to go back to my room. As I passed by the hotel bar, I heard someone call my name, "Hey, John! Come in here." As I walked into the bar, I was greeted by a raucous crowd of revelers, who slapped me on the back and told me how much they liked my music. As we laughed and talked, I asked them if they knew the Lord. Everyone did—in his or her own mind—but they all had their stories about how they used to be in church but this or that had caused them to slip away. It ended up being a wonderful time of witnessing that would never have been available to me if the anointing of the worship had not drawn these lost hearts in.

As God restores the tabernacle of David, the anointed music that comes forth will draw the Gentiles in, not drive them away. As we let God repair the tabernacle's breaches and enthrone Himself on our praises, the demonic powers that have blinded the world will be dismantled and people will be drawn in.

Once, while I was leading worship in an auditorium on a college campus, I was told that students were coming up and dancing on the steps of the building during the worship service. As a moth is drawn to the light, those who are called by His name are drawn by the anointing. Their natural aversion to "religion" is dismantled and they come under the convicting power of the Holy Spirit. This happened to me as I was attempting to sow my wild oats in college. Even though I fought the conviction of the Holy Spirit for months, it had gotten its foothold in me and finally I came—heart and soul—into the Kingdom.

It remains for the Church to answer the Bridegroom's call to come out into His kingdom, to become dissatisfied with church as usual and to enter the ranks of God's army. We have to wake up, and we are waking up. We are like the little boy who never spoke a word until he was six years old. Finally one night at the dinner table the boy said, "This bread tastes stale." The family was shocked. The mother finally gathered her senses and said, "Honey, you can speak perfectly. Why haven't you said anything before now?" The boy replied, "Up 'til now, everything's been all right." We, as the Church, have been silent too long. Maybe, up 'til now, we have thought everything has been all right, or that if it wasn't, there wasn't anything we could do about it.

The Man in the Arena

This is the season to step into our calling as God's manifested sons and daughters and redeem His creation. If it means standing in the gap and warring for His purposes in our worship, then we must do it. No longer will we be content to stay in the chamber while the Bridegroom goes out into the kingdom. We will risk our comfort, our ease and our status quo. Many will shout at us to get back in the boat. Many will call us radical and extremist. Many will judge us and sneer at our mistakes along this new path. I am reminded of the words of Theodore Roosevelt in a speech he made in France back in 1910:

> It is not the critic who counts; not the man who points out how the strong man stumbled, or where the doer of deeds could have done them better. The credit belongs to the man who is actually in the arena, whose face is marred by dust and sweat and blood; who strives valiantly, who errs and comes short again and again; who knows the great enthusiasms, the great devotions; who spends himself in a

worthy cause; who at the best, knows in the end the triumph of high achievement, and whom, at the worst, if he
fails, at least fails while daring greatly, so that his place
shall never be with those timid souls who know neither
victory or defeat.[10]

We were not created to be bystanders, "timid souls who know
neither victory nor defeat." We are the center of God's creation,
and He has always tried to draw us out into His larger world. Although we are capable of failure—and indeed have "come short
again and again" and our faces have often been "marred by dust
and sweat and blood"—God seems to take immense pleasure in
using the likes of us to advance His kingdom on earth. Let the crit-
ics point where we have stumbled or where we could have done
better, but we are the Church, Lord Sabaoth's warrior bride: we are
"in the arena" and we are not getting out! Joseph Garlington says,
"The glory of the Church is not to be cowering in some corner
while we fearfully wait for the rapture to rescue us from the bad
old devil."[11]

"Change, It's Here to Stay"

That's a favorite saying of my friend Jim Hodges. Jim ministers
around the world and is in a position to see changes in worship as
they develop. He observes:

We are now witnessing a worship-shift in the 21st century
Church. This shift, like previous ones, is the result of the
unfolding revelation of God's restorative purposes. Whenever the Holy Spirit illuminates the truths of the Bible,
change occurs in the Body of Christ and in the earth![12]

Change is difficult. Mindsets die hard. What we have gotten
used to sometimes keeps us from entering into the new things
God has for us. Just when we get settled down in the last move
God brought, we find ourselves facing a new one. Each new move
of God brings a new revelation in worship. It is like the four living

beings before the throne of God, crying, "Holy, holy, holy." Each time they are about to recover their composure, they are thrown into a new revelation of some aspect of God and fall back down, crying, "Holy, holy, holy" all over again. New revelation brings new flows of worship.

When Martin Luther came into the revelation that "The just shall live by faith," his life was changed, the world was later changed and worship came into a new glory. It wasn't a new truth; it was just new to him and the people of his day. It's the same today. The revelation we are receiving now is not new. It's just new to us. David walked in it 3,000 years ago. Dr. Jonathan David says:

> The world has changed dramatically and will continue. The specific successful methods used by the churches throughout the ages in the past may not directly apply to the future. Thus we must keep looking intently for underlying timeless fundamental concepts and patterns that might apply across eras.[13]

Those "timeless fundamental concepts and patterns" that Dr. David mentioned are the ones God released to us in David's tabernacle. Our challenge is to make our lives and our mindsets change to line up with what has been true all along. Worship is not just the warm and friendly time we have on Sunday morning before the preacher comes; it is the throne on which the very government of God rests. We are participants in that government as we worship and enthrone Him. As such, we must redeem every resource, lay aside every old mindset and throw ourselves into the apostolic worship that will facilitate His purposes.

Bringing in the Ark Again

Our High-Tech Oxcart
We have been very successful bringing in the Ark in our day and age. The Philistines of the Dark Ages have given it up and we are excited to have it back. We have brought it in with great celebration.

We have danced before it with all our might. Everyone has gathered to the gala. This is great! This has been God's plan, and I believe He is very pleased with our progress.

I also believe we still have the Ark on an oxcart, so to speak. But up until now that has been all right. Just as the Israelites brought the Ark in on the most fashionable, upscale, high-tech mode of transport available to them in that day, the oxcart, we have brought the Ark in on the best of our talent and technology. We offer the Lord no less than our most proficient musicians, our most gifted singers and dancers, and our most high-tech sound systems and recording equipment run by our most accomplished technicians. And we have done it with all our might. I am not saying this is bad, but it is still an oxcart. We have revered our "art" and the excellence with which we have brought our praises to God, but Bob Sorge wrote:

> Someone has likened our giving to God the most excellent music we can produce to the little boy who brings home a drawing from second grade. His mother tells him how wonderful it is, and after gazing proudly at his childish scribble, she posts the work on the refrigerator door to be frequently admired. Even the very best we can offer God is no more than just a "scribble" to him. Therefore, whether our music is at its best or worst is quite irrelevant from God's perspective. But to us it makes a tremendous amount of difference![14]

In the early charismatic movement, many of the songs were simple choruses and Scripture songs, but they were sung from the heart. Even so, there became a stigma over the simplicity of the songs compared to the more accomplished music of the world. As we moved into the 1980s, Christian musicians began to bring Christian music into a level of excellence: the songs became more elaborate and the chord structures became more complex. Our ability to present our music became more and more sophisticated. Today our Christian music is second to none, and I believe God is pleased that we want to give Him our best. But I have sometimes seen the quest for excellence take the place of the heart of worship. That's when we have to back off and realize that even our best is just a "scribble" to Him. If there is no heart of worship, then our excellence does not make a difference. If there is no communion and sacrifice, then there is nothing for Him to enthrone Himself upon. David was willing to be "undignified" if that's what it took to release his heart of worship.

The Bridegroom has called us to His larger world. God is restoring David's tabernacle. The oxcart, no matter how fancy, has been found wanting. Like David, we must bear the Ark—the Presence of the Lord—on the shoulders of consecrated ministers. We will certainly give God our most excellent offering; but more than just excellence, we will give Him our consecrated hearts in our worship. God is enthroning Himself on the praises of His people; and from that throne, He is warring to bring in the fullness of the harvest. We are His worship warriors.

Unless the Lord Builds the House

It is important to note that it is God who is rebuilding the tabernacle of David, not us. We cannot run out and duplicate some aspect of the tabernacle and say, "Behold, the tabernacle of David, rebuilt!" The thing for us to do in this season is to keep our eyes open, because the tabernacle of David is literally unfolding before our very eyes. The Lord Himself is restoring it. Our responsibility is to allow God to invade our concepts of worship. As we minister to Him in the chamber, we must be willing to come with Him out into His larger world. We must open ourselves to the models of apostolic worship that make a way for the government of God. "Unless the LORD builds the house, they labor in vain who build it" (Ps. 127:1, NASB). We can but open our hearts to His continuing revelation of worship. Kevin J. Conner says:

> For around 500 years the Church has been coming out of the Dark Ages and has seen a continual unfolding of Truth being restored and new light shining on the Church's pathway.[15]

Let us therefore walk in that unfolding light and enter into the fullness of His desire for us. *Halal!*

THE HARVEST NOW AND TO COME
CHUCK D. PIERCE

We have entered a new worship season in the earth. I call this "The Season of Harvest Songs"! This is an apostolic season. An apostolic season is where we receive our call and are sent into the fields that have been prepared for harvest. We have a mentality of celebration, work, war and triumph, all expressed through worship. The harvest is a picture of God's judgment. Jesus used this as a metaphor to make us realize that there will come a time when He gathers those who believe. The harvest has already begun. It began when Jesus first came and now is maturing rapidly. Yet there is a tug-of-war in heavenly places over who will control the harvest and bring the resources into the storehouse. In Luke 10:2, Jesus says, "Therefore pray the Lord of the harvest to send out laborers into His harvest."

Worshiping in Spirit and truth is necessary to enter the war in the earth realm for a Kingdom Harvest. There are many fields and all are being prepared for the harvesters—the worshipers—to enter. Storehouses are being prepared. The final theater of war will be the War of Harvest. Harvest time is when we are at the end of a season, the crops have matured and there must be a gathering. Revelation 14:15-16 says, "Another angel came out of the temple, crying with a loud voice to Him who sat on the cloud, 'Thrust in Your sickle and reap, for the time has come for You to reap, for the harvest of the earth is ripe.' So He who sat on the cloud thrust in His sickle on the earth, and the earth was reaped."

In my book *God's Unfolding Battle Plan*, I share the following:

We face a multitude of wars in various dimensions and from every front. In the next 20 years, all nations will reconcile around Israel, while some will arise to become dominant on the world scene. The United States of America will attempt to find its voice new and fresh but will not be heard as loudly as in the past. Mammon will be the greatest influencing force of rule in the world. Bloodlines will continue to conflict with other bloodlines simply because nations are comprised of people with unredeemed blood. The carnal mind will continue, as always, to be in enmity with God and resist His knowledge. Antichrist will continue to have a plan to rule the earth. However, the earth—again, as always—will still be the Lord's and the fullness thereof![16]

Because the earth is the Lord's and He has a plan of fullness, He has a plan of harvest. *Harvest is a process.* The grain must be cut with a sickle. What has been cut is then gathered into sheaves and taken to the threshing floor where tools or animals are used for the threshing. The grain is winnowed and tossed into the air, where the wind separates and blows away the chaff from the heavier kernels of the harvest. The last phase of harvest is the storage. This occurs when the kernels are shaken in a sieve so that the harvest can be stored. The war dynamic of harvest is maturing at this time over this point of the process. We are in a shaking process. What can be shaken will be shaken. The Lord is shaking away the iniquities in our lives, corporate gatherings, cities and nations that would make us less "marketable."

The key to our harvest is the weight of His glory. In the winnowing stage, the weightier kernels do not blow away. In the season ahead there will be many issues that cause us to be tossed to and fro. Without the weight of His glory resting upon us, we will be blown away and not complete the harvesting process that God has released into the earth. We can only receive this key to harvest if we learn to worship in Spirit and truth. Not only are we being harvested, but we are also the harvesters for the future! Dr. Robert Heidler, the incredible teacher that I serve with, recently wrote me the following:

Two nights ago, I had a dream. In the dream, Linda had been out shopping and came home with a cardboard box. In the box was a rattlesnake. She said, "The Lord told me if we would bring this rattlesnake into our house and keep it there for three weeks that we would enter into a season of endless harvest." So we did. We put the poisonous snake in the garage and kept the door closed to make sure it couldn't get into the main house. We were very careful how we went into the garage because we knew we had a rattlesnake in the house. I awakened and remembered that when we were commissioned and sent, or *apostolos*-ed, we were given authority over serpents and scorpions. The problem is that the Church has been so frightened of the world that we won't let ourselves get anywhere near its contamination. But if we will put aside our fear and bring the world into our homes, not to become "of it" but to convert and sanctify all the culture for God's purposes, we will see that we do have authority over the power of the enemy.

I heard the Lord say: *"Some of you are resisting bringing the enemy under your feet. That's what is keeping your next level of portion from being unlocked. The harvest is yours. Do not fear the enemy when I give you the enemy. Ask Me for your desire on your enemy. If you'll ask Me for your desire on your enemies, what I will do is bring that enemy in and within three weeks everything that the enemy has held up, confiscated or taken from you, I will give you. The storehouse the enemy was guarding, you will now own the key!*

"There is a time that harvest comes! Even if your harvest season was once captured, in My plan and in My season I can cause a harvest season to come back around again. Open your eyes. Open your eyes of faith. Open your eyes of expectation! I am a God that is able to bring harvest back to you. If you are willing to seek Me, if you are willing to set your face like flint, I can bring the windows of heaven back over you so that what you've lost, what has been walled up and stored away from your use in one season, can be released now! You can see the harvest come in and secured for this day.

"Worship Me in Spirit and truth and I can cause cities and cultures that knew Me not to be transformed in a day. Hear My

songs of heaven. New songs break old cycles. Harvest songs are being released. Sing with heaven and I will send hosts to assist you in the harvest."

For Study and Reflection
Read Revelation 14. Meditate on Isaiah 32 and
memorize Matthew 10:2.

Endnotes

Preface: Worship as It Is in Heaven: The Ladder from Heaven to Earth!
1. "Shield Up!" *Scientific American*, May 2010, pp. 17-18.

Introduction
1. C. Peter Wagner, *Changing Church* (Ventura, CA: Regal, 2004), p. 10.
2. C. Peter Wagner, *Apostles and Prophets* (Ventura, CA: Regal, 2000), p. 10.
3. Wagner, *Changing Church*, p. 10.
4. Rick Joyner, *The Apostolic Ministry* (Fort Mill, SC: MorningStar Publications, Inc., 2004), p. 7.
5. Wagner, *Changing Church*, pp. 14-15.
6. Ibid., p. 14 (reference #2: David B. Barnett and Todd M. Johnson, "Annual Statistical Table of Global Missions," *International Bulletin of Missionary Research*, January 2003, p. 25). Barrett assured the author (C. Peter Wagner) in a private correspondence dated December 14, 2003, that the author's terminology and his refer to the same global phenomenon.
7. David B. Barrett and Todd M. Johnson, *International Bulletin of Missionary Research*, January 2008.
8. Joyner, *The Apostolic Ministry*, p. 9.
9. Dr. Jonathan David, *Apostolic Blueprints for Accurate Building* (Muar, Johor, Malaysia: Jonathan David, 2008), p. x.
10. Wagner, *Changing Church*, p. 10.

Chapter 1: What Happens When We Worship
1. Matt Redman, *The Unquenchable Worshipper* (Ventura, CA: Regal Books, 2001), p. 18.
2. *Merriam-Webster Dictionary* (Springfield, MA: Merriam-Webster, Inc. 2001), s.v. "synergism."
3. Chuck D. Pierce with John Dickson, *The Worship Warrior* (Ventura, CA: Regal, 2002), p. 160.
4. *Merriam-Webster Dictionary*, s.v. "throne."
5. *Biblesoft's New Exhaustive Strong's Numbers and Concordance with Expanded Greek-Hebrew Dictionary* (Biblesoft, Inc. and International Bible Translators, Inc., 2003), OT #3427, *yashab*.
6. Cindy Jacobs, *Possessing the Gates of Your Enemy* (Tarrytown, NY: Chosen Books, 1994), p. 56.
7. Chuck D. Pierce, *Interpreting the Times* (Lake Mary, FL: Charisma House, 2008), p. 120.
8. Robert Gay, *Silencing the Enemy* (Lake Mary, FL: Creation House, 1993), p. 44.
9. *Biblesoft's New Exhaustive Strong's Numbers and Concordance with Expanded Greek-Hebrew Dictionary*, OT #4294, *matteh*.
10. Chuck Pierce, Worship Warrior Conference brochure.
11. Joseph L. Garlington, *Worship: The Pattern of Things in Heaven* (Shippensburg, PA: Destiny Image Publishers, 1997).
12. Jim Hodges, *Releasing the Sounds of Heaven on Earth* (Denton, TX: Glory of Zion International Ministries, 2004).

Chapter 2: In Heaven As It Isn't on Earth
1. *Biblesoft's New Exhaustive Strong's Numbers and Concordance with Expanded Greek-Hebrew Dictionary* (Biblesoft, Inc. and International Bible Translators, Inc., 2003), OT #1984, *halal*.
2. Ibid, OT# 3034, *yadah*.
3. Mark Twain (aka Samuel Clemens), *Letters from the Earth* (New York: Harper & Row Publishers, 1938), p. 18.
4. Barbara Wentroble, *Praying with Authority* (Ventura, CA: Regal, 2003), p. 86.

5. Joseph L. Garlington, *Worship: The Pattern of Things in Heaven* (Shippensburg, PA: Destiny Image Publishers, 1997), p. 93.

6. Jim Hodges, *Releasing the Sounds of Heaven on Earth* (Denton, TX: Glory of Zion International Ministries, 2004), p. 15.

7. Greg Otis, teaching at the Federation of Churches and Ministries Worship Conference, June 2004.

8. Bob Sorge, *Exploring Worship: A Practical Guide to Praise and Worship* (Greenwood, MO: Oasis House, 2001), p. 71.

9. LaMar Boschman, *Future Worship* (Ventura, CA: Regal, 1999), p. 52.

10. Robert Heidler, sermon at Glory of Zion Outreach Center, October 20, 2005.

Chapter 3: The Power of Music

1. LaMar Boshman, *Future Worship* (Ventura, CA: Regal, 1999), p. 57.

2. Jack Hayford, *Worship His Majesty* (Ventura, CA: Regal, 2000), p. 25.

3. Richard C. Leonard, "Music and Worship in the Bible," *Scholarship and Publishing in Worship Studies and Biblical Theology* (Hamilton, IL: Laudemont Ministries, 1997)..

4. Martin Luther, quoted in "A Mighty Fortress Is Our God," *Christian History Institute's Glimpses Bulletin Inserts*, no. 65, 2004.

5. Peter Yarrow, quoted in *Off the Record: Songwriters on Songwriters* (Kansas City, MO: Andrews McMeel Publishing, 2002), pp. 199-200.

6. Ibid.

7. Robert Gay, *Silencing the Enemy* (Lake Mary, FL: Creation House, 1993), p. 31.

8. Boshman, *Future Worship*, p. 132.

9. Bob Sorge, *Exploring Worship* (Greenwood, MO: Oasis House, 2001), p. 7.

10. Jim Hodges, *Releasing the Sounds of Heaven on Earth* (Denton, TX: Glory of Zion International Ministries, 2004), p. 28.

11. Sorge, *Exploring Worship*, p. 18.

12. Boshman, *Future Worship*, pp. 54-55.

13. Marsha Mueller, "PYRO 101: Basic Considerations," *Technologies for Worship*, January/February 2005, vol. 14, no. 1.

14. Pastor Bob Rognlien, "Wired for Divine Experience: Jesus' Dream for Our Worship," *Worship Leader Magazine*, June 2005.

15. Phillip Schaff, *History of the Church, Volume 3: Nicene and Post Nicene Christianity (a.d. 311-590)*, chapter 7, part 74.

16. Chuck Pierce, speaking at the Prosperity Conference in Baltimore, Maryland, March 27, 2004.

17. Ernest B. Gentile, *Worship God* (Portland, OR: City Bible Publishing, 1994), p. 125.

18. Hayford, *Worship His Majesty*, p. 246.

Chapter 4: Bringing in the Ark

1. Charles Swindoll, "Principles vs. Precepts," *Day by Day Devotional*, June 7-8, 2008. http://bible.oneplace.com/devotionals/Day_by_Day/11576986/.

2. Caz Taylor, *David's Tabernacle: Patterns for New Testament Worship* (Greenwood, MO: Oasis House, 2004), p. 80.

Chapter 5: Bringing in the Ark Again

1. Jim Hodges, *Releasing the Sounds of Heaven on Earth* (Denton, TX: Glory of Zion International Ministries, 2004), p. 54.

2. Derek Prince, *War in Heaven* (Grand Rapids, MI: Chosen Books, 2003), p. 57.

3. Billye Brim, *The Blood and the Glory* (Tulsa, OK: Harrison House, Inc., 1995), p. 30.

4. Prince, *War in Heaven*, p. 58.

5. *Biblesoft's New Exhaustive Strong's Numbers and Concordance with Expanded Greek-Hebrew Dictionary* (Biblesoft, Inc. and International Bible Translators, Inc., 2003), OT #2555, *chamac*.

6. Ibid., OT #5329, *natsach.*

7. W.E. Vine, *Vine's Expository Dictionary of Biblical Words* (Nashville, TN: Thomas Nelson, 1985), OT #8334, *sharat.*

8. *Biblesoft's New Exhaustive Strong's Numbers and Concordance with Expanded Greek-Hebrew Dictionary,* OT #2145, *zakar.*

9. Ibid., OT #3034, *yadah.*

10. Ibid., OT #1984, *halal.*

11. Kevin J. Conner, *The Temple of Solomon* (Portland, OR: City Bible Publishing, 1988), p. 18.

12. Chuck D. Pierce, *Interpreting the Times* (Lake Mary, FL: Charisma House, 2008), p. 126.

Chapter 6: The Glory of Zion

1. Joseph L. Garlington, *Worship: The Pattern of Things in Heaven* (Shippensburg, PA: Destiny Image Publishers, 1997), p. 116.

Chapter 7: Rebuilding the Tabernacle

1. Kevin J. Conner, *The Tabernacle of David* (Portland, OR: City Bible Publishing, 1976), p. 49.

2. Ernest B. Gentile, *Worship God* (Portland, OR: City Bible Publishing, 1994), p. 250.

3. Andrew Murray, "The Two Covenants," PC Study Bible formatted electronic database, 2003.

4. Gordon Rattray Taylor, *Sex in History* (New York; Vanguard Press, 1954), chapter 14.

5. Clement of Alexandria, *Stromata,* book 7:7.

6. Gregory Thaumaturgus, quoted in Eugène Louis Backman, *Religious Dances in the Christian Church and in Popular Medicine* (London, UK: Allen & Unwin, 1952), p. 22

7. Basileios, quoted in Backman, *Religious Dances in the Christian Church and in Popular Medicine,* p. 22.

8. Ibid.

9. Bob Sorge, *Following the River, A Vision for Corporate Worship* (Greenwood, MO: Oasis House, 2004), p. 50.

10. Robert D. Heidler, *The Messianic Church Arising!* (Denton, TX: Glory of Zion Ministries, 2000), p. 7.

11. Eusebius, *The Conversion of Constantine,* chapter XXVIII.

12. Eusebius, *Church History,* book X, chapter V, no. 1-17.

13. Ibid., chapter VI, no. 1-4.

14. Finley Hooper, *Roman Realities* (Detroit, MI: Wayne State University Press, 1979), p. 505.

15. Eusebius, *The Life of the Blessed Emperor Constantine,* chapter 1, part 6; chapter 2, part 5; chapter 8, part 12.

16. Phillip Schaff, *History of the Church, Volume 3: Nicene and Post Nicene Christianity (a.d. 311-590),* chapter 7, part 74.

17. Moses Hadas, *Imperial Rome* (New York: Time Incorporated, 1965), p. 159.

18. Schaff, *History of the Church, Volume 3: Nicene and Post Nicene Christianity (a.d. 311-590),* chapter 7, part 74.

19. Ibid.

Chapter 8: Rebuilding the Tabernacle Again

1. LaMar Boschman, *Future Worship* (Ventura, CA: Regal, 1999), p. 115.

2. Ernest B. Gentile, *Worship God* (Portland, OR: City Bible Publishing, 1994), p. 149.

3. Madeleine Forell Marshall, "Why the Church of England Disliked Hymns," *Christianity Today,* 1993, no. 31.

4. Thomas Symmes, *Utile Dulci* (1723), quoted in Linda R. Ruggles, "The Regular Singing Controversy: The Case Against Lining-Out," Archiving Early America website. http://www.earlyamerica.com/review/fall97/sing.html.

5. Richard M. Riss, *A Survey of 20th Century Revival Movements in North America* (Peabody, MA: Hendrickson Publishers, 1988), p. 11.

6. Gerald R. McDermott, "The 18th-Century Awakening: A Reminder for American Evangelicals in the 1990s," *Christian Word Ministries,* 2006. http://www.christianword.org/revival/wakeup.html.

7. Reverend Dr. Alan C. Clifford, "Charles Wesley (1707–1788)," Heath Christian Book Shop Charitable Trust, 1997. http://www.igracemusic.com/hymnbook/authors/charles_wesley.html).

8. Lydia Bolles Newcomb, "The Yankee Tunesmiths and Other Early American Composers," *The New England Magazine,* December 1895, vol. 19, no. 4. http://www.nationwide.net/~amaranth/billings.htm.

9. Robert D. Johnston, *The Middling Sorts: Explorations in the History of the American Middle Class* (New York: Routledge, 2001), p. 127.

10. Ibid.

11. Bob Sorge, *Exploring Worship* (Greenwood, MO: Oasis House, 2001), p. 2.

12. Johnston, *The Middling Sorts,* p. 127.

13. "An Outline of American History (1994)," From Revolution to Reconstruction, October 20, 2004. http://www.let.rug.nl/~usa/H/1994/ch4_p13.htm.

14. "The Second Great Awakening," Glimpses Bulletin Inserts, no. 40. http://chi.gospelcom.net/GLIMPSEF/Glimpses/glmps040.shtml.

15. Lucinda Coleman, "Worship God in Dance," *Renewal Journal,* 1995, pp. 35-44. http://www.pastornet.net.au/renewal/journal6/coleman.html. Lucinda Coleman, a high school teacher, has been a dance coordinator at Gateway Baptist Church in Brisbane and now lives in Port Hedland, Western Australia. This article is adapted from her research on "Dance in the Church," written as part of her studies at the Queensland University of Technology. It briefly traces the history of dance in worship. Renewal in the Church in recent decades has rediscovered dance, including liturgical dance and spontaneous dance. As with all other forms of worship, it can give glory to the performer, or it can give glory to God.

16. Johnston, *The Middling Sorts,* p. 130.

17. Ibid.

18. Alexis de Tocqueville, *Democracy in America,* 1835.

19. Frances Trollope, *Domestic Manners of the Americans,* 1832, chapter VIII.

20. "Jesus Loves Me," *Christian History Institute's Glimpses Bulletin Inserts,* 2004, no. 62.

21. "The American Gospel Song," Smith Creek Music, 2001. http://www.smithcreekmusic.com/Hymnology/Ame . . . hymnody/WhatIsAGospelHymn.html.

22. "Fanny Crosby: Queen of American Hymn Writers," *Christian History Institute's Glimpses Bulletin Inserts,* 2004, no. 30.

23. Larry Eskridge, "Slain by the Music," *The Christian Century,* March 7, 2006, pp. 18-20. Larry Eskridge is associate director of the Institute for the Study of American Evangelicals at Wheaton College in Illinois. http://www.religion-online.org/showarticle.asp?title=3326.

24. Ibid.

25. Paul Harvey, *Freedom's Coming: Religious Culture and the Shaping of the South from the Civil War Through the Civil Rights Era* (Chapel Hill, NC: The University of North Carolina Press, 2005).

26. Robert Bahr, *Least of All Saints: The Story of Aimee Semple McPherson* (Englewood Cliffs, NJ: Prentice Hall, 1979), p. 267.

27. Bill Hamon, *Prophets and the Prophetic Movement* (Shippensburg, PA: Destiny Image, 1990), pp. 117-118.

28. C. Peter Wagner, *Discovering Your Spiritual Gifts* (Ventura, CA: Regal, 2002), p. 22.

29. *Charisma* magazine, February 1994, p. 30.

Chapter 9: Pursuing the Bridegroom

1. Greg Otis, teaching at the Federation of Churches and Ministries Worship Conference, June 2004.
2. Chuck Pierce, quoted in C. Peter Wagner, ed., *Destiny of a Nation* (Colorado Springs, CO: Wagner Publications, 2001), p. 45.
3. Dr. Jonathan David, *Apostolic Blueprints for Accurate Building* (Johor, Malaysia, 2008), p. x.
4. C. Peter Wagner, *Changing Church* (Ventura, CA: Regal Books, 2004), p. 91.
5. LaMar Boschman, *Future Worship* (Ventura, CA: Regal, 1999), p. 25.
6. Watchman Nee, *Song of Songs* (Fort Washington, PA: Christian Literature Crusade, 1955), p. 139.
7. Ramsey MacMullen, *Christianizing the Roman Empire (a.d 100–400)* (New Haven, CT: Yale University Press, 1984), p. 112.
8. Chuck D. Pierce, *God's Unfolding Battle Plan* (Ventura, CA: Regal, 2007), p. 40.
9. *Merriam-Webster Dictionary* (Springfield, MA: Merriam-Webster, Inc. 2001), s.v. "phlegmatic."
10. Jon Hodges, quoted in Pierce, *God's Unfolding Battle Plan,* p. 40.

Chapter 10: How Then Must We Worship?

1. Chuck D. Pierce, *Interpreting the Times* (Lake Mary, FL: Charisma House, 2008), p. 210.
2. C. Peter Wagner, *Changing Church* (Ventura, CA: Regal, 2004), p. 112.
3. Robert Stearn, *Prepare the Way* (Lake Mary, FL: Charisma House, 1999), p. 108.
4. Cindy Jacobs, *The Voice of God: How God Speaks Personally and Corporately to His Children Today* (Ventura, CA: Regal, 2004), p. 195.
5. Chuck D. Pierce, *The Future War of the Church* (Ventura, CA: Regal, 2001), p. 23.
6. LaMar Boschman, *The Prophetic Song* (Dallas, TX: The Worship Institute Publishers, 1986), pp. 1-2.
7. Ibid., p. 34.
8. Jacobs, *The Voice of God,* p. 194.
9. Ibid.
10. Ibid., p. 145.
11. Barbara Wentroble, *Prophetic Intercession* (Ventura, CA: Regal, 2003), p. 67.
12. Jacobs, *The Voice of God,* pp. 193-194.
13. Bob Sorge, *Following the River: A Vision for Corporate Worship* (Greenwood, MO: Oasis House, 2004), p. 6.
14. Ibid., pp. 14-15.
15. Chuck D. Pierce and Rebecca Wagner Sytsema, *Possessing Your Inheritance* (Ventura, CA: Regal, 1999), p. 88.

Chapter 11: The Apostolic Perspective

1. Jimmy Dunn, "An Introduction to Ancient Egyptian Musical Instruments," Tour Egypt. http://www.touregypt.net/featurestories/music.htm.
2. Philip Schaff, *The Schaff-Herzog Encyclopedia of Religious Knowledge,* vol. 2 (Grand Rapids, MI: Baker Book House, 1952), p. 1702.
3. Ernest B. Gentile, *Worship God* (Portland, OR: City Bible Publishing, 1994), p. 178.
4. Reverend Jon McClintock and James Strong, *McClintock and Strong's Encyclopedia,* vol. VI (New York: Harper & Brothers, 1887), p. 762.
5. OT #8596 *toph* (tofe); from OT #8608 contracted; a tambourine. OT #8608 *taphaph* (taw-faf"); a primitive root; to drum, i.e. play (as) on the tambourine. *Biblesoft's New Exhaustive Strong's Numbers and Concordance with Expanded Greek-Hebrew Dictionary* (Biblesoft, Inc. and International Bible Translators, Inc., 2003).
6. Joseph Otten, *The Catholic Encyclopedia,* vol. X (New York: Robert Appleton Company, 2003).

7. Larry Eskridge, "Slain by the Music," *The Christian Century*, March 7, 2006, pp. 18-20. Used by permission. http://www.religion-online.org/showarticle.asp?title=3326.

8. Bill Click, "A Brief History of 20th Century Religious Time," River of Power Ministries Newsletter, March 16, 2006.

9. Paul Harvey, *Freedom's Coming: Religious Culture and the Shaping of the South from the Civil War Through the Civil Rights Era* (Chapel Hill, NC: The University of North Carolina Press, 2005).

10. Theodore Roosevelt in a speech titled, "The Man in the Area," delivered at the Sorbonne in Paris, France, on April 23, 1910.

11. Joseph L. Garlington, *Worship, the Pattern of Things in Heaven* (Shippensburg, PA: Destiny Image Publishers, 1997).

12. Jim Hodges, *Releasing the Sounds of Heaven on Earth* (Denton, TX: Glory of Zion International Ministries, 2004), p. 11.

13. Dr. Jonathan David, *Apostolic Blueprints for Accurate Building* (Muar, Johor, Malaysia: Jonathan David, 2008), p. ix.

14. Bob Sorge, *Exploring Worship* (Greenwood, MO: Oasis House, 2001), p. 164.

15. Kevin J. Conner, *The Tabernacle of David* (Portland, OR: City Bible Publishing, 1976), p. 164.

16. Chuck D. Pierce, *God's Unfolding Battle Plan* (Ventura, CA: Regal, 2007).

ALSO FROM CHUCK D. PIERCE

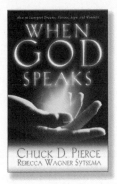

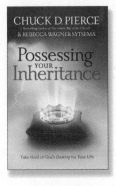

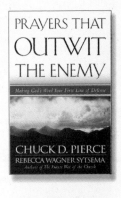

When God Speaks
How to Interpret Dreams,
Visions, Signs and Wonders
*Chuck D. Pierce and
Rebecca Wagner Sytsema*
ISBN 08307.37073
ISBN 978.08307.37079

Possessing Your Inheritance
Take Hold of God's
Destiny for Your Life
*Chuck D. Pierce and
Rebecca Wagner Sytsema*
ISBN 08307.51165
ISBN 978.08307.51167

Prayers that Outwit the Enemy
Making God's Word Your
First Line of Defense
*Chuck D. Pierce and
Rebecca Wagner Sytsema*
ISBN 08307.31628
ISBN 978.08307.31626

Restoring Your Shield of Faith
Reach a New Dimension
of Faith for Daily Victory
*Chuck D. Pierce and
Robert Heidler*
ISBN 08307.32632
ISBN 978.08307.32630

The Future War of the Church
How We Can Defeat Lawlessness
and Bring God's Order to the Earth
*Chuck D. Pierce and
Rebecca Wagner Sytsema*
ISBN 08307.44142
ISBN 978.08307.44145

God's Unfolding Battle Plan
A Field Manual for
Advancing the Kingdom of God
Chuck D. Pierce
ISBN 08307.44703
ISBN 978.08307.44701

Available at Bookstores Everywhere!
Go to **www.regalbooks.com** to learn more about your favorite
Regal books and authors. Visit us online today!

God's Word for Your World™
www.regalbooks.com